REALIZING *BAKKE*'S LEGACY

REALIZING
BAKKE'S LEGACY

Affirmative Action, Equal Opportunity,
and Access to Higher Education

Edited by

Patricia Marin & Catherine L. Horn

STERLING, VIRGINIA

COPYRIGHT © 2008 BY
STYLUS PUBLISHING, LLC.

Published by Stylus Publishing, LLC
22883 Quicksilver Drive
Sterling, Virginia 20166–2102

Library of Congress Cataloging-in-Publication-Data
Realizing Bakke's legacy : affirmative action, equal opportunity, and access to higher education / edited by Patricia Marin & Catherine L. Horn.
   p. cm.
  Includes bibliographical references and index.
  ISBN 978–1-57922–267–3 (hardcover : alk. paper)—ISBN 978–1-57922–268–0 (pbk. : alk. paper)
   1. Discrimination in higher education—United States. 2. Affirmative action programs in education—United States. 3. Educational equalization—United States. 4. Bakke, Allan Paul. I. Marin, Patricia, Ph.D. II. Horn, Catherine L.
LC212.42.R43 2008
379.2'60973—dc22   2008000728

13-digit ISBN: 978–1-57922–267–3 (cloth)
13-digit ISBN: 978–1-57922–268–0 (paper)

Printed in the United States of America

All first editions printed on acid free paper
that meets the American National Standards Institute
Z39–48 Standard.

Bulk Purchases

Quantity discounts are available for use in workshops and for staff development.
Call 1–800–232–0223

First Edition, 2008

10 9 8 7 6 5 4 3 2 1

This book is dedicated to
John T. Yun and John T. Clegg
for supporting us unconditionally.

For Ryan, Harper, and Alexander—
to encourage you to make the world a better place.

CONTENTS

PART THREE: POLICY AND PRACTICE

TABLES

CHAPTER 8: *BAKKE* AT 30
A History of Affirmative Action in U.S. Law Schools

FIGURES

CHAPTER 7: IS 1500 THE NEW 1280?
The SAT and Admissions Since *Bakke*

CHAPTER 8: *BAKKE* AT 30
A History of Affirmative Action in U.S. Law Schools

ACKNOWLEDGMENTS

This book would not exist without the support of many. We thank Caroline Chauncey for her encouragement and belief in our work, and for all the feedback she provided in the early stages of this project. We also thank Amaury Nora for encouraging us to contact Stylus Publishing when we were looking for a home for the book.

We are grateful to John von Knorring for his support of this project from the beginning and for all his guidance along the way. We also thank the staff at Stylus Publishing for their contributions to making this book a reality.

We gratefully acknowledge the hard work and commitment of our contributors. We are honored to work with colleagues dedicated to improving educational opportunities for all students.

We also want to thank John T. Clegg for his graphic design input, John T. Yun for substantive feedback, Angelo N. Ancheta for legal clarifications, and Zoe McCoy for yeoman's work on table and figure layout and on overall book logistics.

We thank our colleagues at the University of California, Santa Barbara and the University of Houston for their professional and intellectual support in this process.

Finally, we thank our families and friends who provided critical emotional support throughout this process and without whom we could not have finished.

Patricia Marin and Catherine L. Horn

I

REALIZING THE
LEGACY OF *BAKKE*

Catherine L. Horn and Patricia Marin

When the Supreme Court issued its June 28, 1978, ruling on the *Regents of the University of California v. Bakke,* Justice Thurgood Marshall, the only African American among the justices, concluded, "I doubt that there is a computer capable of determining the number of persons and institutions that may be affected by the decision in this case" (Greider, 1978, p. A1). Three decades later, just as Marshall intimated, the landscape of postsecondary education could hardly be described absent recognition of *Bakke's* touch. Most typically, *Bakke* is credited with establishing a legal framework upon which to consider race and ethnicity in higher education admissions decisions. To understand *Bakke* only in that context, however, would be to limit understanding of its full scope. This book brings together social scientists and legal experts to represent a broader picture of the ways in which *Bakke* has profoundly altered this country's elementary, secondary, postsecondary, and professional school landscape.

The issues addressed in the chapters of this book include a historical understanding of the case, new discussions and analysis of the impact of *Bakke* on the 30th anniversary of the decision, and, finally, consideration of what the future holds in light of *Bakke* and its reaffirmation in recent Supreme Court opinions. Simultaneously including and extending beyond issues of affirmative action, we believe the research in this book expands the public discourse about the future of affirmative action and higher education and contributes to efforts to expand access, equal opportunity, and success in postsecondary education among traditionally underserved students. This introduction serves several purposes. First, we mark the *Bakke* decision by remembering the case and considering racial/ethnic diversity specifically in the context of medical school admissions and completions, the professional school under consideration in the original trial. We also examine *Bakke*'s influence more broadly, including its relationship to the elementary and secondary pipeline, the ways in which it has framed understanding of race/ethnicity and the postsecondary experience, and its reach far beyond the admissions door. Although the 30th anniversary gives us an artificial marker at which to pause and consider this landmark case, the full extent of its influence needs to be systematically acknowledged.

The *Bakke* Case

In 1974, Allan Bakke, a White applicant to the University of California, Davis, medical school, filed suit against the university after having his medical school application denied for the second year in a row. He contended that the component of the admission policy that reserved 16 of 100 slots for non-White students was in violation of both the Equal Protection Clause of the Fourteenth Amendment and Title VI of the Civil Rights Act. The California Superior Court ruled that UC Davis's admissions practices were illegal but failed to grant Bakke admission into the medical school, arguing that he had not adequately met the burden of demonstrating he would have been admitted to Davis but for the policy. On appeal, the California Supreme Court affirmed the trial court's decision about the admissions program, but ordered that UC Davis admit Bakke. The university immediately appealed to the Supreme Court, which agreed to hear oral arguments in the fall of 1977 (*Bakke,* 1978). In his deciding opinion for a divided Court, Justice Lewis Powell affirmed that the Davis policy was illegal and that Bakke should be admitted. However, he disagreed that race could not be used in an admissions policy. He found that, although race cannot act as a primary determinant of admission under the Fourteenth Amendment and Title VI, "attainment of a diverse student body . . . is a constitutionally permissible goal for an institution of higher education" (*Bakke,* 1978, p. 311–312).[1] Specifically, "In such an admissions program, race or ethnic background may be deemed a 'plus' in a particular applicant's file, yet it does not insulate the individual from comparison with all other candidates for the available seats" (p. 317).

Grutter 25 Years After *Bakke*

Although authors in this volume discuss the uncertainty surrounding the *Bakke* decision since it was issued, there is consensus among all that the 2003 *Grutter v. Bollinger* ruling solidified Justice Powell's deciding opinion in *Bakke*. As such, *Grutter*'s relationship to *Bakke* is important for several reasons. First, in her majority opinion, Justice Sandra Day O'Connor reestablished the legally compelling interest of the educational benefits of a diverse student body first described in *Bakke*. In doing so, she gave credence to the rationale that many colleges and universities had been using for 30 years to justify their admissions practices. In upholding the Michigan law school's admission policy, her decision also supported the practice of using race as a plus factor.

Equally important, O'Connor admonished institutions of higher education about their continued use of race-conscious admissions policies:

> It has been 25 years since Justice Powell first approved the use of race to further an interest in student body diversity in the context of public higher education. Since that time, the number of minority applicants with high grades and test scores has indeed increased. . . . We expect that 25 years from now, the use of racial preferences will no longer be necessary to further the interest approved today. (*Grutter,* 2003, p. 343)

Using *Bakke* as a marker, Justice O'Connor's decision outlined a great challenge for the elementary, secondary, and postsecondary education systems in this country. And although scholars disagree about the extent to which her caution is legally binding, many groups have already begun to treat it as a fait accompli by ending or revising programs and policies absent any direct legal pressure to do so.

Considering Race in Admissions

Those who support the use of race-conscious admissions policies do so for many reasons well-captured by Bowen and Bok (1998):

> The relative scarcity of talented [minority] professionals is all too real. It seems clear to a number of us . . . that American society needs the high-achieving [minority] graduates who will provide leadership in every walk of life . . . We agree emphatically with the sentiment expressed by Mamphela

Ramphele, vice chancellor of the University of Cape Town in South Africa, when she said: "Everyone deserves opportunity; no one deserves success." But we remain persuaded that present racial disparities in outcomes are dismayingly disproportionate. . . . There is everything to be said . . . for addressing the underlying problems in families, neighborhoods, and primary and secondary schools that many have identified so clearly. But this is desperately difficult work, which will, at best, produce results only over a very long period of time. Meanwhile, it is important . . . to do what can be done to make a difference at each educational level, including colleges . . . Turning aside from efforts to help larger numbers of well-qualified [minorities] gain the educational advantages they will need to move steadily and confidently into the mainstream of American life could have extremely serious consequences. (pp. 283–286)

Bowen and Bok (as well as many others) believe that affirmative action allows our society to progress in a way that would not be possible otherwise and, as such, is essential.

Opponents of race-conscious admissions policies often base their criticisms around four key points. Considering race/ethnicity in admissions decisions is arguably an anathema because it

- Makes generalizations about people on the basis of immutable characteristics;
- Creates resentment among many of those who lose out because of this "discrimination";
- Stigmatizes the so-called beneficiaries of the preferences—both in the eyes of others and in their eyes; and
- Compromises the mission of the university making intellectual ability a "secondary attribute." (Clegg, 1999)

Although each of these criticisms gives reason for pause, it is the fourth point that seems to resonate most among those who would like to see a fully race-neutral system in place. Entrenched in the idea that intellectual ability is compromised when race/ethnicity is considered is the notion of merit. This argument assumes that individual merit can be accurately measured and that it can often be measured by a single test, such as the SAT. "The SAT exam and the vocabulary of 'worthiness' that tends to be used in connection with it create an artificial environment that reinforces the myth that individual merit and intelligence can only be measured by scores on such tests" (Moses, 1999, p. 272). There is often a belief that tests such as the SAT are infallible predictive measures of success, unaffected by the circumstances surrounding the test-taker's preparation.

Regardless of position, it is important to note that the current legal, social, and political climate that surrounds discussions of the admission of traditionally underserved minorities to higher education is vastly different from that of 30 years ago when Justice Powell issued his landmark opinion. As Trent (1991) notes, the following changes are especially pronounced. First, the "racial crisis" that used to focus solely on the demands and needs of Blacks has now broadened to encompass Latinos, Native Americans, and women. Further, "the debate regarding higher education and race was occurring in an atmosphere of heightened expectations for equal opportunity and social justice. Today we monitor urban infant mortality rates that exceed those of third world countries" (Trent, 1991, p. 108). Finally, three decades ago the Supreme Court was seen as an ally in the struggle for civil rights. Today's more conservative Court does not hold that same reputation.

The Medical School Story

In understanding the realization of *Bakke*'s legacy, it would be remiss of this book not to acknowledge the professional school at the center of the court case—a medical school. Among the more than 42,000 applicants to medical school in 1974, roughly 82% were White compared with Asians, Blacks, and Latinos who comprised 3%, 5%, and 2% of the pool, respectively (Association of American Medical Colleges [AAMC], 2005). Thirty years later, however, the applicant pool represented a different racial/ethnic makeup; in 2004, 62% were White and 20% Asian. Blacks and Latinos each composed 8% of the pool (AAMC, 2005). This change, in many ways, marks an important shift, as admission and, ultimately, completion trends can only be considered in the context of who applies. The 2004 matriculants, for example, were similar in racial/ethnic makeup to the applicant pool from which they were selected (AAMC, 2005). With respect to the result of such shifts, the AAMC notes,

> A diverse student body brings a wealth of ideas, helps students challenge
> their assumptions, and broadens students' perspectives regarding racial,

ethnic, and cultural differences. Diverse educational environments have also been found to contribute to improved intellectual and social outcomes. Moreover, diversity in group settings has been linked to greater cognitive outcomes for all group members. (2005, p. 9)

Bakke, then, has given medical schools an important tool to help reap the educational benefits of a racially diverse class.

Bakke and the Changing Landscape of Admissions and Beyond

Beyond the direct relationship to medical schools, *Bakke*'s broadest impact has been on admission policies writ large. Although it did not put to rest the legal, social, or policy debate regarding race-conscious decision making in college admissions, *Bakke* has remained the cornerstone of discussion around subsequent legal challenges such as *Hopwood v. Texas* (1996) and *Grutter v. Bollinger* (2003) and the discussion of educational benefits of diversity and the admission policies that have been created to support that notion. Before *Bakke,* higher education did not have a clear framework for affirmative action, relying largely on an employment model for considering race/ethnicity in college admissions. With the 1978 decision, the Supreme Court provided specific guidelines for university admissions policies, both narrowing (through the finding that quotas were illegal) and expanding (by allowing race/ethnicity to be included as part of holistic review) how race/ethnicity could be considered. In particular, Justice Powell's opinion reshaped the discussion of race/ethnicity in college admissions from one of remedies for the present effects of past institutional discrimination to one of educational benefits of diversity, establishing a philosophy that continues to drive admission practices today.

What makes this book unique is that it does not simply stop at the admission door when considering *Bakke*'s influence. In reality, the Supreme Court's decision has informed and guided many issues, among them the debate about the purpose of affirmative action in college admissions, the formulation and systemic influence of identity politics, and underlying assumptions about the fundamental right to postsecondary access. Unlike other education cases (e.g., *Brown v. Board of Education* [1954]), *Bakke* was not a watershed moment but, instead, initially a codification of practice across a range of policies. At a fundamental level, *Bakke* has provided educational institutions with the language to clearly articulate some of their most central goals and practices and has contributed to the discussion about the purpose and benefits of higher education and access to education at all levels, from elementary to graduate school. The *Bakke* rationale has also been used to develop and justify myriad supplemental programs and policies intended to expand access and equity for underrepresented students. Race-conscious scholarships, recruitment practices that attend to race, and summer bridge programs are but a few of the interventions that have made effective use of *Bakke*.

Timed to coincide with the 30th anniversary of the U.S. Supreme Court's 1978 *Regents of the University of California v. Bakke* decision, this edited volume explores the complex set of legal and educational policy circumstances established by this critical court decision that continue to simultaneously frame, narrow, and confound our understanding of affirmative action in higher education admissions specifically and issues of equity in education broadly. The book is guided by three frames: *Bakke*'s legal and philosophical lineage; the educational pipeline: past, present, and future; and policy and practice. Broadly described, the book provides a historical analysis of the legal and policy parameters defined and excluded by the 1978 *Bakke* decision and highlights the legal and social fissures that exist related to affirmative action and college admissions. Further, the volume discusses in detail the philosophical underpinnings of affirmative action as a catalyst for reaping the benefits of diversity, taking care to attend to how key policy levers (e.g., testing, financial aid) shape the pipeline of students flowing to colleges and influence the effects of affirmative action, regardless of definition. The book also takes on an understanding of how practices across institutional, state, and national levels have continued to respond to and challenge *Bakke,* especially in light of the 2003 *Gratz v. Bollinger* and *Grutter v. Bollinger* cases and the resulting politics of fear cultivated by key advocacy groups working to end race-conscious decision making.

The book begins with Angelo Ancheta's chapter, "*Bakke,* Antidiscrimination Jurisprudence, and the Trajectory of Affirmative Action Law," which provides an important legal lens through which to understand this historical case. As Ancheta describes, *Bakke* fundamentally established the legal framework that has been used to justify and implement affirmative action in higher education admissions for more than 30 years. But Ancheta also suggests that affirmative action was dealt a serious blow in *Bakke,* as societal discrimination was rejected by Justice Powell as a compelling interest, leaving the weaker version of diversity to carry the day. In the chapter by Michele Moses, "Can We Find Common Ground on Affirmative Action 30 Years After *Bakke?*," the affirmative action debate is presented as an example of an enduring moral disagreement. In that context, Moses explores why this disagreement has persisted and whether it is possible to find a middle ground upon which to create policy that upholds the spirit of *Bakke.* Moses concludes that, building on several basic shared ideals, there may be at least opportunity for dialogue and understanding between those who support and oppose affirmative action.

The next section of the book examines the educational pipeline through which students flow toward and through higher education. It begins with John Yun and Chungmei Lee's chapter, "O'Connor's Claim: The Educational Pipeline and *Bakke.*" These authors examine the feasibility of achieving Justice O'Connor's goal of eliminating the need for affirmative action by 2028 (25 years after *Grutter* and 50 after *Bakke*) by considering the progress that has been made in narrowing the educational achievement gap. Their findings that students are more racially isolated now than they were during the immediate aftermath of *Bakke* and that resources and educational outcomes remain starkly different among White, Black, and Latino students suggests that there should be a tempered approach to ending the ability of colleges and universities to use race-conscious means to create their diverse learning environments.

Using O'Connor's suggestion that an improved elementary and secondary pipeline may eliminate the need for affirmative action in college admissions by 2028, Donald Heller's work in "Educational Attainment in the States: Are We Progressing Toward Equity in 2028?" demonstrates that there are currently large differences in the rates at which White, Black, and Latino students navigate through the educational pipeline toward completion of a baccalaureate degree. Heller's study further emphasizes the fact that the effects of leakage from the educational pipeline are cumulative. When a student leaves the standard path toward BA completion, it is incredibly difficult to resume that journey later in life, a particularly troubling conclusion in the context of O'Connor's 25-year sunset clause.

Michal Kurlaender and Erika Felts extend the work in Heller's chapter by reminding us that to the extent that *Bakke* sought to preserve the ability of colleges and universities to diversify their student bodies for both short- and long-term benefits, its lasting impact must be evaluated beyond the college door. Although discussion about affirmative action in education for the past 30 years has been largely around issues of access to college for underrepresented groups, *Bakke* also offers important commentary on the role of a diverse student body to post-admission outcomes. The chapter, "*Bakke* Beyond College Access: Investigating Racial/Ethnic Differences in College Completion," descriptively considers in detail patterns of college completion during the last three decades.

Catherine Horn and John Yun open the final section of the book, "Policy and Practice," with their chapter, "Is 1500 the New 1280? The SAT and Admissions Since *Bakke*." Their work analyzes the changing significance of standardized testing policies, particularly the use of the SAT, on applicant pools at elite colleges since *Bakke*. Horn and Yun's work highlights the complex role of testing in the creation of elite and diverse campuses and suggests that this dichotomy of high academic standards and the creation of a campus that reaps the educational benefits of diversity is a false one. Horn and Yun conclude with the argument that institutions need to move toward (or return to) a reconceptualization of merit. William Kidder extends the consideration of admission policy with the work presented in his chapter, "*Bakke* at 30: A History of Affirmative Action in U.S. Law Schools." His review of the history of law school affirmative action leading up to *Bakke* and during the three decades subsequent illuminates how important, yet fragile, the forward-looking gains of affirmative action have been. Kidder documents a complex history of affirmative action in law school admission, and concludes that *Bakke*'s influence must be understood in the context of the changing demand and supply for a law school education and in relation to an evolving social, political, and legal environment.

Karen Miksch's chapter, "Institutional Decision Making and the Politics of Fear 30 Years After *Bakke*," documents the evolving role of the university general counsel and also the emergent politics of fear being cultivated by anti-affirmative action groups and through mainstream media outlets. Miksch notes that the increasingly legalized environment of higher education, and the concomitant expanding role of the general counsel's office, means that university attorneys are key actors in the affirmative action debate. Her chapter offers critical insight for campus administrators seeking to preserve institutional autonomy and avoid litigation. Miksch notes that collaboration between and among university attorneys, administrators, and academics may ultimately lead to better informed decisions regarding race-conscious policies and programs. Patricia Marin and Stella Flores conclude this section with "*Bakke* and State Policy: Exercising Institutional Autonomy to Maintain a Diverse Student Body." This chapter considers some of the external limits on an institution's academic freedom and what institutions have to or can do to creatively exercise their autonomy, within these existing parameters, to admit a diverse student body as per *Bakke*. In the current climate that is generally hostile to race-conscious policies, Marin and Flores argue that institutions interested in achieving the benefits of a diverse student body must act intentionally as policy evaluators as well as policy actors to successfully achieve their goals. We conclude the book with "The Future of *Bakke*," suggesting legal, social science, and policy efforts still needed to inform work on access and equity in higher education. The chapter challenges institutions to actively claim the rights granted to them under *Bakke* in their pursuit of equal opportunity.

Conclusion

The Supreme Court's 2003 *Grutter* decision upheld *Bakke*'s affirmation of diversity as a legally compelling interest. That decision did not, however, erase the multiplicity of voices still debating the fundamental issues of *Bakke;* the authors in this book capture that complexity. The benefits of diversity are not simply conceived. As racial divisions in the country are sharpening and as educational outcomes continue to be directly related to race and poverty, we believe that the research in this book helps inform the discussions and decisions by federal and state policymakers, educational providers, civil rights advocates, and other interested stakeholders to bring about the changes that lead to equal opportunity in postsecondary education. Ultimately, this book seeks to provide a vision for considerations of affirmative action in the 21st century.

    Bakke continues to serve as a touchstone for our understanding of racial equity in postsecondary education. Sadly, however, the disproportionate underrepresentation of minorities in higher education—especially at selective institutions—remains and must be attended to if, as the research suggests, attendance at and graduation from such institutions appreciably improves professional advancement (Bowen & Bok, 1998). The work found in this volume documents the continued inequities throughout the elementary, secondary, and postsecondary system, making the possibility of a strictly race-neutral admissions process that garners a racially and ethnically diverse student body unlikely. As Trent (1991) writes, "While the complexity of the problem of underrepresentation in higher education requires local, state and national efforts that exceed the scope of higher education, the efforts of the universities and colleges are crucial if not central" (p. 110). Perhaps the most direct and effective means of addressing this access and equity crisis within the higher education system is through the realization of *Bakke*'s legacy.

Note

1. Powell's conception of diversity was not simply defined by race and ethnicity, although much of how *Bakke* has been used has come under these auspices.

References

Association of American Medical Colleges. (2005). *Minorities in medical education: Facts and figures 2005.* Washington, DC: Author.

Bowen, W., & Bok, D. (1998). *The shape of the river: Long term consequences of considering race in college and university admissions.* Princeton, NJ: Princeton University Press.

Brown v. Board of Education of the City of Topeka, 347 U.S. 483 (1954).

Clegg, R. (1999). Racial and ethnic preferences in higher education. *Phi Kappa Phi Journal, 79*(1), 32–35.

Gratz v. Bollinger, 539 U.S. 244 (2003).

Greider, W. (1978, June 29). The scene: An hour of history, yes, but without the thunderclap. *The Washington Post*, p. A1.

Grutter v. Bollinger, 539 U.S. 306 (2003).

Hopwood v. Texas, 78 F.3d 932 (5th Cir.), *cert. denied,* 518 U.S. 1033 (1996).

Moses, Y. (1999). Race, higher education, and American society. *Journal of Anthropological Research, 55,* 265–277.

Regents of the University of California v. Bakke, 438 U.S. 265 (1978).

Trent, W. (1991). Student affirmative action in higher education: Addressing underrepresentation. In P. Altbach & K. Lomotey (Eds.), *The racial crisis in American higher education* (pp. 107–132). Albany: State University of New York Press.

PART ONE

BAKKE'S LEGAL AND PHILOSOPHICAL LINEAGE

2

BAKKE, ANTIDISCRIMINATION JURISPRUDENCE, AND THE TRAJECTORY OF AFFIRMATIVE ACTION LAW

Angelo N. Ancheta

The U.S. Supreme Court's famously divided decision in *Regents of the University of California v. Bakke* (1978) is a landmark case in constitutional history for a number of reasons. First, it established the fundamental legal framework that has been used to justify and implement affirmative action in higher education admissions for more than 30 years. Second, it shifted the course of the Supreme Court's case law on race-conscious legal remedies and public policies from one of general endorsement to one of increasing skepticism and disapproval. Third, its multiple opinions crystallized the longstanding and deep-seated conflict that has pervaded Supreme Court decision making in the area of race—the tension between norms that address inequality through policies that employ race and norms that seek to end discrimination through measures that are race-neutral and "colorblind."[1]

The controversy over race consciousness versus race neutrality at the heart of the affirmative action debate was not laid to rest by *Bakke,* or by *Grutter v. Bollinger* (2003), the Supreme Court case upholding race-conscious admissions at the University of Michigan. Nor is the controversy likely to be resolved in the near future. Debates are widespread and cover major sectors of law addressing racial inequality in American life. Even contemporary interpretations of *Brown v. Board of Education of the City of Topeka* (1954), hailed as the most defining court decision of the 20th century, reveal deeply contradictory perspectives on the role of race in the law, with some arguing that the integration ideal of *Brown* mandates race-conscious remedial action by government and others arguing that *Brown* requires an absolute bar on governmental considerations of race.

The *Bakke* case is central to understanding the history and trajectory of antidiscrimination law because it sits at the midpoint, both literally and figuratively, of the Supreme Court's modern jurisprudence on race, starting with *Brown* and moving forward to the present. This chapter offers a historical analysis of Supreme Court developments in affirmative action law, focusing on the central role of *Bakke* in setting the course for the Court's decisions during the last three decades. The first section of this chapter frames the debate about affirmative action in terms of competing norms in antidiscrimination jurisprudence—a contrast regarding what can be labeled *antisubordination* norms versus *anticlassification* norms. The next section examines how these norms are displayed in the multiple opinions of the *Bakke* case. The final section traces the development of post-*Bakke* affirmative action law, with special attention to the Court's decisions in its most recent higher education affirmative action cases, *Grutter v. Bollinger* (2003) and *Gratz v. Bollinger* (2003), and the Court's dividing lines in the K–12 educational case *Parents Involved in Community Schools v. Seattle School District No. 1* (2007).

Antidiscrimination Norms

Although affirmative action debates are often portrayed in rudimentary terms as tensions between race-conscious and colorblind policies or as disputes about labels such as "preferences" and "reverse discrimination," the issues are considerably more complex. The differences extend to disagreements about policy options and to questions of legal philosophy and jurisprudence, standards of constitutional interpretation, normative values of equality, and basic understandings of the role of race in American society (Edley, 1996). As major players in the field of affirmative action law, the courts are at the storm center of these debates, and the opinions of Supreme Court justices and judges of the lower courts inevitably reflect competing ideologies and policy preferences. Judges are not neutral arbiters when racial policies are at stake; they, like everyone else who ponders questions of racial justice in American society, have strong beliefs and predilections.

In their role as interpreters of the Constitution—in particular the meaning of the Equal Protection Clause of the Fourteenth Amendment—the courts are charged with establishing and applying legal tests to assess the constitutionality of affirmative action policies. Inevitably, judicial standards and the ultimate outcomes in litigation are determined not simply by relevant evidence and the specific facts of cases but by a set of underlying norms—a core antidiscrimination jurisprudence—that shapes judicial decision making. Although they can be phrased in different ways, the dominant norms that have influenced judicial decision making since *Bakke* can be divided into two basic categories: *anticlassification* norms and *antisubordination* norms (Balkin & Siegel, 2003; Siegel, 2004).

Anticlassification norms can be characterized by their emphasis on protecting individual rights and using the intentional and differential treatment of individuals as the primary measure of inequality (see table 2.1). According to these norms, the Equal Protection Clause exists to ensure formal equality, and race-conscious actions by the state, if not prohibited outright, are subject to the deepest skepticism by the courts. As a consequence, policies designed to benefit members of racial minority groups should be subject to the same standards and legal tests as are policies designed to harm members of racial

TABLE 2.1
Anticlassification vs. Antisubordination Norms

Anticlassification Norms	*Antisubordination Norms*
• Primacy of Individual Rights	• Recognition of Group-Based Rights
• Normative Race-Neutrality (Colorblindness)	• Tolerance for Race-Conscious Measures
• High Sensitivity to Burdens on Nonminorities	• Low Sensitivity to Burdens on Nonminorities
• Standards of Judicial Review Consistent Across Governmental Motives	• Different Standards of Review Based on Governmental Motives (Recognition of "Benign" vs. "Invidious" Classifications)
• Little or No Institutional Deference	• Deference Based on Context
• Remediation Limited to Identified and Specific Actors	• Remediation Extends to Systemic Discrimination and Broad Range of Institutions

minority groups. The mere act of racial classification, regardless of the under-lying motives of the state actors, makes a public policy presumptively uncon-stitutional. Justifications for race-conscious policies are, thus, rare; aside from specific remedies for fully documented discrimination by a particular public institution, very few governmental interests are sufficiently important to jus-tify the use of race.

Antisubordination norms, on the other hand, view the Equal Protection Clause as more protective of minority rights, offering a greater tolerance for group-based remedies and the use of race to address multiple forms of racial inequality and subordination (see table 2.1). Unintentional harms by the state that result in disparate effects on racial minorities are cognizable injuries that should be redressed under the law, and motives, when considered, are subject to differential standards based on whether they benefit or burden racial minority groups. Like anticlassification norms, antisubordination norms propose that policies that subjugate and exclude minorities should be presumptively unconstitutional, but inclusive policies designed to promote greater opportunities for minorities should be subject to reduced judicial scrutiny. Deference to important institutions becomes acceptable when con-sidering the constitutionality of policies designed to promote inclusion, and a range of state interests beyond remediation by a single institution can jus-tify race-conscious policies. And, although the burdens that may fall on non-minorities because of race-conscious policies are not irrelevant in constitutional inquiries, the benefits and costs weighed in the legal calculus tilt more strongly in favor of protecting minority rights.

There are, of course, both strong and weak versions of these norms, with strong forms of anticlassification leading to an almost automatic disapproval of race-conscious policies (the exceptions being court-ordered remedies for clear violations of constitutional or statutory rights), and strong versions of antisubordination showing tolerance for policies such as minority set-aside programs. Weaker versions of each norm may lead to convergence and agree-ment on a particular set of facts—for instance, both a modest anticlassifica-tion norm and a modest antisubordination norm might lead judges to agree that limited uses of race in a competitive selection process designed to pro-mote diversity would be constitutionally acceptable.

The multiple opinions in *Bakke* are classic illustrations of the tension between anticlassification and antisubordination norms, and the *Bakke* rul-ing itself set the basic trajectory of the Supreme Court's three decades of

affirmative action jurisprudence—a jurisprudence that continues to dominate judicial decisions in the area of racial justice.

The *Bakke* Opinions

The *Bakke* case is renowned for its fragmented decision and its multiple
opinions.[2] Justice Lewis Powell was joined by Justices William Brennan,
Byron White, Thurgood Marshall, and Harry Blackmun to uphold the prospective use of race in higher education admissions, but was joined by Chief
Justice Warren Burger and Justices John Paul Stevens, Potter Stewart, and
William Rehnquist to strike down the particular minority set-aside program
at the medical school of the University of California, Davis—a program that
limited competition for 16 out of 100 seats in the entering class to disadvantaged minority students. Although a "plus-factor" admissions program such
as those debated in the University of Michigan cases was not before the
Court, Justice Powell's controlling opinion proposed that an admissions program that employed race as a plus-factor among several factors in choosing
an educationally diverse—and not merely racially diverse—student body
would satisfy strict judicial scrutiny.

The importance of Justice Powell's opinion in articulating the diversity
rationale for race-conscious admissions cannot be gainsaid. The Powell opinion set the basic framework for selective university admissions programs
throughout the country through the 1990s, and the Supreme Court's 2003
decision in *Grutter* reaffirmed the Powell opinion as constitutional canon.
But the division among the justices in *Bakke* is just as important as the
Powell opinion in understanding how competing norms have affected Supreme Court case law and the justices' votes in affirmative action cases since
Bakke.

Antisubordination and the Brennan Opinion

The Brennan bloc would have upheld the UC Davis medical school admissions policy under the Equal Protection Clause. Justice Brennan's constitutional analysis proceeded in two steps, both of which illuminate his reliance
on antisubordination rather than anticlassification norms. First, he concluded that the standard of review applicable to race-conscious affirmative
action programs, although careful and searching, did not have to be strict
scrutiny—the standard that had been applied to governmental policies that

employed race to exclude minorities from participation in public life. Second, he concluded under this more relaxed standard that the Davis policy was justified by a sufficiently important interest in addressing the effects of past discrimination in society; moreover, the policy did not stigmatize or overburden any particular group.

Standard of Review: Intermediate Scrutiny

In articulating the standard of review to assess the Davis program, Justice Brennan navigated a course between strict scrutiny and rationality review, the far more deferential standard of review employed when assessing most economic and social legislation. Justice Brennan concluded that rationality review, which requires only that a policy bear some rational relationship to a legitimate interest, was inapplicable because "The mere recitation of a benign, compensatory purpose is not an automatic shield which protects against any inquiry into the actual purposes underlying a statutory scheme" (*Bakke,* 1978, p. 358–359). But strict scrutiny was equally inapplicable because of the lack of stigma associated with the program; Whites as a class had not been saddled with the same disabilities associated with discrimination against minorities, nor had they been "subjected to such a history of purposeful unequal treatment, or relegated to such a position of political powerlessness as to command extraordinary protection from the majoritarian political process" (p. 357).

Instead, Justice Brennan articulated an intermediate standard of review, borrowing from the Court's equal protection case law in the areas of gender discrimination and discrimination against illegitimate children. Race, like the other categories, had been "inexcusably utilized to stereotype and stigmatize politically powerless segments of society" and affirmative action programs could present a risk of stigma because "they may promote racial separatism and reinforce the views of those who believe that members of racial minorities are inherently incapable of succeeding on their own." In addition, race is "an immutable characteristic which its possessors are powerless to escape or set aside" (*Bakke,* 1978, p. 360).

The appropriate test for Justice Brennan was, therefore, one that required an interest to be important—but not "compelling," as required under strict scrutiny—and one that avoided the harms of stereotyping and stigma:

> Because of the significant risk that racial classifications established for ostensibly benign purposes can be misused, causing effects not unlike those

created by invidious classifications, it is inappropriate to inquire only whether there is any conceivable basis that might sustain such a classification. Instead, to justify such a classification an important and articulated purpose for its use must be shown. In addition, any statute must be stricken that stigmatizes any group or that singles out those least well represented in the political process to bear the brunt of a benign program. (*Bakke,* 1978, p. 361)

Justice Brennan thus concluded that programs that had been designed to promote inclusion rather than subordination—including the subordination of Whites—could pass constitutional muster under a more lenient equal protection test.

Satisfying Intermediate Scrutiny

Employing intermediate scrutiny, Justice Brennan concluded that the Davis program did indeed advance an important interest and did not stigmatize any individual or group. Justice Brennan relied on school desegregation and employment discrimination case law, as well as empirical data on the underrepresentation of minorities in medicine, and fully accepted the university's interest in remedying societal discrimination:

Davis' articulated purpose of remedying the effects of past societal discrimination is, under our cases, sufficiently important to justify the use of race-conscious admissions programs where there is a sound basis for concluding that minority underrepresentation is substantial and chronic, and that the handicap of past discrimination is impeding access of minorities to the Medical School. (*Bakke,* 1978, p. 362)

Moreover, neither Allan Bakke, the plaintiff, as an individual nor Whites as a group had suffered any stigma because of the program:

Unlike discrimination against racial minorities, the use of racial preferences for remedial purposes does not inflict a pervasive injury upon individual whites in the sense that wherever they go or whatever they do there is a significant likelihood that they will be treated as second-class citizens because of their color. This distinction does not mean that the exclusion of a white resulting from the preferential use of race is not sufficiently serious to require justification; but it does mean that the injury inflicted by such a policy is not distinguishable from disadvantages caused by a wide range of government actions, none of which has ever been thought impermissible for that reason alone. (*Bakke,* 1978, p. 375)

The Davis program was reasonable in light of its objectives, did not equate minority status with disadvantage, and did not necessarily violate the Constitution because it set aside a predetermined number of seats for disadvantaged minority students. A set-aside program was not distinct in a constitutional sense from a plus-factor program, Justice Brennan argued, because both programs afforded special consideration to minority applicants that could result in the exclusion of a White student.

Antisubordination and the Marshall and Blackmun Opinions

Justice Marshall concurred with Justice Brennan, but wrote separately to express his fear that the Court had come "full circle" (*Bakke,* 1978, p. 402) since the passage of the Fourteenth Amendment, the judicial curtailing of Reconstruction-era rights, the Jim Crow decades of segregation, the Court's desegregation decision in *Brown,* and the era of affirmative action to erect new constitutional barriers to equality for minorities. Drawing on both the social and legal history of African Americans in the United States, Justice Marshall's opinion stated,

> For it must be remembered that, during most of the past 200 years, the Constitution as interpreted by this Court did not prohibit the most ingenious and pervasive forms of discrimination against the Negro. Now, when a State acts to remedy the effects of that legacy of discrimination, I cannot believe that this same Constitution stands as a barrier. (*Bakke,* 1978, p. 387)

Reflecting a strong antisubordination stance, Justice Marshall went on to state,

> It is more than a little ironic that, after several hundred years of class-based discrimination against Negroes, the Court is unwilling to hold that a class-based remedy for that discrimination is permissible. In declining to so hold, today's judgment ignores the fact that for several hundred years Negroes have been discriminated against, not as individuals, but rather solely because of the color of their skins. It is unnecessary in 20th-century America to have individual Negroes demonstrate that they have been victims of racial discrimination; the racism of our society has been so pervasive

that none, regardless of wealth or position, has managed to escape its impact. (p. 400)

Justice Blackmun's opinion reflects similarly strong antisubordination currents in his treatment of equal protection jurisprudence. Reacting to Justice Powell's view that the Fourteenth Amendment had expanded beyond its original concept of guaranteeing equal citizenship to African Americans to include broader principles that might ban affirmative action, Justice Blackmun wrote,

> This enlargement does not mean for me, however, that the Fourteenth Amendment has broken away from its moorings and its original intended purposes. Those original aims persist. And that, in a distinct sense, is what "affirmative action," in the face of proper facts, is all about. (p. 405)

Justice Blackmun then went on to state the need to address past discrimination:

> In order to get beyond racism, we must first take account of race. There is no other way. And in order to treat some persons equally, we must treat them differently. We cannot—we dare not—let the Equal Protection Clause perpetuate racial supremacy. (p. 407)

Anticlassification and the Stevens Opinion

Justice Stevens, joined by Chief Justice Burger and Justices Stewart and Rehnquist, agreed with Justice Powell that the medical school admissions policy at the University of California, Davis was illegal, but relied solely on a federal statute—Title VI of the Civil Rights of 1964—to invalidate the program and did not reach the question of what standard of review should be used in assessing the program under the Equal Protection Clause. His analysis, while limited to statutory interpretation, reflects anticlassification norms of formal equality, individualized rights to equal treatment under the law, and colorblindness.

Title VI states in part, "No person in the United States shall, on the ground of race, color, or national origin, be excluded from participation in, be denied the benefits of, or be subjected to discrimination under any program or activity receiving Federal financial assistance" (42 U.S.C. § 2000d). While Justice Stevens declined to rule on the doctrinal question of whether

Title VI and the Fourteenth Amendment were coextensive—that their prohibitions were identical—he argued that "the proponents of Title VI assumed that the Constitution itself required a colorblind standard on the part of government" (*Bakke,* 1978, p. 416).

Legislative history, according to Justice Stevens, revealed that Congress' "answer to the problem of federal funding of segregated facilities stands as a broad prohibition against the exclusion of any individual from a federally funded program 'on the ground of race'" (p. 413). Quoting from the legislative record, Justice Stevens wrote,

> The word "discrimination" has been used in many a court case. What it really means in the bill is a distinction in treatment . . . given to different individuals because of their different race, religion or national origin. . . .
>
> The answer to this question [what was meant by "discrimination"] is that if race is not a factor, we do not have to worry about discrimination because of race. . . . The Internal Revenue Code does not provide that colored people do not have to pay taxes, or that they can pay their taxes 6 months later than everyone else.
>
> If we started to treat Americans as Americans, not as fat ones, thin ones, short ones, tall ones, brown ones, green ones, yellow ones, or white ones, but as Americans. If we did that we would not need to worry about discrimination. (p. 415)

Thus, for Justice Stevens, colorblindness and proscriptions on individual differential treatment emerged as primary values under Title VI—and by inference the Equal Protection Clause. Taking a literal approach to Title VI's prohibitions, the Stevens bloc voted to strike down the Davis admissions program: "The University, through its special admissions policy, excluded Bakke from participation in its program of medical education because of his race. . . . The plain language of the statute therefore requires affirmance of the judgment below" (p. 412). Although Bakke had not been prohibited from applying and being admitted to the medical school—the other 84 seats in the class remained available to him—exclusion from the 16 minority-reserved slots was sufficient to cause a Title VI violation.

Justice Stevens' analysis of Title VI commanded only four votes, and both Justice Brennan and Justice Powell argued that Title VI was indeed coextensive with the Equal Protection Clause—although Justices Brennan and Powell disagreed about what would be permissible under the Equal Protection Clause. The Stevens opinion is considerably briefer than the Powell and Brennan opinions, but its analysis of a major federal antidiscrimination statute is revealing nonetheless: colorblindness and formal equality emerge as dominant standards in antidiscrimination law, and the burdens of racial classification are magnified through a focus on individuals rather than groups or institutions.

Anticlassification and the Powell Opinion

Justice Powell's opinion in *Bakke* has been enshrined in constitutional law and educational policy making—as well as in popular culture—as a Solomonic middle ground between the Brennan and Stevens blocs. Over time, the diversity rationale has become undeniably important, embraced not only in higher education but in the public and private employment sectors as well; without question, the gains in minority participation achieved through diversity programs have been widespread and meaningful. But Justice Powell's opinion, despite its endorsement of diversity and race as a plus-factor, is strongly animated by anticlassification values. Strict scrutiny is Justice Powell's standard for analyzing racial classifications, and notions of minority inclusion and social justice are watered down by his reliance on *educational* diversity, not racial diversity, to justify race-conscious admissions. Only the special context of higher education and its attendant academic freedoms lead him in *Bakke* to create an exception to a general prohibition on racial classifications.

Individual Rights and the Standard of Review

Both the legal analysis and rhetoric of Justice Powell's opinion are illuminating. In addressing the nature of rights under the Equal Protection Clause, Justice Powell states,

> It is settled beyond question that the "rights created by the first section of the Fourteenth Amendment are, by its terms, guaranteed to the individual. The rights established are personal rights." . . . The guarantee of equal protection cannot mean one thing when applied to one individual and something else when applied to a person of another color. If both are not accorded the same protection, then it is not equal. (*Bakke*, 1978, p. 289)

Stating, "The clock of our liberties . . . cannot be turned back to 1868" (p. 295) and to the original intent of the Fourteenth Amendment, Justice Powell goes on to conclude there is no fundamental difference between "invidious" and "benign" racial classifications:

> *All* state-imposed classifications that rearrange burdens and benefits on the basis of race are likely to be viewed with deep resentment by the individuals burdened. The denial to innocent persons of equal rights and opportunities may outrage those so deprived and therefore may be perceived as invidious. (p. 295)

Addressing the question of what standard of review should apply to race-conscious affirmative action programs, Justice Powell's opinion states, "Once the artificial line of a 'two-class theory' of the Fourteenth Amendment is put aside, the difficulties entailed in varying the level of judicial review according to a perceived 'preferred' status of a particular racial or ethnic minority are intractable" (p. 295). Racial preferences, according to Justice Powell, are not always clearly benign, may reinforce stereotypes that certain groups are unable to achieve success without special protection, and can force innocent persons to bear the burdens of redressing grievances that were not of their making. Therefore, strict scrutiny necessarily applies to race-conscious affirmative action programs as well.

Strict Scrutiny and Admissions Programs

Applying strict scrutiny by requiring a highly substantial interest and a necessary means to advance that interest, Justice Powell recognized four goals of the program—(1) reducing the historic deficit of minorities in medical schools and the medical profession, (2) countering the effects of societal discrimination, (3) increasing the number of doctors who will serve in underserved communities, and (4) obtaining the educational benefits of a racially and ethnically diverse student body. He then rejected the first three, while accepting, with an important modification, the diversity rationale as sufficiently important.

Under Justice Powell's reasoning, reducing the deficit of minority physicians is a facially invalid goal because it establishes a specified percentage of minority students simply for its own sake. Societal discrimination, unlike identified discrimination against a particular actor, is "an amorphous concept of injury that may be ageless in its reach into the past" (p. 306), and "To hold otherwise would be to convert a remedy heretofore reserved for violations of legal rights into a privilege that all institutions throughout the

Nation could grant at their pleasure to whatever groups are perceived as victims of societal discrimination" (p. 310). And Justice Powell found virtually no evidence in the record that could justify the university's use of its special admissions program to promote better health care among underserved citizens.

Educational Diversity

Although the university's diversity rationale focused on racial and ethnic diversity, Justice Powell made clear that "ethnic diversity . . . is only one element in a range of factors a university properly may consider in attaining the goal of a heterogeneous student body" (p. 314). Thus, the rationale that he found to be constitutionally permissible is a broader diversity that encompasses factors such as race, ethnicity, geography, and cultural advantage or disadvantage, and is tied to "The freedom of a university to make its own judgments as to education [and] the selection of its student body" (*Bakke,* 1978, p. 312). Supported by the First Amendment interest in academic freedom, a university must be "accorded the right to select those students who will contribute the most to the 'robust exchange of ideas'" (p. 313).

However, in assessing whether the Davis program was necessary to advance its interest in diversity, Justice Powell rejected the program, which he concluded "focused *solely* on ethnic diversity," and "would hinder rather than further attainment of genuine diversity" (p. 315). Turning to an example of a permissible policy—the Harvard College admissions policy that had been detailed in an *amicus curiae* brief before the Court—Justice Powell concluded that race or ethnicity could be used as a plus factor, along with other factors such as geography, personal talents, experience, leadership potential, or a history of overcoming disadvantage. Such a policy would treat applicants as individuals and not insulate them from comparison with other applicants.

Summarizing his position and relying heavily on anticlassification norms, Justice Powell concluded,

> The fatal flaw in petitioner's preferential program is its disregard of individual rights as guaranteed by the Fourteenth Amendment. . . . Such rights are not absolute. But when a State's distribution of benefits or imposition of burdens hinges on ancestry or the color of a person's skin, that individual is entitled to a demonstration that the challenged classification is necessary to promote a substantial state interest. Petitioner has failed to carry this burden. (p. 320)

The Powell opinion thus laid the groundwork for major shifts in the law of racial discrimination and affirmative action. Diversity in higher education became an acceptable state interest and opened the door in theory to forward-looking interests designed to promote important social goals, rather than simply redressing past injuries. But affirmative action was dealt a serious blow in *Bakke,* one from which it has never recovered. Societal discrimination, despite its powerful effects on opportunities for minority advancement, was rejected by Justice Powell as a compelling interest, and a watered-down version of diversity was enshrined as a talisman for affirmative action policy making.

The Supreme Court and Post-*Bakke* Affirmative Action Law

Although the Supreme Court has struggled with affirmative action law in the decades since *Bakke*—with inconsistent case law emerging during the 1980s and early 1990s because of shifting alignments among the justices—anticlassification jurisprudence now dominates Supreme Court decision making. Recent cases have confirmed that strict scrutiny applies to all race-conscious affirmative action programs, regardless of the level of government or the underlying motives of state institutions. Antisubordination norms still emerge in leading decisions, but the recent composition of the Court has led to the adoption of a strong anticlassification jurisprudence and the relegation of antisubordination norms largely to dissenting opinions. The latest Supreme Court opinion involving voluntary school desegregation policies shows that a near-majority of the Court now endorses a virtual zero-tolerance approach to race-conscious policies, and sees Justice Powell's *Bakke* opinion (and its reaffirmation in *Grutter*), as a unique exception to a general prohibition on race-conscious policies.

Case Law in the 1980s and 1990s

A comprehensive review of the Supreme Court's affirmative action case law is beyond the scope of this chapter, but even a cursory survey of the leading equal protection cases demonstrates the tension between the two antidiscrimination norms and the increasing entrenchment of anticlassification jurisprudence. For example, in *Wygant v. Jackson Board of Education* (1986), the Court ruled by a 5–4 vote that a race-conscious policy in a public school teachers' collective bargaining agreement designed to protect minority teachers from layoffs—and to preserve the integrity of an earlier affirmative action plan—violated the Equal Protection Clause. Writing for a plurality that included Chief Justice Burger and Justices Rehnquist and Sandra Day O'Connor (Justice White concurred in the judgment but did not join any other opinion), Justice Powell concluded, "The level of scrutiny does not change merely because the challenged classification operates against a group that historically has not been subject to governmental discrimination" (*Wygant,* 1986, p. 273) and applied strict scrutiny to strike down the policy. In doing so, he rejected both the interest in addressing societal discrimination and the interest in providing teacher role models for students; he further concluded that the policy was not narrowly tailored because it imposed too heavy a burden—layoff from work—on nonminority teachers.

Writing in dissent, Justice Marshall, joined by Justices Brennan and Blackmun, concluded that the challenged plan would satisfy any level of scrutiny, including strict scrutiny, because the state interest in "preserving the integrity of a valid hiring policy—which in turn sought to achieve diversity and stability for the benefit of *all* students—was sufficient, in this case, to satisfy the demands of the Constitution" (p. 306). Moreover, no alternative would have attained the stated goal in a narrower or more equitable fashion. Justice Stevens, also dissenting, stated, "Race is not always irrelevant to sound governmental decisionmaking," (p. 314) and

> In the context of public education, it is quite obvious that a school board may reasonably conclude that an integrated faculty will be able to provide benefits to the student body that could not be provided by an all-white, or nearly all-white faculty. (p. 315)

He added,

> There is . . . a critical difference between a decision to *exclude* a member of a minority race because of his or her skin color and a decision to *include* more members of the minority in a school faculty for that reason. . . . The inclusionary decision is consistent with the principle that all men are created equal; the exclusionary decision is at war with that principle. (p. 316)

Yet, the outcome of affirmative action cases during the 1980s and early 1990s was far from predictable. In two cases, *Fullilove v. Klutznick* (1980) and

Metro Broadcasting, Inc. v. Federal Communications Commission (1990), the Court upheld affirmative action programs where federal powers were traceable directly or indirectly to Congress. In *Fullilove,* the Court by a 6–3 vote rejected a constitutional challenge to a congressional set-aside program designed to benefit minority contractors. Chief Justice Burger, joined by Justices White and Powell, concluded that the program satisfied either intermediate or strict scrutiny because it was rooted in Congress' special powers; Justice Marshall, joined by Justice Brennan and Blackmun, urged an intermediate standard of review but also concluded that the program would readily satisfy strict scrutiny. Dissenting Justices Stewart, Rehnquist, and Stevens argued, however, that colorblindness was the overarching norm of the Equal Protection Clause, and that "the government may never act to the detriment of a person solely because of that person's race" (*Fullilove,* 1980, p. 525).

In *Metro Broadcasting,* the Court by a 5–4 vote upheld two FCC plans designed to increase opportunities for minorities in the awarding of radio and television broadcast licenses. Writing for the majority, Justice Brennan held that the plans were mandated by Congress and that deference should be granted because of congressional powers; accordingly, an intermediate standard of review was appropriate. Justice Brennan concluded that the plans were substantially related to the important interest in promoting the diversity of broadcast viewpoints. Justice O'Connor, joined by Justices Rehnquist, Antonin Scalia, and Anthony Kennedy, dissented and argued that both congressional and state racial classifications should be subject to strict scrutiny; the FCC plans failed strict scrutiny because broadcast diversity was "simply too amorphous, too insubstantial, and too unrelated to any legitimate basis for employing racial classifications" (*Metro Broadcasting,* 1990, p. 612).

The Supreme Court also upheld affirmative action policies in the 1980s where the lower courts were exercising their powers to remedy severe racial discrimination. In *Local 28, Sheet Metal Workers International Association v. Equal Employment Opportunity Commission* (1986), the Court by a 5–4 vote upheld a lower court's efforts to require an intransigent union that had engaged in long-standing discrimination to remedy its discrimination through hiring goals and other measures. And in *United States v. Paradise* (1987), the Court by a 5–4 vote upheld a court-ordered plan that included hiring and promotions quotas designed to remedy extensive discrimination in the Alabama Department of Public Safety. In both *Local 28* and *Paradise,* the Court could not settle on a standard of review, but the plurality opinions in each would have upheld the programs under even strict scrutiny.

In 1989, the Court in *City of Richmond v. J.A. Croson Company* settled the basic question of what standard of review should apply to state and local affirmative action policies. In a 6–3 decision, the Court struck down a minority set-aside program in municipal contracting, with five justices agreeing that strict scrutiny was the appropriate standard of review. The *Croson* Court ruled that the City of Richmond had made inadequate findings of its own past discrimination to justify a remedial plan, and the set-aside program was not narrowly tailored to an interest in remedying the City's past discrimination. Although Justice O'Connor's opinion made clear that a municipality could have compelling interest in remedying the effects of its past discrimination, a "strong basis in evidence" would be necessary, and the City of Richmond had failed to satisfy that standard.

Writing in dissent, Justice Marshall, joined by Justices Brennan and Blackmun, proposed that the Court's decision marked "a deliberate and giant step backward in this Court's affirmative-action jurisprudence" (*Croson*, 1989, p. 529) and criticized the adoption of the strict scrutiny standard in no uncertain terms:

> In concluding that remedial classifications warrant no different standard of review under the Constitution than the most brutal and repugnant forms of state-sponsored racism, a majority of this Court signals that it regards racial discrimination as largely a phenomenon of the past. (p. 553)

Instead, intermediate scrutiny was the appropriate standard of review and the City of Richmond had easily satisfied it.

Six years later, in *Adarand Constructors, Inc. v. Peña* (1995), the Court by a 5–4 vote extended strict scrutiny to *all* racial classifications, including ones by Congress, and effectively overruled *Metro Broadcasting*. In *Adarand*, Justice O'Connor announced three fundamental propositions to govern racial classifications: (1) *skepticism*: meaning that racial classifications are inherently suspect and must be subject to strict scrutiny; (2) *consistency*: meaning that equal protection principles applied to all classifications regardless of motive—invidious or benign—and regardless of the group affected; and (3) *congruence*: meaning that strict scrutiny applied to all levels of government, whether to state and local government through the Fourteenth Amendment or to the federal government via the due process clause of the Fifth Amendment.

The anticlassification norms of the majority opinion were further reinforced by concurring opinions in *Adarand*. Justice Scalia, for instance, offered a quintessential statement of colorblindness: "In the eyes of government, we are just one race here. It is American" (*Adarand*, 1995, p. 239). Similarly, Justice Clarence Thomas in his concurring opinion wrote, "In my mind, government-sponsored racial discrimination based on benign prejudice is just as noxious as discrimination inspired by malicious prejudice. In each instance, it is racial discrimination, plain and simple" (p. 241).

The *Adarand* dissenters, on the other hand, employed antisubordination reasoning to support arguments for a lower standard of review. For example, Justice Stevens, joined by Justice Ruth Bader Ginsburg, stated,

> The Court's concept of "consistency" assumes that there is no significant difference between a decision by the majority to impose a special burden on the members of a minority race and a decision by the majority to provide a benefit to certain members of that minority notwithstanding its incidental burden on some members of the majority. In my opinion that assumption is untenable. There is no moral or constitutional equivalence between a policy that is designed to perpetuate a caste system and one that seeks to eradicate racial subordination. (*Adarand*, 1995, p. 243)

He added, "The consistency that the Court espouses would disregard the difference between a 'No Trespassing Sign' and a welcome mat. . . . An interest in 'consistency' does not justify treating differences as though they were similarities" (p. 245).

Although the Court's major affirmative action cases during the 1980s and 1990s did not address higher education admissions, the Court made clear by the time of its *Adarand* ruling that strict scrutiny would have to be applied to all racial classifications, even those involving key governmental institutions such as Congress and even when goals and policies implicated other constitutional interests, such as academic freedom under the First Amendment. Because of the intervening case law between *Bakke* and *Adarand*, the courts were increasingly skeptical of affirmative action policies, but the Supreme Court's revisiting of the diversity rationale in its most recent affirmative action cases has shown that affirmative action is surviving, although it may have a life that ultimately survives in only particular environments and with certain preconditions.

Recent Cases

The Supreme Court's most recent higher education affirmative action decisions in *Grutter v. Bollinger* (2003) and *Gratz v. Bollinger* (2003), as well as its voluntary school desegregation ruling in *Parents Involved in Community Schools v. Seattle School District No. 1* (2007), further demonstrate the tension between anticlassification and antisubordination norms and the ascendancy of anticlassification jurisprudence.

Grutter *and* Gratz

Because post-*Bakke* case law had cast increasing doubt on the legality of affirmative action policies, the Supreme Court revisited the question of whether diversity-based admissions policies in higher education were constitutional.[3] The Court, by a 5–4 vote in *Grutter,* upheld a race-conscious admissions policy at the University of Michigan's law school that paralleled the Harvard undergraduate admissions policy cited by Justice Powell in *Bakke.* In doing so, Justice O'Connor's majority opinion reaffirmed the basic conclusions of Justice Powell that academic freedom provided a special basis for colleges and universities to advance an interest in obtaining diverse student bodies. However, in *Gratz,* decided by a 6–3 vote, the Court struck down a University of Michigan undergraduate admissions policy that employed a numerical point system and granted automatic points to members of underrepresented minority groups; such a system, the Court ruled, was overly mechanical and lacked the flexibility to be narrowly tailored to the interest in diversity.

The Court employed strict scrutiny in both cases, but Justice O'Connor's opinion in *Grutter* emphasized the importance of context, so that her version of strict scrutiny was considerably more deferential than the strict scrutiny employed in earlier cases such as *Croson.* Justice O'Connor underscored that the university's interests in academic freedom required a more relaxed evaluation of its diversity interest, and she deferred in *Grutter* to the law school's good faith actions in satisfying the narrow tailoring requirements of strict scrutiny. As a consequence, anticlassificationist norms were especially strong in the dissenting opinions in *Grutter.* Justice Rehnquist, writing for himself and Justices Scalia, Kennedy, and Thomas, stated, "The

Court, in an unprecedented display of deference under our strict scrutiny analysis, upholds the Law School's program despite its obvious flaws" (*Grutter,* 2003, p. 387). Justice Thomas added in his dissent,

> The Constitution abhors classifications based on race, not only because those classifications can harm favored races or are based on illegitimate motives, but also because every time the government places citizens on racial registers and makes race relevant to the provision of burdens or benefits, it demeans us all. (p. 353)

And Justice Scalia's dissent concluded, "The Constitution proscribes government discrimination on the basis of race, and state-provided education is no exception" (p. 349).

In contrast, antisubordination norms were advanced in dissenting opinions of the *Gratz* case. For instance, Justice Ginsburg wrote,

> Our jurisprudence ranks race a "suspect" category, "not because [race] is inevitably an impermissible classification, but because it is one which usually, to our national shame, has been drawn for the purpose of maintaining racial inequality." . . . But where race is considered "for the purpose of achieving equality," . . . no automatic proscription is in order. (*Gratz,* 2003, p. 301)

Justice Stephen Breyer, although concurring in the *Gratz* judgment, added,

> In implementing the Constitution's equality instruction, government decisionmakers may properly distinguish between policies of inclusion and exclusion, . . . for the former are more likely to prove consistent with the basic constitutional obligation that the law respect each individual equally. (p. 282)

Parents Involved in Community Schools

The *Parents Involved* case did not address an affirmative action plan, but the Court relied on affirmative action case law to address the constitutionality of voluntary desegregation plans, which were designed to promote racial diversity and to avoid racial isolation and resegregation, in Seattle, Washington, and Jefferson County, Kentucky.[4] All of the justices agreed that *Grutter* was still good law, but the Court limited *Grutter*'s applicability to K–12 education by stressing the uniqueness of higher education and the absence of academic freedom interests in elementary and secondary education.

Applying strict scrutiny, the Court by a 5–4 vote struck down the voluntary plans on narrow tailoring grounds. The Court concluded that the racial classifications employed in each of the school districts were not necessary to advance their asserted interests, and that the districts had not adequately considered race-neutral alternative policies. A plurality composed of Chief Justice John Roberts and Justices Scalia, Thomas, and Samuel Alito also rejected the school districts' compelling interest arguments, proposing that they were simply interests in "racial balancing"—seeking racial proportionality for its own sake. But Justice Kennedy, who cast the fifth vote to strike down the plans, disagreed fundamentally with this argument and found the interests in avoiding racial isolation and promoting educational diversity (paralleling the higher education diversity interest) to be compelling.

Although the *Parents Involved* case imposes serious limits on the ability of school districts to advance desegregation goals voluntarily, the case is perhaps most remarkable for the extraordinary contrasts in antidiscrimination jurisprudence advanced by Chief Justice Roberts' plurality bloc and the remaining justices. Indeed, their differences run to the very core of the Equal Protection Clause and the legacy of *Brown,* revealing contrasting visions of racial integration that reflect individual rights and colorblindness on one hand and group-based rights and race-conscious remediation on the other.

In his plurality opinion, Chief Justice Roberts proposed an especially strong anticlassification interpretation of *Brown,* arguing, "It was not the inequality of the facilities but the fact of legally separating children on the basis of race on which the Court relied to find a constitutional violation in 1954" (*Parents Involved,* 2007, p. 2767). In determining which side is "more faithful to the heritage of *Brown*" (p. 2767), Chief Justice Roberts's opinion went on to quote the *Brown* plaintiffs' brief, which stated in part that the Fourteenth Amendment prohibits differential treatment on the basis of children's color or race, and to quote from the oral argument of Robert L. Carter, who argued for the *Brown* plaintiffs, to suggest that "no State has any authority under the equal-protection clause of the Fourteenth Amendment to use race as a factor in affording educational opportunities among its citizens" (pp. 2767–2768).

Equating *Brown* with the Seattle and Jefferson County litigation, the Chief Justice's opinion continued,

> Before *Brown,* children were told where they could and could not go to school based on the color of their skin. The school districts in these cases

have not carried the heavy burden of demonstrating that we should allow this once again—even for very different reasons. (p. 2768)

Chief Justice Roberts then concluded his opinion with a cogent anticlassification statement: "The way to stop discrimination on the basis of race is stop discriminating on the basis of race" (p. 2768).

The remarkable language in the Roberts opinion led the other justices to distance themselves from the plurality's analysis. Justice Kennedy stated, "Parts of the opinion by The Chief Justice imply an all-too-unyielding insistence that race cannot be a factor in instances when, in my view, it may be taken into account" and "To the extent the plurality opinion suggests the Constitution mandates that state and local school authorities must accept the status quo of racial isolation in schools, it is, in my view, profoundly mistaken" (p. 2791). Passages in the *Parents Involved* dissenting opinions are even more critical, with Justice Stevens stating, "There is a cruel irony in The Chief Justice's reliance on our decision in *Brown v. Board of Education*" (p. 2797), and "The Chief rewrites the history of one of this Court's most important decisions" (p. 2798). Justice Breyer's opinion, joined by Justices Stevens, David Souter, and Ginsburg, contains more excoriating language:

> It is a cruel distortion of history to compare Topeka, Kansas, in the 1950's [*sic*] to Louisville and Seattle in the modern day—to equate the plight of Linda Brown (who was ordered to attend a Jim Crow school) to the circumstances of Joshua McDonald (whose request to transfer to a school closer to home was initially declined). (p. 2836)

The incidental cost of using a race-conscious label in the Seattle and Louisville cases, Justice Breyer added, "does not approach, in degree or in kind, the terrible harms of slavery, the resulting caste system, and 80 years of legal racial segregation" (p. 2836).

As an alternative, Justice Breyer proposed a more deferential standard of review based on governmental motives: "The Equal Protection Clause, ratified following the Civil War, has always distinguished in practice between state action that excludes and thereby subordinates racial minorities and state action that seeks to bring together people of all races" (pp. 2835–2836). Justice Breyer offered a strong antisubordination justification for the school districts' plans:

The compelling interest at issue here, then, includes an effort to eradicate the remnants, not of general "societal discrimination," . . . but of primary and secondary school segregation . . . ; it includes an effort to create school environments that provide better educational opportunities for all children; it includes an effort to help create citizens better prepared to know, to understand, and to work with people of all races and backgrounds, thereby furthering the kind of democratic government our Constitution foresees. If an educational interest that combines these three elements is not "compelling," what is? (p. 2823)

Because Justice Breyer and the other dissenting justices agreed with Justice Kennedy that the interests in avoiding racial isolation and promoting diversity could be compelling, the Court's ruling in *Parent Involved* was effectively tempered, and five members of the Court provided a basis for school districts to employ other types of race-conscious policies that could advance compelling interests in avoiding racial isolation and in promoting diversity. Justice Kennedy's opinion also offered school districts specific, albeit limited, options for creating constitutionally compliant policies, such as plus-factor student assignment policies that parallel higher education admissions policies, as well as race-neutral policies such as creating magnet schools and drawing attendance zones that are mindful of racial demographics.

Mediating Antidiscrimination Norms: The Court's Center

Justice O'Connor's opinion in *Grutter* and Justice Kennedy's opinion in *Parents Involved,* while adhering to the strict scrutiny standards endorsed by anticlassification jurisprudence, represent moderating and centrist perspectives on an increasingly polarized Court. The O'Connor and Kennedy opinions blunted the more extreme views espoused by blocs such as the Roberts plurality in *Parents Involved,* and they suggest a constitutional analysis of race that, in at least some instances, is more receptive to elements of antisubordination jurisprudence characterized by the Brennan bloc in *Bakke* and the dissenters in more recent affirmative action decisions.

Justice O'Connor employed a version of strict scrutiny that was deferential to institutions of higher education and approached, as a practical matter, the intermediate level of scrutiny for racial classification espoused by adherents of antisubordination jurisprudence. In doing so, she also employed powerful rhetoric reminiscent of earlier antisubordination-focused opinions:

"Ensuring that public institutions are open and available to all segments of
American society, including people of all races and ethnicities, represents a
paramount government objective." . . . And, "Nowhere is the importance
of such openness more acute than in the context of higher education." . . .
Effective participation by members of all racial and ethnic groups in the
civic life of our Nation is essential if the dream of one Nation, indivisible,
is to be realized. (*Grutter,* 2003, pp. 331–332)

Similarly, Justice Kennedy in *Parents Involved* stated, "This Nation has a
moral and ethical obligation to fulfill its historic commitment to creating an
integrated society that ensures equal opportunity for all of its children" (*Parents Involved,* 2007, p. 2797).

Nevertheless, the "centrism" exhibited by Justices O'Connor and Kennedy may be limited to special settings such as public education and must
be placed in the context of a Court that has become increasingly disapproving of racial classifications since *Bakke* and continues to employ strict scrutiny to assess affirmative action policies. In 2006, Justice O'Connor was
replaced by Justice Alito, a member of the Roberts bloc in *Parents Involved,*
and a majority of the current Court views racial classifications with a high
degree of skepticism, if not outright condemnation. Justice Kennedy, while
employing broad rhetoric to endorse school districts' interests in addressing
racial isolation and promoting diversity, still voted to strike down the voluntary desegregation policies on narrow tailoring grounds, and his *Parents Involved* opinion offers schools districts only a small space for developing
constitutionally compliant policies. One can expect that the future decisions
of the Court, as in earlier cases, will feature close votes and divided opinions,
and that the tensions between anticlassification and antisubordination norms
will stay as strong as ever.

Conclusion

In the three decades since the Supreme Court's ruling in *Bakke,* affirmative
action case law has gone through a variety of stages, with early inconsistencies and ultimate clarifications in the standards of review and the likely outcomes of cases. Yet, the fundamental tensions inherent in the multiple *Bakke*
opinions remain, not only in the courts but in public debates and public
policies that attempt to address contemporary racial inequality. The broad
goals of social justice that accompanied early affirmative action policies have

clearly been diluted since *Bakke,* largely because the diversity rationale has replaced social and institutional remediation as the most legally and politically viable justification for affirmative action. Justice Powell's *Bakke* opinion recast race-conscious affirmative action as a public policy to which the highest standards of judicial review must be applied, and in doing so, established the diversity rationale as a rare exception under which racial considerations might be tolerated; institutions both inside and outside of higher education, averse to the risks of future litigation and political outcry, have simply followed suit. *Bakke*'s role in shifting the terms of the affirmative debate is unquestionable, and the limited space that the Court has provided for affirmative action in recent years clearly pivots around the diversity rationale espoused by Justice Powell. And the ascendancy of anticlassification jurisprudence, reflected in the Powell opinion and later Court majorities, has been cemented in the Court's current membership. In the future, the Court may move in different directions, but much will depend on its composition and the norms espoused by the sitting justices. Neither anticlassification norms nor antisubordination norms are likely to disappear altogether, and the dynamic between the two schools of antidiscrimination jurisprudence will continue to animate debates for years to come.

Notes

1. The terms *race-conscious* and *race-neutral* do not have a fixed meaning in the law, but the terms offer a useful dichotomy to describe public policies that employ race explicitly as a factor in the design and implementation of a policy—race-consciousness—versus those that do not employ race explicitly—race-neutrality. When placed under the lens of constitutional analysis, race-conscious policies trigger close scrutiny by the courts, and race-neutral policies will be presumptively constitutional. Even though governmental actors may be aware of relevant information such as the racial composition of a population in race-neutral policy making, their policies would still be assessed under a lower standard of review.

2. Six separate opinions were filed in the *Bakke* case. Justice Powell announced the judgment of the Court striking down the special admissions policy at the medical school of the University of California, Davis, but upholding the use of race in higher education admissions. Justice Stevens, joined by Chief Justice Burger and Justices Stewart and Rehnquist, voted to strike down the admissions policy under Title VI of the Civil Rights Act of 1964. Justice Brennan, joined by Justices White, Marshall, and Blackmun, voted to uphold the use of race in admissions and would have upheld the Davis policy as constitutional under the Equal Protection Clause. Justices White, Marshall, and Blackmun each wrote separate opinions.

3. In *Hopwood v. Texas* (1996), a lower federal appeals court struck down a race-conscious law school admissions policy at the University of Texas and concluded that affirmative action case law since *Bakke* had effectively overruled the case. The Supreme Court chose not to hear an appeal of *Hopwood* and did not address the constitutionality of higher education admissions policies until the University of Michigan cases in 2003.

4. The Supreme Court issued a single opinion in the Seattle and Jefferson County decisions, although the litigation involved two separate cases: *Parents Involved in Community Schools v. Seattle School District No. 1* (2007) and *Meredith v. Jefferson County Board of Education* (2007).

References

Adarand Constructors, Inc. v. Peña, 515 U.S. 200 (1995).

Balkin J., & Siegel, R. (2003). The American civil rights tradition: Anticlassification or antisubordination? *University of Miami Law Review, 58,* 9–34.

Brown v. Board of Education of the City of Topeka, 347 U.S. 483 (1954).

City of Richmond v. J.A. Croson Company, 488 U.S. 469 (1989).

Edley, C. (1996). *Not all Black and White: Affirmative action, race, and American values.* New York: Hill and Wang.

Fullilove v. Klutznick, 448 U.S. 448 (1980).

Gratz v. Bollinger, 539 U.S. 244 (2003).

Grutter v. Bollinger, 539 U.S. 306 (2003).

Hopwood v. Texas, 78 F.3d 932 (5th Cir.), *cert. denied,* 518 U.S. 1033 (1996).

Local 28, Sheet Metal Workers International Association v. Equal Employment Opportunity Commission, 478 U.S. 421 (1986).

Meredith v. Jefferson County Board of Education, 127 S. Ct. 2738 (2007).

Metro Broadcasting, Inc. v. Federal Communications Commission, 497 U.S. 547 (1990).

Parents Involved in Community Schools v. Seattle School District No. 1, 127 S. Ct. 2738 (2007).

Regents of the University of California v. Bakke, 438 U.S. 265 (1978).

Siegel, R. (2004). Equality talk: Antisubordination and anticlassification values in constitutional struggles over *Brown? Harvard Law Review, 117,* 1470–1547.

Title VI of the Civil Rights Act of 1964, 42 U.S.C. § 2000d.

United States v. Paradise, 480 U.S. 149 (1987).

Wygant v. Jackson Board of Education, 476 U.S. 267 (1986).

3

CAN WE FIND COMMON GROUND ON AFFIRMATIVE ACTION 30 YEARS AFTER *BAKKE*?

Michele S. Moses

mericans cannot seem to agree about affirmative action. The public conversation about affirmative action is laden with contradictions regarding issues of race-conscious education policy and equality of educational opportunity. Consider that the Supreme Court decision in *Regents of the University of California v. Bakke* (1978) and—25 years later—the *Gratz v. Bollinger* (2003) and *Grutter v. Bollinger* (2003) decisions have not quelled the public debate even as they have supported the constitutionality of and provided the legal contours for affirmative action in higher education admissions. Consider also that Justices John Roberts and Samuel Alito, the newest members of the Supreme Court, were confirmed without sharing their stances on affirmative action. Indeed just four years after the *Gratz* and *Grutter* decisions, a newly constituted high court ruled against the voluntary K–12 racial integration plans in Louisville, Kentucky, and Seattle, Washington.[1] Political candidates and appointees also waffle on issues related to affirmative action, not wanting to alienate potential supporters. Individual universities curb affirmative action and related race-conscious programs even as they call for increased diversity on campus (Schmidt, 2004). In 2006,

---

An earlier version of a portion of this chapter appeared in *Educational Policy.*

voters in the state of Michigan approved a ballot initiative that effectively abolished affirmative action programs even after the state's flagship university had spent substantial resources defending affirmative action (*Detroit News,* 2006). In 2007, affirmative action opponents began actively campaigning to have similar ballot initiatives in five other states (i.e., Arizona, Colorado, Missouri, Nebraska, and Oklahoma) for the 2008 vote. What is going on here? The disagreement about affirmative action must be more profound than we currently understand it to be. It cannot be simply about access to higher education, or racism, or discrimination. It is, of course, about those things, but it is also—importantly, I argue—a *moral* disagreement. In fact, the affirmative action debate is an example of an enduring moral disagreement, one that arouses profound conflict over fundamental moral ideals such as equality, liberty, and diversity.

This chapter explores affirmative action as a moral disagreement to answer the following questions: Why has the disagreement over affirmative action stubbornly persisted, even though the *Bakke* Supreme Court case made a reasoned decision on affirmative action in higher education admissions? What fuels people's entrenched opinions about affirmative action, even as opposing sides use similar language and terms in defending their positions (e.g., equality, liberty, and diversity)? Political philosophy provides the theoretical underpinning for this inquiry. To clarify the moral disagreement over affirmative action, I examine the broad philosophical perspectives that dominate the scholarly debate, relying on Gutmann and Thompson's (1996, 2004) deliberative democratic theory as the lens of analysis. Gutmann and Thompson provide provocative theoretical ideas about moral disagreement in a democratic society such as the United States and how we might come to better understand opposing sides and ultimately resolve deep disagreements.

In what follows, I first provide background on how the *Bakke* decision has influenced current affirmative action policy. Next, to identify underlying principles and assumptions within the diverse political positions, I draw on ideas about the nature of moral disagreement (e.g., Gutmann & Thompson, 1996, 2004; Milo, 1986; Rawls, 1971), as well as a combination of philosophical and policy scholarship from varying perspectives that challenge race-conscious policies (e.g., Garfield, 2006; Schuck, 2003a; Wood, 2003) or support race-conscious policies (e.g., Dworkin, 2000; Feinberg, 1998). My overall aim is to obtain a deeper understanding of the affirmative action debate as a moral disagreement—that is, of the moral values and ideals invoked by both supporters and opponents of affirmative action. As such, I bring to light the ideals and principles common to both, and question whether it is possible to find some middle ground from which to formulate policy that upholds the spirit of the *Bakke* ruling.

Bakke's Influence on the Current Affirmative Action Policy Context

In June 1978, the Supreme Court held 4–1–4 in *Regents of the University of California v. Bakke* that "(a) the minority-admissions program of the University of California Medical School in Davis had discriminated illegally against a white male applicant, but (b) that universities could legally consider race as a factor in admissions" (Sobel, 1980, p. 145). Justices Warren Burger, John Paul Stevens, Potter Stewart, and William Rehnquist decided in favor of Allan Bakke on both counts; conversely, Justices William Brennan, Byron White, Thurgood Marshall, and Harry Blackmun ruled in support of the medical school on both. In the swing vote, Justice Lewis Powell decided *against* the Davis policy that allotted specific quotas but *in favor of* the constitutionality of using race as a factor in admissions decisions. Because he was the deciding vote for both sides, Powell's became the Court's majority opinion. This type of split decision showed that the justices were as divided as the nation. The four justices who were against both Davis's quotas and the constitutionality of considering race viewed affirmative action as degrading to the ideal of equality. The four justices in favor of affirmative action policy saw it as a legitimate way to further equality. Justice Powell's deciding opinion stated that universities should be allowed to admit any students whom they believe will add most to the robust exchange of ideas on campus; the search for a diverse student body, Powell explained, is a constitutionally acceptable goal (O'Neill, 1985). Thus, race could be a legitimate factor to consider in admissions decisions. (For further discussion about this from a legal standpoint, see Ancheta, this volume.)

One especially enduring justification for affirmative action policies, the diversity rationale, came from Justice Powell's *Bakke* opinion. The legacy left by *Bakke* provides the legal guidelines for affirmative action policy, now updated and bolstered by *Gratz* and *Grutter*. Justice Powell had appended Harvard College's affirmative action program to his opinion as a guide to the constitutionality of such admissions programs. Within the plan, diversity was held as the most important rationale for affirmative action. Harvard officials believed that a diversity of students enhanced their student body and the educational experience (Sindler, 1978). With this in mind, the admissions committee looked at myriad activities, heritages, talents, and career objectives in selecting students for admission. This way of understanding the educational benefits of diversity undergirds the diversity rationale invoked in the *Bakke* decision. Although the diversity rationale for the use of affirmative action in higher education admissions remains in place within the legal framework, that has not precluded legal challenges to *Bakke*.

In both of the cases against the University of Michigan, the defense relied most heavily on *Bakke* and used the benefits of diversity rationale to justify affirmative action in its undergraduate and law school admissions policies (Elgass, 2000). Like Allan Bakke's lawyers in 1978, the plaintiff's Center for Individual Rights lawyers maintained that the University of Michigan's use of race as a factor in admissions violated the Equal Protection Clause of the Fourteenth Amendment and Title VI of the Civil Rights Act. In the final decision in these cases, issued June 23, 2003, the Supreme Court upheld Justice Powell's opinion in *Bakke* that student diversity is a compelling state interest. By upholding the University of Michigan Law School admissions policy as narrowly tailored, the Court endorsed policies that follow its guidelines in letter and spirit. In the *Grutter* majority opinion, Justice Sandra Day O'Connor noted that policies could focus on a range of attributes including applicants' varied talents and experiences and possible contributions to the learning environment, as well as academic ability. The key would be to assess each applicant individually (*Grutter,* 2003).

After the 2003 Supreme Court rulings, opponents of race-conscious education policies seemed to feel a renewed urgency to prohibit the consideration of race and ethnicity in higher education admissions and related programs. Immediately after the rulings in *Gratz* and *Grutter* were announced, Ward Connerly, Chair of the American Civil Rights Coalition, announced that he would propose an amendment to Michigan's state constitution opposing affirmative action. Proposal 2, known as the Michigan Civil Rights Initiative (MCRI), passed in November 2006 with 58% of the vote. Like both California and Washington before it, the state of Michigan is now prohibited from "discriminating or granting preferential treatment based on race, sex, color, ethnicity, or national origin" (MCRI, 2004, n.p.). After

Proposal 2 passed, Connerly's group announced similar campaigns in several other states aimed at the important 2008 presidential-year ballot.

Such efforts suggest that not only is the debate over affirmative action complex, but the way it manifests in the policy arena is complex as well. Voters also do not seem to be swayed by arguments for affirmative action based on the concept of equality. In fact, opponents of affirmative action use the concept of equality as the backbone of their campaigns *against* affirmative action programs. Other opponents of affirmative action even uphold the ideal of diversity as important for U.S. society. Perhaps it is a question of interpretations. I argue that people coming from conflicting ideological perspectives are using the ideals of diversity, equality, and liberty in very different ways, thus fueling the deep disagreement about affirmative action policy.

Given the recent political developments surrounding race-conscious education policies, it is important to try to understand the roots of the moral and political disagreement over such policies. In the next section, I first describe what makes a particular disagreement a moral one. This discussion provides the context necessary to understand the most prominent moral and political ideals at issue in the debate about affirmative action. Differing political theories of justice, such as egalitarian theory and libertarian theory, each seem to agree on the importance of the moral ideal of basic equality, and yet vehemently disagree about whether affirmative action is a defensible policy to help bring about basic equality.

Defining Moral Disagreement

What is moral disagreement? How is it important for examining affirmative action policy? Fittingly for a discussion on disagreement itself, there is no easy agreement among theorists about what exactly constitutes a *moral* disagreement. There is even little agreement on what such disagreements ought to be called; the terms *radical moral disagreement, partial moral disagreement, moral conflict, intractable controversy, internal moral disagreement, irreconcilable moral disagreement,* and *reasonable disagreement* are among those present within the scholarly literature.

So, what makes a particular disagreement a moral one? Moral disagreements—as opposed to individual, personal disputes—concern enduring, contested public issues involving values, relationships, and ideals (Gutmann & Thompson, 1996). There can certainly be personal disputes embedded in larger moral disagreements, but disagreements become moral ones when they center on public issues with broad social consequences. The affirmative action debate is an example of a moral disagreement, one that arouses profound conflict regarding fundamental moral ideals such as equality and liberty. Moral disagreements are qualitatively different from disagreements based on factual issues or differences of opinion, taste, or style. Two people may disagree about whose car reached the stop sign first after a fender-bender, or they may disagree about whether to root for the Mets or the Yankees. These are not moral disagreements. But if two people disagree or two political perspectives conflict about the state's role in providing public aid for people living in poverty, this is likely a *moral* disagreement. For at root, this is a disagreement about what priority should be given to the fundamental moral ideals of equality and liberty in a democratic society such as that of the United States. Moral disagreements are based largely on the conceptual schemes and theories of justice that underlie people's views.

Moral disagreements endure despite significant agreement about factual and even moral considerations. Some disputants may agree about factual claims and moral values, but disagree in their moral evaluations, that is, about what to *do* about the disagreement. So, in the case of such race-conscious education policies as affirmative action, there exists a persistent moral disagreement despite ostensible *agreement* about the importance of basic moral ideals such as freedom and equality. Of course, the opposing sides do not agree on all moral ideals. Agreement about moral basics does not mean that there will be the same moral beliefs about certain kinds of disagreements. For example, those with an egalitarian perspective may believe that affirmative action is needed to foster equality, whereas those who hold libertarian political theory to be tenable can value equality, but believe that affirmative action is not the means to that end.[2] But is there an irreconcilable disagreement (i.e., a moral deadlock)? There is a difference of moral opinion to be sure, and different moral priorities. Moral deadlock, Milo (1986) allowed, can be the result of this type of moral disagreement. It can stem from bad reasoning or conflicting interpretations of shared moral ideals. For instance, both egalitarian and libertarian theories of justice, which underlie the main opposing positions in the public moral disagreement over affirmative action, may claim to value the basic moral ideals of liberty and equality. But how each ideal is interpreted and prioritized within these theories of justice differs substantially. In addition, the motives behind the claims can be questioned. Thus is born a persistent moral disagreement despite seemingly shared central moral and political ideals.

Accordingly, Gutmann and Thompson (1996) called moral disagreement the most formidable challenge to democracy today; they lamented that we have no adequate way to cope with fundamental value conflicts. Their answer was to conceive of a democracy that has a central place for moral discussion in political and public life—what they and others call deliberative democracy. A central part of good deliberation is gaining a more nuanced understanding of the nature of the disagreement, the moral ideals involved, and the political commitments invoked.

Serious debate occurs over policy, but generally, scant attention is paid to the moral principles and political commitments that underlie it. Too often this results in an unreflective acceptance of ideas and policies that claim to uphold such principles as if they are uncontroversial. In American society, it is difficult to argue against broad and often vague concepts such as justice, equality of opportunity, liberty, and so forth. Milo (1986) maintained that productive moral disagreement is only possible if there is substantial agreement between opposing sides about what the relevant issues and principles are within the debate. Otherwise there is no basis for even a conversation, much less any resolution. From what I have discussed so far, the debate about affirmative action policy constitutes a moral disagreement, one in which there is agreement by both sides about the relevance of the moral and political ideals of equality, liberty, and even diversity. There is, at the very least, basis for a conversation, one that may lead to better understanding.

The Roots of the Disagreement Over Affirmative Action

I argue that illuminating the moral and political roots of the disagreement about affirmative action is important for gaining a more profound understanding of how to best inform public discussion of such race-conscious policies. These roots concern most centrally the moral ideals of equality and liberty, which often have been viewed as fundamentally opposed to each other.

Specific conceptions and political uses of the moral ideals of equality and liberty characterize the political commitments central to egalitarian and libertarian theories of justice. With the firm acknowledgement that there is substantial complexity and overlap within and among prominent theories of justice along the political spectrum, I have purposefully chosen to focus this examination on the opposing commitments of egalitarian political theory and libertarian political theory. Either explicitly or implicitly, these two theories underlie much practical policy debate in the United States.[3] Whereas egalitarian political theory tends to underlie many "liberal"—as popularly understood—policy positions, libertarian political theory underlies a good portion (though certainly not all) of "conservative"—again, as popularly understood—policy positions. In this section, I endeavor to clarify what the prominent ideals mean within egalitarian and libertarian theory and how those meanings inform policy views. How are such important ideals as equality and liberty defined and interpreted, respectively, by egalitarians and libertarians?

The Priority of Equality Within Egalitarian Theory

All persons are purportedly equal under the law. As a result, a discussion of equality at a high level of abstraction may be unproblematic regardless of one's underlying theory of justice. Differences arise more readily at a more practical level, especially in interpretation of central concepts (Rosenfeld, 1991). Egalitarianism is characterized by a concern for *social* justice, in contrast to the libertarian concern for *individual* justice. Whereas social justice is inextricably bound up with equality, individual justice is intertwined with personal autonomy and liberty. Egalitarianism emphasizes both equality itself and equality of opportunity.

Egalitarian theory has held that equality is *the* fundamental moral ideal (Dworkin, 2000; Kymlicka, 1992). Dworkin (2000) articulated this perspective well: "Equal concern," he wrote, "is the sovereign virtue of political community—without it government is only tyranny—and when a nation's wealth is very unequally distributed, as the wealth of even very prosperous nations now is, then its equal concern is suspect" (p. 1). For people to be treated with equal concern, they need to have equality of resources. By resources, Dworkin means something akin to opportunities and possibilities for flourishing. For a theory of justice to be taken seriously, each person has to matter equally, to be treated as equal. Of significant note here is that *treatment as equals* does not necessarily imply getting the *same* treatment. For example, the Supreme Court's ruling in *Lau v. Nichols* (1974) held that for limited English proficient students to be treated as equals within the public education system, they needed to be treated differently from students whose primary language is English; that is, they needed to receive instruction in their native languages. In this case, receiving the *same* treatment resulted in vast *inequality* of educational opportunity for limited English proficient students. Regarding higher education, supporters of affirmative action in admissions argue that the treatment of students of color as equals in the admissions system sometimes requires different treatment than White students, such as the consideration of race or ethnicity as one qualifying factor for admission.

Egalitarianism also emphasizes equality of opportunity and "justice as fairness" (Rawls, 1971, 1993, 2001). Consequently, treatment as equals requires equality of opportunity. Each person has a right to equal basic liberties, professional positions and offices are open to all under the principle of fair equality of opportunity, and inequality is permissible so long as any inequalities result in maximizing the position of the worst off—that is, those with the fewest primary goods. For Rawls (1971), persons' talents, abilities, and initial life circumstances are morally arbitrary and, as such, are an unfair basis from which to delineate their life chances. It would follow, then, that affirmative action policies are permissible to ensure that students of color are granted equal basic liberties and fair equality of opportunity.

Unlike egalitarians, libertarians assign a higher priority to the moral ideal of liberty than to equality. Historically, which moral ideals and democratic principles are assigned higher priority and used to justify views and policy decisions have been key distinctions between egalitarian and libertarian theories.

The Priority of Liberty Within Libertarian Theory

Libertarians characterize the moral and political ideal of liberty as "requiring that each person should have the greatest amount of liberty commensurate with the same liberty for all" (Sterba, 1992, p. 5). The role of the state is to protect human rights that are centered on liberty. Hospers (1974) names three human rights as central to a libertarian theory of justice: the right to life (to protect people from force and coercion, unjust killing), the right to liberty (to protect freedom of speech, press, assembly, ideas), and the right to property (to protect material and intellectual property from theft, fraud, slander, etc.). This understanding of liberty excludes certain rights as falling under "human rights," such as the right to receive public aid. Similarly, the right to property is considered a right to acquire goods and resources by fair means, rather than a right to receive goods from others who are better off in order to promote one's own welfare.[4]

The libertarian interpretation of liberty does not mean that libertarians do not care whether less advantaged people have their basic needs met; instead, it means that libertarians believe that the state has no duty to provide for those needs. Social welfare is, therefore, the requirement of charity, not of justice. One contemporary example of this idea in practice was George W. Bush's administration's call for faith-based charities and organizations to lead in the provision of social services for needy people. This call is justified through the belief that under a free market system and a minimal state, the least advantaged will have access to adequate opportunities and resources to make sure that their basic needs are met.

Nozick (1974), long held as the representative of libertarian political philosophy,[5] put forward a libertarian theory of "justice as entitlement." This view is characterized by respect for rights of ownership of self and property, which allows persons the freedom to choose how they want to live their lives without the intrusion of the state. Why should any goods acquired within the free market be redistributed when one's talents, abilities, work ethic, and possessions are one's own? Libertarianism holds that vast structural inequalities could be just, that is, could come about in a just manner. There might be bad luck involved in people's starting places in life—even unfairness—but not injustice. So long as people's property rights are respected and the state fosters liberty and is not coercive, then the distribution of goods that results can be considered just. As a result, a formalist notion of opportunity that calls for equal access (i.e., no official or legal barriers) to education is considered just. This contrasts with compensatory and participatory conceptions of opportunity held by some egalitarians emphasizing that mere access to opportunities is not enough. Also required are remedial policies to compensate for people's unequal starting places in life, a concern for outcomes, and the inclusion of disadvantaged stakeholders in deciding what is just and unjust (Howe, 1997).

There is often agreement between political theories about the principle of basic equality—that persons should be treated as equals and that the state ought to treat persons with equal concern and respect (Dworkin, 1978). This nominal agreement is positive, yet a conflict still occurs in defining what *treatment as equals* means. For libertarians, treatment as equals means that we respect a person's property ownership—her or his self as well as her or his material goods. That such a primary principle may result in vast socioeconomic inequality is unproblematic within libertarian political theory, as long as property rights and procedures for the acquisition and transfer of property are fair. As the previous two sections have shown, there are substantial differences between egalitarian and libertarian political theory; nevertheless, there are commonalities to be considered as well. I move now to an examination of an important shared ideal.

Basic Equality as a Shared Ideal

Even though an egalitarian theory of justice considers equality of opportunity and resources to be a prerequisite for treating people as equals and a libertarian theory of justice deems the right to one's own work, effort, and property as requirements for treating people as equals, both theories invoke the ideal of basic equality. Competing political theories may not agree about how to define and interpret such concepts as equality, yet they are still invoking the concept positively; at the very least, such a positive reliance on the concept holds promise for finding some basic agreement from which to move forward in better understanding each others' positions and emerging policy compromises. Kymlicka (1992) pointed out that, traditionally, theorists have believed that there is a continuum of political theories of justice from the left to the right, and that each of these appeals to a different ultimate foundational value. The theories, therefore, have been seen as incompatible, their differences as incapable of resolution. However, he followed Dworkin (1978) in saying that a regard for *basic equality* (characterized not by an equal distribution of income and wealth, but by the more abstract idea of treating people as equals) is what should be viewed as the *ultimate* foundational value held by political theories from the left to the right. Kymlicka's (1992) point is this: "A theory is egalitarian in this sense if it accepts that the interests of each member of the community matter, and matter equally. . . . This more basic notion of equality is found in Nozick's libertarianism as much as Marx's communism" (p. 4).

This is a key point. The ideal of basic equality holds an important place in both egalitarian and libertarian political theory. Some citizens, educators, researchers, and other policy actors may feel clear about how they interpret and prioritize the moral and political ideals that guide their policy positions. Nevertheless, the ideals and their place in the conceptual schemes that drive positions are often implicit, which makes it difficult to make informed choices about policy prescriptions. To make the most knowledgeable, coherent, and consistent choices, citizens and policy actors need to be clear about their moral ideals as well as have an understanding of the moral ideals held dear within opposing views. There is, of course, no guarantee that a more profound understanding of one's own views as well as the views of one's opponents will lead one to change her or his positions on policy issues. Many factors other than rational deliberation and argument make up conceptual schemes and influence policy views. What is important to take away from the preceding discussion is that, regardless of the motivations, there is at least some agreement over basic ideals. The moral disagreements about policy stem from a combination of contrasting prioritization, interpretation, and application of the salient principles. Within libertarianism, basic equality is perceived as necessary for enhancing liberty. As a result of the different ideas of what liberty and equality involve, justice for libertarians may require laws and policies that conflict with what justice requires for egalitarians. But there is hope to be found. Because there are important similarities in basic moral ideals, deeper understanding of the ideals and how they affect policy controversies may enhance the public's ability to deliberate about the complex moral disagreement regarding affirmative action. The next section discusses another shared ideal: diversity.

Diversity as a Shared Ideal

Diversity has become a very visible cultural ideal in the United States, one that holds "a special, almost sacrosanct place in our public discourse" (Schuck, 2003b, p. B10). Both supporters and opponents of affirmative action have expressed support for the ideal of diversity. For example, former president Bill Clinton has said, "Our rich texture of racial, religious and political diversity will be a Godsend in the 21st century" (Clinton, 2001, n.p.). President George W. Bush has said that he "strongly support[s] diversity of all kinds, including racial diversity in higher education" (Bush, 2003, n.p.). Certainly, the term *diversity* itself is contested; it can have various meanings and is quite controversial in that those on both sides of the affirmative action debate may support "diversity." At the most basic level, however, *diversity* means variety or heterogeneity. In discussions centering on affirmative action, people tend to focus on race/ethnicity. For the purpose of this chapter, diversity is characterized by a variety of races, ethnicities, colors, cultures, ages, religions, socioeconomic backgrounds, sexes, sexual orientations, gender identities, abilities, languages, and so on. These are qualities people hold that cannot easily be changed. In the context of educational benefits, diversity also includes things that can be changed, such as values, beliefs, moral ideals, intellectual understandings, and political ideologies.

As with the ideals of equality and liberty, there are varying interpretations of the ideal of diversity and what it means for education policy. From a libertarian political perspective, diversity is an ideal with some value, but it problematically has ascended in importance to match the concepts of equality and liberty (Schuck, 2003a; Wood, 2003). Wood (2003) especially lauds the ideal of liberty and is concerned that the ideal of diversity not overshadow liberty or individual equality. Another more practical concern for libertarians is that considering racial diversity in college admissions serves to disadvantage low-income students and students in poverty (Garfield, 2006).

Libertarians are particularly concerned that emphasizing the ideal of diversity not derail attempts at national unity. Misunderstanding what proponents of contemporary diversity believe to be real equality, Wood (2003) asserts, "Real equality, according to diversicrats, consists of parity among groups, and to achieve it, social goods must be measured out in ethnic quotas, purveyed by group preferences, or otherwise filtered according to the will of social factions" (p. 14). In actuality, as noted earlier, egalitarian proponents of the ideal of diversity—historically and now—understand real equality to be characterized by treatment of people as equals.

According to the libertarian perspective, the ideas that bolster the diversity rationale have trumped an older (and to them, more acceptable) notion of diversity, which emphasized unity forged from multiple identities and assimilation (Ravitch, 1995; Wood, 2003). By contrast, they would argue that the contemporary diversity rationale stresses particularity for its own sake, highlighting the group at the expense of the whole. Wood (2003), for example, is concerned that the diversity rationale is founded on the untenable "*belief* that the portion of our individual identity that derives from our ancestry is the most important part, and a *feeling* that group identity is somehow more substantial and powerful than either our individuality or our common humanity" (p. 11). Thus, libertarians do not believe that the ideal of diversity can be used to justify what they deem as special—largely unearned—and divisive privileges for racial and ethnic groups.

Egalitarian theory sees that unity and common humanity can actually be fostered by diversity. For example, Nussbaum argued that diversity is crucial for the proper education of global citizens. As she explained,

> Many of our most pressing problems require for their intelligent, cooperative solution a dialogue that brings together people from many different national and cultural and religious backgrounds . . . A graduate of a U.S. university or college ought to be the sort of citizen who can become an intelligent participant in debates involving these differences, whether professionally or simply as a voter, a juror, a friend. (1997, p. 8)

The ideas of unity and diversity need not be mutually exclusive; indeed individual and group diversity that is sustained over time can contribute to greater mutual human understanding and respect. Too often, the unity for which Wood and similar critics are nostalgic suppressed the very diversity from which it came. Students, Nussbaum (1997) argued, need to be able to reflect on themselves, their culture, community, and nation—critically—to achieve an education for democracy and world citizenship.

Conclusion

A recent study has confirmed that students who are the first in their families to attend college are more often low-income students or students of color than are other students (Guess, 2007). These findings remind us of the importance of increasing access to and meaningful opportunities for higher education. To improve the deliberation regarding affirmative action and retain hope for a mutually acceptable resolution of the moral controversy, stakeholders in the policy process must be able to understand the moral and political underpinnings of the debate about such policies as affirmative action. I hope this chapter will shed some light on the nature of the enduring moral disagreement about affirmative action that began before *Bakke* and continues. Perhaps more questions have been raised than answered, but in a democratic society, questions and deliberations can lead us to greater understanding and—I hope—more equitable policy decisions.

So, given support for the ideals of basic equality and (to a lesser extent) diversity, *can* we find common ground about affirmative action 30 years after the *Bakke* opinion ruled that higher education could employ race-conscious admissions policies? This is a very sobering question, especially because there

CAN WE FIND COMMON GROUND?   55

seem to be myriad other examples of impossible moral conflicts. Consider the debates about abortion and euthanasia, the conflict between creationism and evolution, competing claims about the state's responsibility to poor people or undocumented workers; the list could go on. I am afraid that the answer is more complicated than a simple yes or no. I am not at all sure that we can find common ground strong enough to allow agreement on policy prescriptions. But what we can find are some common gateways to dialogue and understanding. As I have shown, both opponents and supporters of affirmative action tend to agree, at least nominally, on an emphasis on the ideals of equality and diversity, yet their interpretations of those concepts differ substantially. This makes it very difficult to reach agreement on affirmative action policy or other means of achieving educational equality and diversity. George (1999) made a cogent point: "To say that a moral question is difficult . . . is in no way to suggest that it admits of no right answer" (p. 186).

Moral disagreements may get reconciled in different ways: (a) moral argumentation (deliberative argument and discussion akin to Gutmann and Thompson's ideas); (b) empirical discoveries (e.g., scientific discoveries about fetuses or second language acquisition); and (c) educational, cultural, or experiential influences (e.g., when a student leaves home believing that affirmative action is wrong, but then in college is exposed to diversity, etc., and changes his or her view) (Silver, 1994). The existence of difficult, intractable moral disagreements need not imply that disputants have divergent worldviews that *cannot* be better understood and perhaps overcome.

That a disagreement persists regarding the use of affirmative action to foster racial and ethnic diversity on college campuses as well as greater social equality should not cause advocates of equality of educational opportunity to hang our heads in defeat or despair. Those who care deeply about equality of educational opportunity and equity in educational access and outcomes can capitalize on the emphasis both supporters and opponents of affirmative action place on the important concepts analyzed here: equality, liberty, and diversity. We are much closer to having more widely acceptable versions of affirmative action in higher education admissions than when Justice Powell wrote his *Bakke* opinion. The Supreme Court gave more guidance with the *Gratz* and *Grutter* decisions. The salience of the diversity ideal shone through as a compelling state interest, but always in the service of the ideals of equality and liberty both. Even though there will continue to be arguments about how we can best foster these democratic ideals, and formulating mutually acceptable policies is a significant challenge, that some basic ideals are embraced in some form by both those on the right and on the left is cause for considerable hope.

Notes

1. It is important to note that even though the K–12 race-conscious student assignment plans have been curtailed by the Supreme Court, the *Bakke* and *Grutter* rulings supporting the idea that the consideration of race and ethnicity in college and university admissions is constitutional remain in place for higher education admissions.

2. Generally speaking, egalitarian theory holds that people should be treated as equals in society in general and under the law in particular. Libertarian political philosophy holds that all persons are autonomous and have freedom of person and property. As such, egalitarian theory places the principle of equality as the paramount democratic principle, whereas libertarian political theory places liberty as the paramount political principle. This key difference provides the basis for the way the theories diverge regarding education (and other) policy decisions.

3. In addition to affirmative action, another salient example is the long-standing debate about social welfare reform. The arguments for social welfare programs and public aid for the needy have a marked egalitarian cast (see Holyfield, 2002). By contrast, the arguments against social welfare programs have a significant libertarian flavor (see Murray, 1984).

4. These are circumscribed by Nozick's (1974) three principles guiding initial acquisition, voluntary transfer, and rectification.

5. Nozick is widely cited as such, despite the complexity of his ideas presented in *Philosophical Explanations* (1981), for example.

References

Bush, G. W. (2003, January 15). *President Bush discusses Michigan affirmative action case.* Retrieved January 16, 2003, from http://www.whitehouse.gov/news/releases/2003/01/

Clinton, W. J. (2001). Second inaugural address. In *Inaugural addresses of the presidents of the United States: From George Washington to George W. Bush.* Washington, DC: U.S. G.P.O. Retrieved October 5, 2007, from http://www.bartleby.com/124/pres65.html

Detroit News. (2006). *The* Detroit News *statewide exit poll.* Retrieved May 8, 2007, from http://info.detnews.com/pix/2006/pdf/elect_props.pdf

Dworkin, R. (1978). *Taking rights seriously.* Cambridge, MA: Harvard University Press.

Dworkin, R. (2000). *Sovereign virtue: The theory and practice of equality.* Cambridge, MA: Harvard University Press.

Elgass, J. R. (2000). University lawsuit gets court hearing. *The University Record.* Ann Arbor: University of Michigan.

Feinberg, W. (1998). *On higher ground: Education and the case for affirmative action.* New York: Teachers College Press.

Garfield, L. Y. (2006). The cost of good intentions: Why the Supreme Court's decision upholding affirmative action admission programs is detrimental to the cause. *Pace Law Review, 27*(1), 15–54.

George, R. P. (1999). Law, democracy, and moral disagreement. In S. Macedo (Ed.), *Deliberative politics* (pp. 184–197). New York: Oxford University Press.

Gratz v. Bollinger, 539 U.S. 244 (2003).

Grutter v. Bollinger, 539 U.S. 306 (2003).

Guess, A. (2007, June 7). *Trends for the first in the family.* Retrieved June 7, 2007, from http://www.insidehighereducation.com/news/2007/06/07/firstgen

Gutmann, A., & Thompson, D. (1996). *Democracy and disagreement: Why moral conflict cannot be avoided in politics and what should be done about it.* Cambridge, MA: Belknap Press of Harvard University Press.

Gutmann, A., & Thompson, D. (2004). *Why deliberative democracy?* Princeton, NJ: Princeton University Press.

Holyfield, L. (2002). *Moving up and out: Poverty, education, and the single parent family.* Philadelphia: Temple University Press.

Hospers, J. (1974). What libertarianism is. In T. Machan (Ed.), *The libertarian alternative* (pp. 3–20). New York: Nelson-Hall.

Howe, K. R. (1997). *Understanding equal educational opportunity: Social justice, democracy, and schooling.* New York: Teachers College Press.

Kymlicka, W. (1992). *Contemporary political philosophy.* Oxford: Clarendon Press.

Lau v. Nichols, 414 U.S. 563 (1974).

Michigan Civil Rights Initiative. (2004). Retrieved December 1, 2004, from http://www.michigancivilrights.org

Milo, R. D. (1986). Moral deadlock. *The Journal of the Royal Institute of Philosophy, 61,* 453–471.

Murray, C. (1984). *Losing ground: American social policy, 1950–1980.* New York: Basic Books.

Nozick, R. (1974). *Anarchy, state, and utopia.* New York: Basic Books.

Nozick, R. (1981). *Philosophical explanations.* Cambridge, MA: Belknap Press of Harvard University Press.

Nussbaum, M. (1997). *Cultivating humanity: A classical defense of reform in liberal education.* Cambridge. MA: Harvard University Press.

O'Neill, T. J. (1985). Bakke *and the politics of equality: Friends and foes in the classroom of litigation.* Middletown, CT: Wesleyan University Press.

Ravitch, D. (1995). Multiculturalism: E pluribus plures. In K. Ryan & J. M. Cooper (Eds.), *Kaleidoscope: Readings in education* (7th ed., pp. 458–464). Boston: Houghton Mifflin.

Rawls, J. (1971). *A theory of justice.* Cambridge, MA: Harvard University Press.

Rawls, J. (1993). *Political liberalism.* New York: Columbia University Press.

Rawls, J. (2001). *Justice as fairness: A restatement.* Cambridge, MA: Belknap Press of Harvard University Press.

Regents of the University of California v. Bakke, 438 U.S. 265 (1978).

Rosenfeld, M. (1991). *Affirmative action and justice: A philosophical and constitutional inquiry.* New Haven, CT: Yale University Press.

Schmidt, P. (2004, February 25). Yale U. opens an orientation program, formerly for minority students only, to all freshmen. *The Chronicle of Higher Education.* Retrieved February 25, 2007, from http://chronicle.com/daily/2004/02/2004022501n.htm

Schuck, P. H. (2003a). *Diversity in America: Keeping government at a safe distance.* Cambridge, MA: Belknap Press of Harvard University Press.

Schuck, P. H. (2003b, May 2). Affirmative action is poor public policy. *The Chronicle of Higher Education,* p. B10.

Silver, M. (1994). Irreconcilable moral disagreement. In L. Foster & P. Herzog (Eds.), *Defending diversity: Contemporary philosophical perspectives on pluralism and multiculturalism* (pp. 39–58). Amherst: University of Massachusetts Press.

Sindler, A. P. (1978). Bakke, DeFunis, *and minority admissions: The quest for equal opportunity.* New York: Longman.

Sobel, L. (Ed.). (1980). *Quotas and affirmative action.* New York: Facts on File.

Sterba, J. P. (1992). *Justice: Alternative political perspectives* (2nd ed.). Belmont, CA: Wadsworth.

Wood, P. (2003). *Diversity: The invention of a concept.* San Francisco: Encounter.

PART TWO

THE EDUCATIONAL PIPELINE:
PAST, PRESENT, AND FUTURE

4

O'CONNOR'S CLAIM

The Educational Pipeline and *Bakke*

John T. Yun and Chungmei Lee

The June 2003 *Grutter v. Bollinger* decision upholding affirmative action in higher education maintained the tenets of *Regents of the University of California v. Bakke* (1978) as well as provided an important connection to the K–12 educational system by linking the use of race-conscious admissions policies to the preparation of underrepresented minority students for admission to higher education. Justice Sandra Day O'Connor's majority opinion in *Grutter,* expanding on *Bakke,* concludes that the benefits of attending a diverse institution are real and necessary for today's global economy and national security. She goes further to say,

> Diffusion of knowledge and opportunity through public institutions of higher education must be accessible to all individuals regardless of race or ethnicity. Effective participation by members of all racial and ethnic groups in the civic life of our nation is essential if the dream of one Nation, indivisible, is to be realized. (*Grutter,* 2003, p. 331)

In affirming diversity as a compelling interest and a foundation for good citizenship, O'Connor was reasserting the spirit of Justice Lewis Powell's opinion in *Bakke,* which expressed the idea that nondiverse learning environments were pernicious to such a "diffusion of knowledge and opportunity."

In her conclusion, O'Connor wrote, "We expect that 25 years from now, the use of racial preferences will no longer be necessary to further the interest approved today" (*Grutter,* 2003, p. 343), linking the viability of a racially/

ethnically diverse postsecondary student body to the possibility of improved academic outcomes of students currently underrepresented in higher education. The concurring opinion of Justice Ruth Bader Ginsberg[1] suggests a specific mechanism for that change. She states that through better and more equitable primary and secondary education, greater numbers of underrepresented minority students would be stronger candidates for admission to the country's most elite institutions of higher education, thus obviating the need for race-consciousness in admissions (*Grutter,* 2003). However, for the mechanism suggested by Justice Ginsberg to operate within O'Connor's 25-year limit (chosen by O'Conner to mark the 25 years since *Bakke* that had passed at the time of the 2003 ruling), substantial progress would have to be made, relatively quickly, to reduce current disparities in educational resources and outcomes among all students, but particularly between White and Asian students relative to Black and Latino students.[2] Specifically, students would need to be virtually indistinguishable on a whole host of observable characteristics (e.g., test scores, writing ability, extra-curricular activities, alumni status, etc.) that colleges and universities use for admissions.

This chapter examines the feasibility of achieving O'Connor's goal by 2028 (25 years after *Grutter* and 50 after *Bakke*) primarily by examining the progress we have made as a country in narrowing the gap between White, Latino, and Black students across several key educational indicators. The extent to which such progress has been made will illuminate the extent to which O'Connor's admonition is tenable. First, we examine the context of educational opportunity, specifically segregation, the concentration of poverty in segregated schools, and their relationship to one another. Second, we consider the equitable distribution of resources applied to education such as qualified teachers, access to Advanced Placement classes, small class sizes, and equitable funding practices. These indicators of educational equity are important because substantial research and policy initiatives suggest that attending to the gaps among racial/ethnic groups in the context of educational opportunity and the equitable distribution of resources may plausibly be related to greater academic achievement for minority students (Brief of AERA, 2007; Card & Krueger, 1996; Greenwald, Hedges, & Laine, 1996; Harknett et al., 2003), potentially leading to a reduction in the need for race-conscious policies in university admissions. Finally, we compare educational outcomes among racial/ethnic groups as measured by test scores and dropout rates. We examine dropout rates and test scores because each has a substantial impact on the question of admissions to postsecondary education: dropout rates since graduation is (generally) necessary to be eligible for higher education at all, and test scores since they are an enduring measure of academic achievement for colleges and universities. Test scores as a measure of achievement are particularly relevant to this study because we are examining the possible impact of these disparities on admissions at schools likely to use race-conscious policies to achieve diverse student bodies, namely selective colleges and universities.[3]

This chapter is not intended to be an exhaustive examination of each of these facets of schooling. Instead, we primarily use existing research to highlight several important aspects of each of these topical areas that may provide some insight into the feasibility of reaching the level of educational equity necessary to make 2028 a goal that is realistic given the progress made in the 30 years since *Bakke*.

The Contexts of Education

The contexts in which students are educated can have several direct and indirect effects on student achievement. For instance, a large body of literature suggests that racially and socioeconomically integrated learning environments are associated with positive learning outcomes such as higher test scores and higher graduation rates (Cook et al., 1984; Crain & Mahard, 1983; Kahlenberg, 2001; Rothstein, 2004; Schofield, 1995, 2001). The magnitude of such effects, however, is a matter for debate; Cook et al. (1984) suggest that there is no statistically significant effect on average mathematics scores for Black students and a modest effect on reading scores, for example. Adding further complexity to the discussion of the relationship between school context and student achievement, several studies have suggested differential effects of segregated environments on high- and low-achieving students. For instance, Hanushek, Kain, and Rivkin (2002) found that high-achieving Black students benefit scholastically from diverse learning environments more than do their low- or moderately-achieving peers after controlling for student socioeconomic status.[4] The consistent findings in the academic literature of some kind of effect, however, is sufficient to consider addressing school contexts an important approach to narrowing the achievement gap between White students and their underrepresented minority peers.

Since 1968, when segregation was largely a Black-White issue, the demographic landscape of public school enrollment has become increasingly multiracial (Reardon, Yun, & Eitle, 2000). This transformation is largely the result of the surge in Latino enrollment, which is up 380% in almost 40 years (table 4.1). White enrollment has dropped 20% since 1968, and Black enrollment has grown by 33%. Given differential birth rates, age structures, and increased immigration, U.S. Census Bureau projections suggest that by the middle of this century, White students will constitute little more than 40% of the school-age population (Hollmann, Mulder, & Kallan, 2000).

The two most populous regions, the South and the West, enroll more than half of the total public school population (table 4.2).[5] Black students are concentrated in a single region more than any of the other racial groups. Almost half (49%) attend schools in the South, which when added to the Midwest, enroll two-thirds of all Black students. Latinos are similarly concentrated in the West with 44%; two regions, the West and the South, account for 77% of the Latino population. Although Asians only constitute about 5% of total public school enrollment, more than two out of every five Asian students attend schools in the West. There is no similar pattern of clustering for White students; the most populous regions are the Midwest (26%) and South (28%), respectively, and the West and the Northeast each enroll a fifth of White students.

The change in public school enrollment over time has not been distributed evenly. Two major demographic changes occurred between 1990 and 2005 (table 4.2): a declining share of White enrollment (from 67 to 57%) and a surge in Latino enrollment (from 12 to 20%). Additionally, a redistribution of students occurred between 1990 and 2005, specifically the migration of Asians from the West to the South and the movement of American

TABLE 4.1
Public School Enrollment, by Race/Ethnicity, 1968–2005 (in Millions)

	1968	1980	1994	1996	1998	2005	Change 1968–2005
Latinos	2.0	3.2	5.6	6.4	6.9	9.6	7.6 (+380%)
Whites	34.7	29.2	28.5	29.1	28.9	27.7	−7.0 (−20%)
Blacks	6.3	6.4	7.1	7.7	7.9	8.4	2.1 (+33%)

Source: Orfield and Lee (2007, p. 15). Reprinted with permission.

TABLE 4.2
Distribution of Students, by Race and Region, 1990 and 2005

Region	% White		% Black		% Latino		% Asian		% American Indian	
	1990	2005	1990	2005	1990	2005	1990	2005	1990	2005
West	20	19	9	9	47	44	53	45	48	43
Border	7	9	8	9	1	2	3	4	20	23
Midwest	29	26	20	17	7	8	13	13	17	16
South	24	28	45	49	30	33	11	18	11	12
Northeast	20	19	18	15	15	12	19	20	4	5
U.S. Total (%)	67	57	16	17	12	20	4	5	1	1
U.S. Total (n)*	25.4	27.7	5.9	8.3	4.7	9.7	1.3	2.4	0.4	0.5

Source: National Center for Education Statistics (NCES) (1990, 2005).
*U.S. Totals listed in millions.

Indians from the West to the Border states. Except for American Indian students, whose concentration in the South remained the same, a growing share of students of all races was attending schools in the South in 2005. In contrast, although substantial proportions of Latinos, Asians, and American Indians are still attending schools in the West (44, 45, and 43%, respectively), these shares have declined since 1990.

Distribution of Students in Segregated Schools

As table 4.3 shows, a great many White and minority students are not attending schools with each other.[6] More than a third each of Black and Latino students attend schools that are 0 to 10% White (also known as intensely segregated minority schools);[7] in stark contrast, only 1% of Whites attend similarly described schools. Close to half of Black students (48%) and more than half of Latino students (54%) attend schools that are fewer than 20% White. These numbers rise to more than three-quarters for the shares of Black (74%) and Latino (79%) students attending predominantly minority schools. At the other extreme, more than a third of White students (37%)

TABLE 4.3
Distribution of Students by Percent White in School and Race/Ethnicity, 2005

White Students in School (%)	White Students (%)	Black Students (%)	Latino Students (%)	Asian Students (%)	American Indian Students (%)
0–10	1	38	40	16	19
11–20	1	10	14	10	6
21–30	2	9	10	9	6
31–40	3	8	8	9	8
41–50	5	9	7	9	9
51–60	7	8	6	10	10
61–70	10	7	6	11	12
71–80	13	6	5	11	12
81–90	21	4	4	10	12
91–100	37	2	2	6	8
Total	100	100	100	100	100

Source: NCES (2005).

attend schools where greater than 90% of the students, on average, are White compared with only 2% of Black and 2% of Latino students, respectively, who are similarly situated. Asian students have a bimodal distribution, where more than a quarter (26%) of Asian students attend schools where fewer than 20% of the students, on average, are White, while 6% of Asians attend intensely segregated White schools. Despite constituting only 5% of the public school enrollment, more than half (53%) of the Asian student population attends predominantly minority schools.

One of the biggest changes since 1990 is that there are fewer Whites attending intensely segregated White schools. Their share dropped from more than half in 1990 (52%) to 37% in 2005 (tables 4.3 and 4.4). The share of Asians attending these intensely segregated White schools dropped from 10 to 6% and the proportion also dropped for American Indians from 12 to 8%. However, it is noteworthy that despite the drop in the share of White students attending intensely segregated White schools, more than two-thirds (71%) attend schools where at least 70% of their peers are White. On the other hand, the share of Black and Latino students attending intensely segregated minority schools has increased since 1990 from 34% for each to 38% and 40%, respectively, in 2005. The percentage of Asian students attending these schools has also grown, from 14 to 16%. Across the board, more students in 2005 were attending predominantly minority schools than were in 1990 (table 4.4).

Differential Desegregation

Some attribute the increasing levels of racial isolation discussed in the previous section simply to changing demographics (Logan, 2004). Some of the trends we see can be attributed to demographic shifts, particularly during the last 30 years. As the population grows increasingly multiracial, it stands to reason that the racial composition of schools attended by the average student will change and that there will be a smaller share of White students in these schools, all else being equal. However, the extent to which students are experiencing these changes varies by race. This suggests that, regardless of the mechanism driving these changes, minority and the remaining White students in these rapidly resegregating schools are becoming much more racially isolated. This isolation creates an even larger gap between the experiences of these students and those students living in more integrated environments.

TABLE 4.4
Distribution of Students by Percent White in School and Race/Ethnicity, 1990

White Students in School (%)	White Students (%)	Black Students (%)	Latino Students (%)	Asian Students (%)	American Indian Students (%)
0–10	0	34	34	14	21
11–20	1	7	12	11	5
21–30	1	7	10	9	4
31–40	2	8	9	9	5
41–50	4	9	8	9	8
51–60	5	9	8	9	8
61–70	7	9	6	9	10
71–80	11	8	5	9	13
81–90	17	5	5	11	14
91–100	52	3	3	10	12
Total	100	100	100	100	100

Source: NCES (1990).

Black and Latino students have experienced different segregation trends over the years relative to their White and Asian counterparts. Active enforcement of the Civil Rights Act of 1964 and a series of Supreme Court decisions led to the drop in percentage of Southern Black students attending intensely segregated minority schools from 78% in 1968 to 24% in 1988 (Orfield & Lee, 2007). Not until a series of Supreme Court rulings in the 1990s[8] dismantling desegregation plans in the South did we begin to see a resegregation of Black students in this region. Currently, about a third (32%) of Black students attend intensely segregated minority schools in the South (Orfield & Lee, 2007). In short, the story of Black segregation is one of intense segregation followed by a period of desegregation until the late 1980s and, in the last decade, one of increasing resegregation.

In contrast, there have been few overt efforts to desegregate Latinos.[9] Since the late 1960s, when data were first collected on Latino segregation, Latino students have experienced steady increasing segregation over the years. Currently, Latinos are most segregated in the Northeast and the West where 45 and 41% of Latino students, respectively, attend intensely segregated minority schools. The greatest increase in segregation has been in the

West, where currently 41% of Latinos attend intensely segregated minority schools, an increase of 29 percentage points since 1968. Another region where there has been a dramatic increase in the segregation of Latinos is the Midwest, where the percentage of Latinos attending intensely segregated schools increased by 19 percentage points (Orfield & Lee, 2007). In fact, Latinos are now the most segregated minority group in the nation.

Relationship Between School Composition and Poverty

Although segregation alone is a serious issue, the strong relationship between highly segregated minority schools and poverty[10] is even more troubling. As demonstrated in tables 4.5 and 4.6, segregation by race and poverty remained strong between 1995 and 2005.[11] Thirty-nine percent of all U.S. schools are intensely segregated White schools, and about 18% of them are also schools of concentrated poverty where more than half of the students are on free or reduced lunch (table 4.5). In contrast, 86% of the students in intensely segregated minority schools are also in high poverty schools.

In the 10 years between 1995 and 2005, the nation's public schools have grown poorer (tables 4.5 and 4.6). Although only 8% of the intensely segregated White schools were also high-poverty (greater than 50% poor) schools in 1995, that share has risen to 18% by 2005. And although the correlation between intense economic and racial/ethnic segregation dropped from 0.66 to 0.59 during this period, there remains a relatively strong correlation between race and poverty, as evidenced by the fact that more than four-fifths

TABLE 4.5
Distribution of Students by School Racial Composition and Poverty, 2005

% Poor in School	% Black and Latino Students in School									
	0–10	11–20	21–30	31–40	41–50	51–60	61–70	71–80	81–90	91–100
0–10	23	19	8	4	4	4	4	4	3	8
11–25	24	27	25	14	7	4	2	1	1	2
26–50	36	35	40	44	37	28	20	10	7	5
51–100	18	19	27	38	52	65	74	84	89	86
% of Schools	39	12	8	6	6	5	4	4	4	11

Source: NCES (2005).
Note. Totals may not add up to 100 because of rounding.

TABLE 4.6
Distribution of Students by School Racial Composition and Poverty, 1995

% Poor in School	*% Black and Latino Students in School*									
	0– 10	*11– 20*	*21– 30*	*31– 40*	*41– 50*	*51– 60*	*61– 70*	*71– 80*	*81– 90*	*91– 100*
0–10	31	21	10	6	6	5	6	5	5	3
11–25	35	37	31	21	12	7	5	4	3	2
26–50	26	33	44	49	45	38	26	16	11	8
51–100	8	9	15	24	37	50	63	76	81	87
% of Schools	47	11	8	6	6	5	4	3	3	8

Source: Orfield and Yun (1999, p. 17). Adapted with permission.
Note. Totals may not add up to 100 because of rounding.

of all intensely segregated minority schools continue to also be high poverty schools.

A large body of educational research documents a strong correlation between segregation by race and segregation by poverty such that high-minority schools tend to also be high-poverty schools (e.g., Orfield & Lee, 2007). The relationship between poor schools and academic performance has been well documented (Kahlenberg, 2001; Natriello, McDill, & Pallas, 1990). Hallinan and Williams (1990), for example, found that one of the factors influencing academic performance has been peer influence. In his study of Southern schools, Rumberger (2003) similarly reported that a major negative impact on academic achievement related to attending a high-poverty school was the absence of a strong positive peer influence.

Several empirical studies have found that attending a middle-class school exposes all students to higher expectations and more educational and career options compared with attending a low-income school (Anyon, 1997; Dawkins & Braddock, 1994; Natriello et al., 1990; Schofield, 1995). In their study of voluntary transfer policies in metropolitan St. Louis, Wells and Crain (1997) observed that minority students who attend middle- and upper-class schools had higher educational achievement and college attendance rates than did their peers in concentrated poverty schools. Eaton (2001) documented that scores of Boston students who attended suburban public schools had access to knowledge and networks that their peers in inner-city Boston lacked and that this experience increased their educational and professional opportunities. Kahlenberg (2001) found,

> The best guarantee that a school will have what various individual reforms seek to achieve—high standards, qualified teachers, less crowded classes, and so on—is the presence of a critical mass of middle-class families who will ensure that these things happen. (p. 4)

A national study conducted by Monk and Haller (1993) found a correlation between the average socioeconomic status of the student body and academic credits that were offered: Schools with higher concentrations of low-income students had less vigorous curricula. In her research on educational resources, Oakes (1990) found that inequality in resources includes students' limited access to basic math courses such as algebra, which is often a prerequisite to higher-level math courses.

The literature and the data presented in this section show that students of different racial/ethnic groups experience very different schooling contexts, and that these differences have not been mitigated during the past 30 years. Rather, strong evidence suggests that these differences have been exacerbated during the past decade. While these different contexts, especially when combined with concentrations of poverty, can seriously affect the educational opportunities of the students in the less diverse, higher poverty settings, they are only part of the picture. Exploring how schooling resources are distributed among racial/ethnic groups is critical to understanding how policy intersects with context to create educational opportunities.

Resources: On Average, Some National Progress

The argument for a connection between school resources and educational achievement is quite straightforward. If, for example, students are faced with unequal opportunities to learn, substandard materials, or larger class sizes, how can we expect outcomes to be equivalent? The empirical foundation for this claim, however, has been hotly debated during the past 25 years. Led by a series of studies by Hanushek (1981, 1986, 1991), early economics-based research suggested that money had very little impact on individual student and average school test scores. However, subsequent research (e.g., Greenwald et al., 1996) suggested that a wide variety of school inputs are positively associated with a variety of outcomes of schooling. Much of the variation in results across these studies rests on the differing notion of what constitutes an input and an output. Hanushek has largely focused on standardized test scores as his critical outputs and on a limited number of schooling inputs such as per pupil expenditures. In contrast, others have focused on a broader set of both inputs and outputs such as pedagogical emphasis and mathematics achievement (Raudenbush, Fotiu, & Cheong, 1998), total public money spent on children and health/behavioral outcomes (Harknett et al., 2003), or pupil–teacher ratios on the outcomes of educational attainment and earnings (Card & Krueger, 1996), and found more positive relationships. At this point in the debate, nearly all engaged agree that money and resources matter for positive outcomes only if it is used well (Rebell, 2007). What remains unclear is what constitutes important resources to allocate and which outcomes are most important.

This section focuses on several educational resources that have been consistently mentioned in the literature as important preconditions for student success. Whether such educative resources made available to students across race and socioeconomic status will improve educational outcomes is not of greatest importance here; what we are most interested in is whether access to these resources has become more equitable across racial groups through 30 years of sustained focus on improving educational outcomes. When examined at the national level, several measures of student resources (per pupil expenditure, Advanced Placement [AP] course access, teacher preparation, etc.) have shown a narrowing of disparities between racial/ethnic groups (Boozer, Krueger, Wolkon, Haltiwanger, & Loury, 1992; Corcoran, Evans, Goodwin, Murray, & Schwab, 2004), yet important disparities still exist both at the national level and more locally where disparities in access to schooling resources are larger than national numbers might suggest (Rebell, 2007).

Per-Pupil Expenditures and Pupil–Teacher Ratio

In a comprehensive analysis of the changing distribution of school finance and resources from 1972 to 1997, Corcoran et al. (2004) found substantial reductions in funding inequality between rich and poor districts across all states, with reductions of between 25 and 40% in the level of that inequality, depending on the metric used. Interestingly, Corcoran et al. (2004) also show that from 1972 to 1992, there was very little difference (only about $100) between the average per pupil expenditure for White and Black students nationally, which suggests that even 35 years ago Black and White students received, on average, similar amounts of per-pupil support.[12] Although this circumstance may seem to be contradictory (reductions in funding inequality with stable average funding levels), the reductions in funding inequality are for all districts regardless of their racial composition. As such, each metric is actually looking at a different aspect of funding disparities.

In addition to this reduction in overall funding inequality, pupil–teacher ratios for Black and White students have been converging since the *Brown v. Board of Education* (1954) decision. According to Boozer et al. (1992), the pupil–teacher ratio for Black students in the South just before the *Brown* decision was larger by four pupils per teacher, but by the mid-1960s that difference was two students per teacher, and by 1989, that difference was completely eliminated. However, even though this difference in pupil–teacher ratio between Black and White students has been eliminated, this change reflects a concerted effort of over 30 years to address a difference of four pupils per teacher. This suggests that even modest progress in closing gaps in resource allocation can take quite some time to be realized.

Access to Advanced Placement Courses

According to Corcoran et al. (2004), from 1972 to 1992, the racial disparity in schools offering at least one AP course by the percentage of Black students enrolled in the school disappeared and, in fact, reversed. Specifically, in 1972, 30% of schools with a Black enrollment of less than 10% offered AP courses, and only 21.4% of schools with a greater than 90% Black share offered at least one AP course. By 1992, that figure had changed substantially with 72.8% of schools with 10% or fewer Black students and 76.7% of schools with 90% or more Black students offering at least one AP course.

Two important things need to be understood in these changes. First, the increase in overall access (an increase of 40 to 50 percentage points for each school type) is quite large and suggests substantial benefits for all students. In addition, in 1992 a lower proportion of schools with low Black shares (fewer then 10%) had at least one AP course compared with schools with large Black enrollment shares (90% or greater), suggesting the possibility of a narrowing of the resource gap. However, we must note that the metric of percent Black in school may result in some misleading results because schools with fewer than 10% Black students may still be heavily non-White given either large Latino or Asian populations. Further, if these heavily non-White (and low-proportion Black schools) are less likely to offer at least one AP course, then schools with low percentages of Black students may show similar AP offering rates when compared with schools with high Black enrollments. Given that the proportion of Latino and Asian students has changed substantially during the past 20 years, this is a confounding factor that these simple statistics do not address. These opportunity numbers also do not consider the extent to which AP courses were offered (e.g., whether 1 or 10 AP courses were available or indeed how many students might have enrolled in such courses), thus even as high percentages of schools offer at least one AP course, some schools may have very few spaces, very low enrollments, or very few types of AP courses, whereas others may have an endless menu of choices. From these data, we simply do not know. Interestingly, in fall 2007, the College Board performed an audit of the syllabi of all AP courses offered, and for the first time ever, the number of schools offering AP courses fell by 2,081 (to 14,383) either because of the lack of rigor reflected in the syllabus, lack of a qualified teacher, or through nonsubmission of a syllabus (Cech, 2007). At this time we cannot determine the distributive impact of this change, but it does suggest that the quality of AP courses varies across schools quite substantially, and pre-2007 increases should be viewed with some caution.

Qualified Teachers

Finally, some data suggest that the disparities by race/ethnicity in access to certified teachers exists but that the difference is not that large. For instance, using the Schools and Staffing Survey data for 1993 to 1994, Corcoran et al. (2004) estimated that in schools that are 50 to 100% Black, approximately 87% of the teachers were certified in the field in which they were teaching. In schools that are 10% or fewer Black, nearly 94% of all teachers were certified in the courses they taught, for a difference of approximately seven percentage points.

Despite these potentially hopeful signs that resource disparities between minority and White children are being addressed, serious concerns remain. First, these national findings may mask extreme local variations that could have broad impacts on the students who experience them. Second, the nature of the measures (such as the existence of at least one AP course at a school or the per-pupil expenditure of districts) may underestimate the quality of the resource or how widely it is being used. Thus, even where disparities have narrowed, there is still some question whether these changes actually have the potential to increase access to quality education for all students— thus contributing to the goal set in *Grutter*. The chapter now turns to these variations in more detail.

The Persistence of Unequal Access: Local Variation

Although, on average, there have been some improvements in narrowing the resource disparities between underrepresented minority students and their White peers, important disparities persist. One facet of the problem is the considerable local and state-by-state variation that exists in some of the very measures we suggested had improved nationally. For example, with regard to qualified teachers, Darling-Hammond (2001) found that in California schools, the share of unqualified teachers is 6.75 times higher in high-minority schools (greater than 90% minority) than in low-minority schools (less than 30% minority). Freeman, Scafidi, and Sjoquist (2002) found that teachers in the state of Georgia who transferred tended to move toward low-poverty schools with higher student achievement and fewer minority students. State-by-state variation is also a problem in school funding. For instance, in New York State during the 2004 school year, rich and poor districts differed by $2,280 per pupil. Looking at the district level, New York City (whose schools have 81% of their students free-lunch eligible and a high proportion of minority students), for example, spent $12,896 per pupil in 2004 while Manhassett (which has only 4% of its students free-lunch eligible and a much lower proportion of minority students) spent $23,344 per pupil. These local large differences challenge the national numbers and suggest that even where aggregate progress has been made, local variation may still produce large differences in opportunities that cannot be ignored.

Although, in general, Corcoran et al. (2004) found many reductions in resource disparities between racial/ethnic groups, one glaring exception was in access to computers and the Internet, a precondition for developing a critical skill, and one that will certainly increase in importance, particularly for those intending to apply to selective institutions of higher education. From

1994 to 2000, the researchers found that between White schools (schools with fewer than 6% minority enrollment) and majority-minority schools (schools with greater than 50% minority enrollment) the disparity in the percentage of classrooms with Internet access grew from 2 percentage points in 1994 (4% and 2%, respectively) to more than 20 percentage points in 2000 (85 and 65%, respectively). Much of this large change may be because the percentage of classrooms with Internet access grew astoundingly during that 6-year period from only 3% overall in 1994 to 77% in 2000. If such growth continues, access might even out over time; however, schools that are poor and segregated might not be able to keep pace with their more integrated and affluent neighbors, creating yet another lasting disparity.

Raudenbush et al. (1998) performed an interesting analysis that focused attention on several nontraditional school resource measures (disciplinary climate, offering algebra in eighth grade, teacher preparation, and teacher emphasis on reasoning) that they found to be strongly correlated with mathematics proficiency, controlling for a number of individual- and school-level covariates. Raudenbush et al. examined whether access to these resources was equal across racial/ethnic groups as well as parental education levels. In their analysis, they found that access to all four resources related to race/ethnicity, with White and Asian students enjoying the greatest access and Black and Latino students enjoying the least. In some cases, access for Black and Latino students was lower by half a standard deviation, quite a large effect.

Although these studies provide no definite answer about whether the past 30 years of educational reform have bought us a more equitable distribution of resources across ethnic/racial groups in the United States because of the extreme variation in such equalization across geography and demographic categories, at least at the aggregate national level, we do see that there has been some progress on a few important resource metrics. However, we still have a long way to go to ensure that the quality of education students can receive does not differ by race/ethnicity.

Educational Outcome Disparities Over Time

Finally, to understand the viability of O'Connor's 25-year sunset admonition in *Grutter*, we must look at educational outcomes. Since the early 1990s, the emphasis on school reform has turned decidedly away from input-based models like Title I or Head Start that sought to equalize educational inputs among racial/ethnic groups and toward outcome-based reforms seeking to equalize the outcomes of education, particularly on such concrete measures as test scores and high school graduation (see Heller, this volume, for a discussion of high school graduation rates). In this chapter, we consider two outcome measures, dropout patterns and test performance, each in turn.

Dropouts

Why are we focusing on dropping out as a measure of education attainment in this context? At its fundamental level, high school completion is a precondition for most postsecondary educational opportunities. Dropping out of school, then, presents a problem of eligibility for student enrollment in many higher education settings. Much like the story of per-pupil expenditures, there has been a great deal of progress in reducing dropout rates at the national level. According to the National Center for Educational Statistics (2007), White students' dropout rates decreased from about 12% in 1972 to 6% in 2005, Latino dropout rates decreased from about 35% in 1972 to about 22% in 2005, and Black dropout rates decreased from 21% in 1972 to about 10% in 2005. Although Latino dropout rates are substantially higher than those of their Black and White peers, in all cases the disparity in dropout rates has decreased, although not as much as one would like.

This clear progression toward greater educational attainment is somewhat less clear when we examine dropout rates across several cities. Although exact numbers are difficult to obtain given different reporting standards and the lack of a national longitudinal tracking system for students, some place graduation rates at anywhere from 21 to 81%, with substantial differences between racial/ethnic groups (Chaddock, 2006). Ultimately, although progress has been made, the continued dropout problem highlights that inequities remain.[13]

For selective postsecondary schools, which are the institutions most likely to use race-conscious admissions policies to achieve diverse classrooms, the marginal high school graduate is not the student most likely to be hurt by the loss of such policies. Instead, the high achieving Black or Latino student, who scores well on standardized examinations but not well enough to be highly competitive for these selective institutions, is at risk. So although the percentage of students who graduate from high school may be an important metric for how well the educational system is educating students across racial/ethnic groups, it does not tell the story of those high achieving students for whom graduation was never in question, but admission to a selective college or university may be.

Standardized Test Scores

Given this variegated background of dropout rates, we can move forward to look at achievement as measured by standardized test scores. In general, the research literature has come to a consensus that the Black-White test score gap has been difficult to narrow on nearly all longitudinal test-based measures of student achievement (Grissmer, Flanagan, & Williamson, 1998). Using National Assessment of Educational Progress (NAEP)[14] data for 17-year-olds over time, the racial/ethnic gap in both mathematics and reading achievement present in the 1970s narrowed substantially during the 1980s and then hit a plateau in the early 1990s until 2004 (see figures 4.1 and 4.2). The figures track the scaled scores on the NAEP mathematics and reading examinations from 1975 to 2004, which represent the 50th, 75th, and 90th percentiles for White students and the 90th percentile for Latino and Black students. Note that the 90th percentile in reading for Latino and Black students is slightly below the 75th percentile for White students (figure 4.1). The disparity is even more stark in mathematics for Black students where their 90th percentile is just a few scaled score points above the 50th percentile for White students (figure 4.2). High-achieving Latino students fare a little better with their 90th percentile close to White students' 75th percentile.

Confirming these general findings, Hedges and Nowell (1998) found that the largest discrepancies between Black and White students were at the top of test score distributions with White high school seniors between 10 and 20 times more likely to be in the top 5% of the national distribution on composite measures of academic skills from nationally representative surveys given in 1962, 1972, 1980, 1982, and 1992 compared with their Black peers. This differential at the top of the distribution is particularly troubling because these are the very students who will be competing for spots at the selective admissions colleges.

If we use the data in figures 4.1 and 4.2 and the total number of 17-year old-students in public schools, we can calculate the numbers of students who would score at or above the 50th and 90th percentile thresholds for their given racial/ethnic group. Given these calculations we are left with some

FIGURE 4.1
NAEP reading scores, by race and percentile, for 17-year-old students, 1975–2004

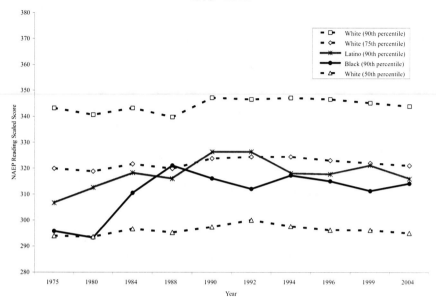

Source: NCES (1975–2004).

troubling results. Approximately 1.4 million White students would be expected to score at or above the 90th percentile for Black and Latino students on the NAEP mathematics examination, representing only 56,000 Black students and 61,000 Latino students. In other words, in mathematics, when applying to college, 1.4 million White students are competing for admission with similar achievement (as predicted by NAEP) as 56,000 Black students and 61,000 Latino students.[15] Similar numbers exist for the NAEP reading examination with 700,000 White students competing with similar reading achievement (as predicted by NAEP) as 56,000 Black and 61,000 Latino students. Assuming all of these students graduate (which is reasonable given the relatively high achievement scores), colleges and universities that use the least restrictive approach to testing and admissions (considering all students who score above a threshold value for admissions, for example) are left with six White students for every Black and Latino student, at best (to the extent that NAEP performance is indicative of college admission test scores). Given

FIGURE 4.2
**NAEP mathematics scores, by race and percentile, for 17-year-old students,
1978–2004**

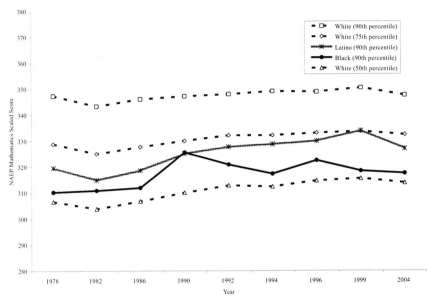

Source: NCES (1975–2004).

such odds, at this stage a race-neutral approach to admissions is sure to produce very segregated higher education learning environments. Without the
race-conscious tools afforded by *Bakke,* selective admissions colleges and universities would be left with few options to create the diverse classes that they
believe to be important to achieve their educational missions.

Conclusion

Justices O'Conner and Ginsberg outline one route to the end of the race-
conscious admissions plans affirmed by *Bakke* and *Grutter.* They suggest,
through O'Connor's majority opinion in *Grutter* and Ginsberg's concurring
opinion, that through more equitable schooling options for underrepresented minority students we could conceivably move away from race-
conscious policies to create the diverse learning environments foreseen by
Bakke by 2028, 25 years after that landmark decision. For this approach to

work, however, applicants of each racial group would need to have equivalent distributions on the metrics colleges and universities use for admissions.

Our examination of how successful schools have been in eliminating disparities in context, resources, and outcomes during the 30 years since *Bakke* give us little reason to be optimistic about the 25-year window. Students are more racially isolated now than they were during the aftermath of the *Bakke* decision. For many resources, there remains a clear educational access differential among White, Black, and Latino students. Where we have seen a narrowing of difference, such as in student–teacher ratios, the changes have been modest (four students per teacher) and have taken a great deal of time to occur (30 years). Finally, when examining educational outcomes, the differences in test scores have been remarkably stable during the past 30 years, with little progress even in understanding why this differential seems to be so intractable.

Eliminating differences in educational attainment and achievement between racial/ethnic groups is a goal to which we should all aspire. However, given the slow pace of educational change, and the high stakes of selective college admissions, there should be a tempered approach when it comes to removing the ability of colleges and universities to use race-conscious means to create their diverse learning environments. Until it becomes clear that we are making substantial progress in educating all students equally, creating yet another barrier to students who already face myriad challenges may fly in the face of the spirit of both *Bakke* and *Grutter,* undermining the very real benefits they sought to guarantee.

Notes

1. Concurring opinions generally agree with the result of a case, but not necessarily with the reasoning offered.

2. Of the five major racial/ethnic categories recognized by the National Center for Educational Statistics (NCES) Common Core of Data (CCD) (White, Asian, Latino, Black, and American Indian), Latino, Black, and American Indian students are generally recognized as underrepresented by race/ethnicity in higher education. Because of their small population, we have omitted American Indian students from this analysis and focused on Black and Latino students. Further, although we are aware that disparities in educational outcomes exist between Southeast Asians and other Asian groups, this is beyond the scope of our chapter.

3. Kane (1998) has documented that race-conscious admission policies are primarily used in highly selective colleges and universities.

4. This finding is particularly relevant to the O'Conner and Ginsberg opinions because high-achieving minority students are exactly the group that would be competitive for institutions with selective admissions and are the students that we will need to focus on because issues of race-conscious admissions policies only have relevance for selective admissions schools (Wilbur & Bonous, 1998).

5. The NCES CCD is listed by school year. In this chapter, we have chosen to list CCD data by the fall of the school year. Thus, 1990 refers to data from the fall of the 1990–1991 school year.

6. We were interested in the distribution of students in regular schools rather than special education, vocational, or other alternative schools where school populations might not be distributed in similar proportions across racial and ethnic groups. Using this criterion, we captured 92% of the public elementary and secondary schools and 98% of the students.

7. For the purposes of this chapter, we define intensely segregated minority schools as those with fewer than 10% White enrollment. Intensely segregated White schools are those with greater than 90% White enrollment. Predominantly minority schools are those with greater than 50% minority enrollment. In reporting research findings of other scholars, we provide their definitions for these terms when they differ from ours.

8. Examples of cases include *Board of Education of Oklahoma City v. Dowell* (1991), *Freeman v. Pitts* (1992), and *Missouri v. Jenkins* (1995).

9. Although there were state and local efforts to desegregate Latinos throughout the 1940s, 1950s, and 1960s, the Supreme Court did not recognize the Latino right to desegregation until 1973 in *Keyes v. School District No. 1, Denver, Colorado*. Segregation of Latino students was often addressed in court on the basis of discrimination by language rather than traditional desegregation laws after the passage of *Lau v. Nichols* (1974).

10. Parts of this section have been adapted from Orfield and Lee (2006).

11. In this chapter, we define poor students as those who are eligible for the federal government's free or reduced lunch program.

12. In 1992, Black students actually received more money than Whites, on average. One reason for such differences may be that Black students disproportionately live in urban areas where the cost of running a school system is higher than it is in suburban and rural areas. Thus, the expenditure numbers for the average Black student could be inflated relative to Whites because of regional differences in the cost of living and the distribution of the populations.

13. For additional discussion on dropouts, see Orfield (2004).

14. The NAEP is often referred to as the "nation's report card" and is part of a testing program that has existed since 1969. The section of the exam we use for our analysis is the long-term trend data, which is intended to measure the basic achievement of students in mathematics and English using a nationally representative sample and consistent questions over an extended period. The examinations use nearly identical assessments year after year, so the changes in achievement on the NAEP

are thought to be good representations of changes in student achievement on these examinations.

15. These numbers were calculated using the total number of 17-year-olds in the country for each racial group using the 2000 U.S. Census. In these calculations, we have assumed that the findings of the NAEP were nationally representative, and that the percentile scores for the sample would be the same for the populations of 17-year-olds in the country who had not yet received a high school diploma. We then multiply that number by the 50th, 75th, or 90th percentile. These student numbers are likely overestimates of each group because a number of dropouts did not contribute to the testing distribution on the NAEP but were included in the estimate of the total number of White, Black, and Latino students scoring at a particular achievement level. In addition, the overestimates are likely to be greater for Black and Latino students because they drop out at higher rates than their White peers.

References

Anyon, J. (1997). *Ghetto schooling: A political economy of urban educational reform.* New York: Teachers College Record.

Board of Education of Oklahoma City v. Dowell, 498 U.S. 237 (1991).

Boozer, M., Krueger, A., Wolkon, S., Haltiwanger, J., & Loury, G. (1992). Race and school quality since *Brown v. Board of Education. Brookings Papers on Economic Activity. Microeconomics, 1992,* 269–338.

Brief of the American Education Research Association as *amicus curiae* in support of respondents, *Parents Involved in Community Schools v. Seattle School District No. 1,* 127 S. Ct. 2738 (2007).

Brown v. Board of Education of the City of Topeka, 347 U.S. 483 (1954).

Card, D., & Krueger, A. (1996). School resources and student outcomes: An overview of the literature and new evidence from North and South Carolina. *Journal of Economic Perspectives, 10*(4), 31–50.

Cech, S. (2007, November 14). Number of schools offering AP falls after first audit of courses. *Education Week,* pp. 1, 13.

Chaddock, G. R. (2006, June 21). U.S. high school dropout rate: High, but how high? *Christian Science Monitor.* Retrieved October 1, 2007, from http://www.csmonitor.com/2006/0621/p03s02-ussc.html

Cook, T., Armor, D. J., Crain, R. L., Miller, N., Stephan, W. G., & Walberg, H. J. (Eds.). (1984). *School desegregation and Black achievement.* Washington, DC: National Institute of Education.

Corcoran, S., Evans, W., Goodwin, J., Murray, S., & Schwab, R. (2004). The changing distribution of education finance, 1972–1997. In K. Neckerman (Ed.), *Social inequality* (pp. 433–466). New York: Russell Sage Foundation.

Crain, R. L., & Mahard, R. E. (1983). The effect of research methodology on deseg-regation-achievement studies: A meta-analysis. *The American Journal of Sociology, 88*(5), 839–854.

Darling-Hammond, L. (2001). Apartheid in American education: How opportunity is rationed to children of color in the United States. In T. Johnson, J. Boyden, & W. Pittz (Eds.), *Racial profiling and punishment in American education* (pp. 39–44). Oakland, CA: Applied Research Center.

Dawkins, M. P., & Braddock J. H. (1994). The continuing significance of desegrega-tion: School racial composition and African American inclusion in American so-ciety. *Journal of Negro Education, 63*(3), 394–405.

Eaton, S. (2001). *The other Boston busing story: What's won and lost across the bound-ary line.* New Haven, CT: Yale University Press.

Freeman v. Pitts, 503 U.S. 467 (1992).

Freeman, C., Scafidi, B., & Sjoquist, D. L. (2002). Racial segregation in Georgia public schools, 1994–2002: Trends, causes, and impact on teacher quality. In J. Boger & G. Orfield (Eds.), *School resegregation: Must the South turn back?* (pp. 148–163). Chapel Hill: University of North Carolina Press.

Greenwald, R., Hedges, L., & Laine, R. (1996). The effect of school resources on student achievement. *Review of Educational Research, 66*(3), 361–396.

Grissmer, D., Flanagan, A., & Williamson, S. (1998). Why did the Black-White score gap narrow in the 1970s and 1980s? In C. Jencks & M. Phillips (Eds.), *The Black-White test score gap* (pp. 182–228). Washington, DC: Brookings Institution Press.

Grutter v. Bollinger, 539 U.S. 306 (2003).

Hallinan, M. T., & Williams, R. A. (1990). Students' characteristics and the peer-influenced characteristics. *Sociology of Education, 63*(2), 122–132.

Hanushek, E. (1981). Throwing money at schools. *Journal of Policy Analysis and Management, 1,* 19–41.

Hanushek, E. (1986). The economics of schooling: Production and efficiency in public schools. *Journal of Economic Literature, 24,* 1141–1177.

Hanushek, E. (1991). When school finance "reform" may not be good policy. *Harvard Journal on Legislation, 28,* 423–465.

Hanushek, E. A., Kain, J. F., & Rivkin, S. G. (2002). *New evidence about* Brown v. Board of Education: *The complex effects of school racial composition on achievement.* Cambridge, MA: National Bureau of Economic Research.

Harknett, K., Garfinkle, I., Bainbridge, J., Smeeding, T., Folbre, N., & McLana-han, S. (2003). *Do public expenditures improve child outcomes in the U.S.? A com-parison across fifty states* [Center for Policy Research Working Paper No. 53]. Syracuse, NY: Maxwell School of Citizenship and Public Affairs.

Hedges, L., & Nowell, A. (1998). Black-White test score convergence since 1965. In C. Jenks & M. Phillips (Eds.), *The Black-White test score gap* (pp. 149–181). Washington, DC: Brookings Institution Press.

Hollmann, F. W., Mulder, T. J., & Kallan, J. E. (2000). *Methodology and assumptions for the population projections of the United States: 1999 to 2100* [U.S. Census Bureau, Population Division Working Paper No. 380]. Retrieved November 14, 2007, from http://www.census.gov/population/www/documentation/twps0038.html

Kahlenberg, R. (2001). *All together now.* Washington, DC: Brookings Institution Press.

Kane, T. (1998). Misconceptions in the debate over affirmative action in college admissions. In G. Orfield & E. Miller (Eds.), *Chilling admissions: The affirmative action crisis and the search for alternatives* (pp. 17–32). Cambridge, MA: Harvard Education Publishing Group.

Keyes v. School District No. 1, Denver, Colorado, 413 U.S. 189 (1973).

Lau v. Nichols, 414 U.S. 563 (1974).

Logan, J. (2004). *Resegregation in American public schools? Not in the 1990s.* Albany, NY: Lewis Mumford Center for Comparative Urban and Regional Research.

Missouri v. Jenkins, 515 U.S. 70 (1995).

Monk, D., & Haller, E. (1993). Predictors of high school academic course offerings: The role of school size. *American Educational Research Journal, 30*(1), 3–21.

National Center for Education Statistics. (1975–2004). *NAEP data explorer.* Washington, DC: U.S. Department of Education. Retrieved October 1, 2007, http://www.nces.ed.gov/nationsreportcard/lttnde/

National Center for Education Statistics. (1990). *Common core of data.* Washington, DC: U.S. Department of Education. Retrieved October 1, 2007, http://www.nces.ed.gov/ccd/pubschuniv.asp

National Center for Education Statistics. (2005). *Common core of data.* Washington, DC: U.S. Department of Education. Retrieved October 1, 2007, http://www.nces.ed.gov/ccd/pubschuniv.asp

National Center for Education Statistics. (2007). *The condition of education, 2007* (NCES 2007–064), Indicator 23. Washington, DC: U.S. Department of Education. Retrieved October 1, 2007, from http://www.nces.ed.gov/programs/coe/2007/section3/indicator23.asp

Natriello, G., McDill, E. L., & Pallas, A. M. (1990). *Schooling disadvantaged children: Racing against catastrophe.* New York: Teachers College Press.

Oakes, J. (1990). *Multiplying inequalities.* Santa Monica, CA: RAND Institute.

Orfield, G. (2004). *Dropouts in America: Confronting the graduation rate crisis.* Cambridge, MA: Harvard Education Press.

Orfield, G., & Lee, C. (2006). *Why segregation matters: Poverty and educational inequality.* Cambridge, MA: The Civil Rights Project at Harvard University.

Orfield, G., & Lee, C. (2007). *Historic reversals, accelerating resegregation, and the need for new integration.* Los Angeles, CA: The Civil Rights Project at UCLA.

Orfield, G., & Yun, J. T. (1999). *Resegregation in American schools.* Cambridge, MA: The Civil Rights Project at Harvard University.

Raudenbush, S., Fotiu, R., & Cheong, Y. (1998). Inequality of access to educational resources: A national report card for eighth-grade math. *Educational Evaluation and Policy Analysis, 20*(4), 253–267.

Reardon, S. F., Yun, J. T., & Eitle, T. (2000). The changing context of school segregation: Multiracial measurement of school segregation from 1987–1997. *Demography, 37*(3), 351–364.

Rebell, M. (2007). Poverty, "meaningful" educational opportunity, and the necessary role of the courts. *North Carolina Law Review, 85,* 1468–1542.

Regents of the University of California v. Bakke, 438 U.S. 265 (1978).

Rothstein, R. (2004). *Class and schools: Using social, economic and educational reform to close the Black-White achievement gap.* Washington, DC: Economic Policy Institute.

Rumberger, R. W. (2003). The causes and consequences of student mobility. *Journal of Negro Education, 72,* 6–21.

Schofield, J. W. (1995). Review of research on school desegregation's impact on elementary and secondary school students. In J. A. Banks & C. A. Banks (Eds.), *Handbook of research on multicultural education* (pp. 595–616). New York: Simon & Schuster Macmillan.

Schofield, J. W. (2001). Maximizing the benefits of a diverse student body: Lessons from school desegregation research. In G. Orfield & M. Kurlaender (Eds.), *Diversity challenged: Evidence on the impact of affirmative action* (pp. 99–110). Cambridge, MA: Harvard Education Publishing Group.

Wells, A., & Crain, R. (1997). *Stepping over the color line: African-American students in White suburban schools.* New Haven, CT: Yale University Press.

Wilbur, S., & Bonous, M. (1998). Testing a new approach to admissions: The Irvine experience. In G. Orfield & E. Miller (Eds.), *Chilling admissions: The affirmative action crisis and the search for alternatives* (pp. 111–123). Cambridge, MA: The Civil Rights Project at Harvard University.

5

EDUCATIONAL ATTAINMENT
IN THE STATES

Are We Progressing Toward Equity in 2028?

Donald E. Heller

I n 1978, the Supreme Court issued its opinion in *Regents of the University of California v. Bakke,* a landmark case that challenged the use of affirmative action in higher education. While striking down the use of racial quotas, as had been used in the medical school at the University of California, Davis, the Supreme Court affirmed the use of affirmative action for the purpose of achieving diversity of the study body. The rationale for the use of affirmative action in the *Bakke* decision was largely based on the perceived benefits of having a diverse student body rather than on the need to remedy the present effects of past discrimination or inequities.[1]

It took a quarter of a century for the Supreme Court to return to the question of affirmative action in college admissions. In 2003, the Court issued its much-awaited opinion in *Grutter v. Bollinger.* By upholding the University of Michigan's right to use affirmative action in its law school admissions process, the Court affirmed its decision in *Bakke.* Echoing its ruling of 25 years earlier, the focus of the Court's decision in *Grutter* was once again on the benefits of diversity in the university, rather than on the use of affirmative action to help address the current effects of past discrimination and present inequities that linger because of that discrimination.

The author acknowledges the research assistance of Jason DeRousie and Samuel Museus in the preparation of the data used in this chapter.

Nevertheless, near the end of her majority opinion in *Grutter,* Justice Sandra Day O'Connor referenced expectations of improvements to existing inequities when she wrote,

> It has been 25 years since Justice Powell first approved the use of race to further an interest in student body diversity in the context of public higher education. Since that time, the number of minority applicants with high grades and test scores has indeed increased. . . . We expect that 25 years from now, the use of racial preferences will no longer be necessary to further the interest approved today. (p. 342)

Marking 25 years since *Bakke,* Justice O'Connor indicates that in that period we have observed improvement in educational outcomes such as grades and test scores. She concludes that in 25 more years, 2028, the improvement will be so great that race-conscious affirmative action will no longer be needed to diversify a student body. In doing so, she expands the discussion from the benefits of diversity emphasized in *Bakke* to a discussion that also emphasizes considerations of equity. This is an important return to issues that many civil rights advocates claim have been missing from the conversation since the benefits of diversity rationale gained prominence in defending affirmative action programs.

To determine whether Justice O'Connor's (and the majority's) professed wish that race-conscious policies will no longer be necessary at some point in the future may come true, it is helpful to understand the current state of equity among the races. For the purpose of this chapter, "equity" is defined as parity in educational attainment among the races. Equity is examined by comparing the rates at which students from different racial groups move through the educational pipeline—beginning in the ninth grade—and into and through postsecondary education. The analysis compares Black and Hispanic students—both of which are groups that historically have had higher drop-out rates and lower high school graduation rates, as well as having been underrepresented in American higher education—to White students nationally and across the states.[2]

I begin the chapter with an outline of the data used along with the methodology employed to examine issues of equity along the educational pipeline. I include a discussion of the inherent limitations of the analysis. Next, I present the results of the analyses, comparing the racial groups within and across the states. In the final section of the chapter, I draw some conclusions from the findings regarding Justice O'Connor's prediction that our society will no longer need affirmative action in 2028—a time that is now only two decades away.

Tracking Progress Through the Pipeline: Data and Methodology

Data for this study were drawn from two databases of the U.S. Department of Education, National Center for Education Statistics (NCES). First, the Common Core of Data (CCD) provides information about public elementary and secondary schools in the nation (NCES, 2006a). Data on enrollments by grade level and race are reported to NCES by individual school districts around the country. The CCD data are used to study enrollment and high school diploma completion in secondary schools.

The second source of data from NCES is the Integrated Postsecondary Education Data System, or IPEDS (NCES, 2006b). All accredited colleges and universities in the country report enrollment and degree-completion data to NCES annually. These data were used to examine enrollments and bachelor's degree completion rates by state and racial group.

The data from the CCD and IPEDS were used to examine measures of progress through five points along the educational pipeline (figure 5.1). The first step is enrollment in the fall of the 9th-grade year. The second step is enrollment in the fall of the 12th grade, which assuming normal progress, should occur 3 years after 9th-grade enrollment. The next step is graduation from high school, normally by the spring following 12th-grade enrollment. Postsecondary enrollment is measured in the fall after graduating from high school. And then, assuming that a student progresses straight through, a bachelor's degree would be received 4 years after graduating from high school.

This model has a number of limitations. First, the data from NCES (both the CCD and IPEDS) are not cohort-based (i.e., they do not measure

FIGURE 5.1
Model of the educational pipeline

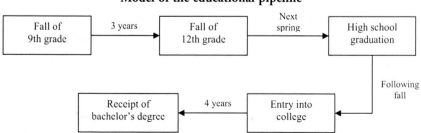

the progress of individual students through the pipeline). Rather, the data are cross-sectional, or a snapshot of enrollments in each school or college in each year. Thus, they do not account for migration of students among districts or colleges, or across state lines. However, the comparison of cross-sectional data has become an often-used method of calculating such educational progress measures as high school graduation rates (Education Trust, 2006; *Education Week,* 2007).

Second, some evidence indicates that the ninth grade becomes a "pile-up" year, where there are an unusually high number of retentions, which would expand the enrollment in this grade (Texas Education Agency, 1995; Wheelock & Miao, 2005). This is particularly true of Black and Hispanic students. The effect of this would be to lower the high school graduation ratio for these students relative to Whites (discussed later in the chapter).

Third, the data from the CCD also exclude students in private secondary schools; in 2003, approximately 8% of all secondary schools students attended private schools (NCES, 2007, Table 52). The IPEDS data do include students in private (not-for-profit and for-profit) higher education institutions. Additionally, another 2% of all students were homeschooled (NCES, 2007, Table 37).

Fourth, the model assumes standard sequential progress through the pipeline, without allowing for stops along the way. For example, as shown in figure 5.1, the model assumes a student is enrolled in the 12th grade 3 years after she was enrolled in the 9th grade. Similarly, the model assumes a student enrolls in college in the fall after graduating from high school, and completes a bachelor's degree approximately 4 years after enrolling in college. Not all students follow this standard pattern. Some students who attend postsecondary education delay their entry for some period after graduating from high school. During the college years, some students stop out for a period or attend school part-time, thus delaying degree completion. For example, data from NCES indicate that approximately 69% of high school graduates enroll in some form of postsecondary education within 12 months of high school graduation (NCES, 2007, Table 187). In addition, approximately one-third of students who ultimately did attend college delayed their entry by at least 12 months (Horn, Cataldi, & Sikora, 2005). Differences in the attendance patterns of students from different racial groups may also contribute to differences in their overall degree attainment rates.

The absence of current, state-level longitudinal data on the progress of students through the educational pipeline (particularly from the K–12 sector through postsecondary education) forces the use of the cross-sectional data used for this analysis. The ideal way to track student progress would be through a longitudinal database that contains records for each student in each year. Although some states have begun to develop student-record data-sets that track individuals through the pipeline, they are in the minority, and there is no national-level equivalent database (Ewell, Schild, & Paulson, 2003). Absent this, however, even with these limitations, the data analyzed in this chapter do allow for comparisons across the states, and among the three racial groups studied.

Factors that affect progress through the pipeline, such as whether a student graduates from high school or attains a college degree within 4 years of high school graduation, can be both independent of the context of the specific state in which the student resides and related to that state context. Thus, differences among the racial groups within a state, as well as differences within a group across states, help provide valuable information about student progress through the pipeline and how far we are from achieving Justice O'Connor's goal of no longer needing affirmative action by 2028.

Four measures were used in this study to track progress through the pipeline. All the measures are based on ratios for the three racial groups studied, rather than raw numbers of students progressing through the pipeline. The use of these ratios to compare the races has been adapted from a study on California higher education conducted in 2003 (Bensimon, Hao, & Bustillos, 2003).[3] The specific measures used here are the following:

> *9th- to 12th-grade progression:* This measures the ratio of 12th-grade enrollments to the 9th-grade enrollment level in the state (and for each of the three racial groups studied—Whites, Blacks, and Hispanics) 3 years earlier. If all ninth graders progressed on time to their senior year in high school, and there was no migration into or out of the state, this ratio would equal 1.0. The ratio compares 12th graders in the fall of 2003 (the most recent data available through the CCD) to 9th graders enrolled in the fall of 2000.
>
> *High school graduation rate:* This measures the ratio of high school diplomas awarded in a state to the enrollment of ninth graders 3 years earlier.[4] If every ninth grader graduated from high school on time, and

there was no migration, this ratio would be 1.0. This ratio compares diplomas awarded in the 2002–2003 school year to ninth graders enrolled in the fall of 1999.

First-time freshmen enrollment rate: This measures the ratio of first-time freshmen enrolled in college in the state in the fall (in both public and private postsecondary institutions) to the number of high school diplomas awarded in the previous school year. "First-time freshmen" are defined by NCES as those students attending some form of postsecondary education for the first time.[5] This ratio compares the number of students attending college in the fall of 2003 to the number of students awarded diplomas in the 2002–2003 school year.

Bachelor's degree rate: This measures the ratio of bachelor's degrees awarded in a state (by both public and private postsecondary institutions) to the number of high school diplomas awarded 4 years earlier. This ratio compares bachelor's degrees awarded in the 2004–2005 academic year (the most recent data available through IPEDS) to high school diplomas awarded in the 2000–2001 school year.

Is There Educational Equity Among Racial Groups?

As described earlier, the focus of this study is to compare the rates of progress of Black and Hispanic students through the educational pipeline with those of White students. Data on each of the measures outlined in the previous section were calculated for the entire nation to establish the national baseline, and then the same measures were calculated for each state. Table 5.1 shows the national measures for each of the three racial groups studied, as well as for all students.

TABLE 5.1
Educational Pipeline Ratios for the Nation

Group Rates	White	Black	Hispanic	All Races*
9th- to 12th-grade progression	0.84	0.61	0.66	0.77
High school graduation	0.77	0.51	0.58	0.69
First-time freshmen enrollment	0.86	0.89	0.66	0.89
Bachelor's degree	0.59	0.41	0.34	0.56

Source: Author's calculations from data drawn from NCES (2006a, 2006b).
*Other racial groups not shown separately are included here.

Overall in the country, the ratio of 12th-grade enrollments in 2003 to 9th-grade enrollments 3 years earlier was 0.77. Approximately 23% of 9th graders never make it to the fall of their senior year in high school. The rate for each racial group ranged from a high of 0.84 for White students to a low of 0.61 for Blacks.

Turning to high school graduation rates, the ratio of the number of high school diplomas issued nationally to 9th-grade enrollments 3 years earlier was 0.69. Whites had the highest rate at 0.77 and Blacks the lowest, at 0.51.[6] The difference between the 9th- to 12th-grade progression rates, and the high school graduation rates (eight percentage points for the total group), is an indicator of the proportion of students who are lost from the pipeline during their senior year of high school.

The entry rates of first-time students into college were very similar for both Whites (0.86) and Blacks (0.89), with Hispanic students lagging behind at 0.66. These rates are relatively high, most likely because the ranks of first-time freshmen students (as counted by NCES) can include adult students who are entering college for the first time. Thus, the numerator of the ratio can be inflated by the adult students, but the denominator is fixed at the number of high school graduates.[7] However, that Black students entered college at a similar rate to that of White students is not inconsistent with other research that has examined the college entry rates of students from different racial groups. This research has found that, controlling for levels of educational achievement, college attendance rates are actually *higher* for Black students than for Whites. One study found, "For similarly skilled individuals, college attendance rates for Blacks exceeded college attendance rates for Whites by 6 to 17 percentage points overall" (Jacobson, Olsen, Rice, & Sweetland, 2001, p. 26).

In other words, if Black and White high school graduates had had similar levels of academic achievement, one would have expected even higher first-time freshmen enrollment rates here for Black students (or lower for White students). Although Blacks and Whites did not necessarily have the same levels of educational achievement in high school, what may be at work here is that graduating from high school for Black students becomes the minimal level of achievement necessary to encourage postsecondary attendance, thus driving up their enrollment rates relative to those of White students.

The rates at which students received bachelor's degrees in 2005 compared with high school graduates 4 years earlier ranged from 0.59 for White students to 0.34 for Hispanics. Overall, the rate was 0.56. Again, as with the entry rates into college, these figures are somewhat inflated because of the presence of older students returning to college and attaining a bachelor's degree. For example, an adult student who attained a bachelor's degree in 2005 would be included in the numerator of the ratio, even though he may have graduated from high school 10 years earlier (and thus would be excluded from the denominator).[8]

These national figures demonstrate that there are large differences across the racial groups in the rate at which they move through the educational pipeline. Figure 5.2 compares the groups at three major points, starting with 100 ninth graders in each group (and all races together). For example, of the 100 White ninth graders, 77 would graduate from high school in 4 years, and 45 would receive a bachelor's degree 4 years after high school graduation. For both Blacks and Hispanics, fewer than half as many students would ultimately receive bachelor's degrees.

Turning to the states, similar patterns are seen. However, there are clear differences across the states, both with respect to how a state performs compared with national averages, as well as when comparing students across the

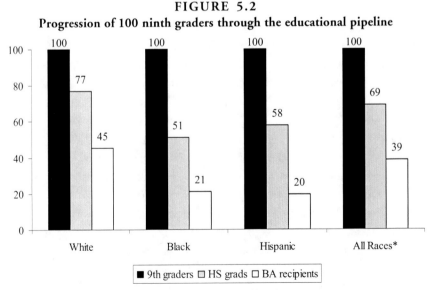

FIGURE 5.2
Progression of 100 ninth graders through the educational pipeline

Source: Author's calculations from data drawn from NCES (2006a, 2006b).
*Other racial groups not shown separately are included here.

three racial groups within the state. To show both of these comparisons, the ratios described earlier were calculated for each racial group in each state, and then the ratios for Black and Hispanic students were each plotted against those of Whites.

Figure 5.3 presents the first comparison, showing the 9th- to 12th-grade progression rates of Black (on the horizontal axis) and White (on the vertical axis) students.[9] Also shown are two sets of reference lines. The dashed diagonal line represents a hypothetical parity line between the two races; a state whose rates for the two races were the same would be on this line. States with the White rate higher than the Black rate appear above and to the left of the parity line; states whose Black students have a higher rate than White students appear below and to the right of this line. For example, Wisconsin had a 9th- to 12th-grade progression rate for White students of 0.94, meaning that there were 94 Whites enrolled in 12th grade in 2003 for every 100 White students enrolled in 9th grade in 2000. In contrast, the Black rate for

FIGURE 5.3

Comparison of White and Black 9th- to 12th-grade progression rates

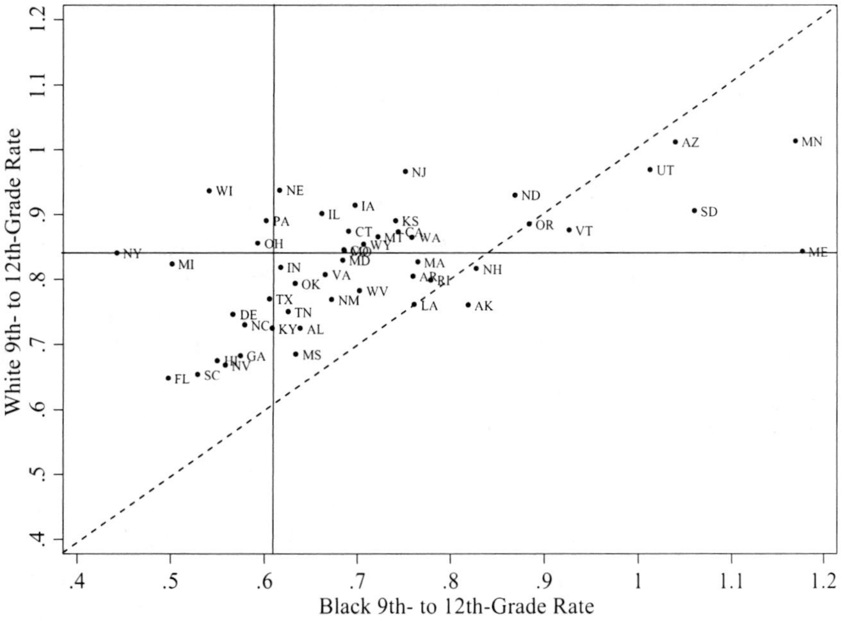

Source: Author's calculations from data drawn from NCES (2006a, 2006b).

Wisconsin was 0.54. A state could have a rate greater than 1.0 because of in-migration from other states or students moving from private schools (or home schools) back to the public schools.

The second set of reference lines is the solid vertical and horizontal lines. The vertical line represents the progression rate for Blacks nationally, and the horizontal line is the same measure for White students.[10] Thus, a state that is plotted above the solid horizontal line has a White progression rate higher than the national rate. A state that falls to the left of the vertical line has a rate for Black students that is lower than the nation as a whole. States in the upper right quadrant outperform the national rate for both Black and White students; students in the opposite (lower left) quadrant lag behind the national averages for both groups. For example, White students in New York progressed from 9th to 12th grade at the same rate as the nation as a whole. Black students in that state, however, progressed at a rate well below the national rate of 0.61. Ohio was very close to the national rate for both groups. States such as Florida, South Carolina, Nevada, and Georgia scored below the national averages for both Whites and Blacks, yet Whites in these states still had higher progression rates than Blacks. Conversely, in states such as Arizona, Utah, and South Dakota, both White and Black students outperformed the national averages, and Blacks had higher progression rates than Whites did.[11]

Figure 5.4 shows the same comparison for Hispanic and White students. Most states with the largest Hispanic populations—Florida, Texas, New Mexico, and New York—had Hispanic rates below the national average. But there were some exceptions; both Arizona and California, with large Hispanic student populations, had progression rates greater than the national average. Both of these states also had rates for White students that were above the national average, so it may be that students from both racial groups benefit from elementary and secondary schools that are higher in quality—or at least do a better job moving students from the 9th grade through to the 12th grade—than in most other states.

Figure 5.5 shows the high school graduation rates of White and Black students across the states. As shown in table 5.1, the rate for Blacks nationally was 0.51 and for Whites it was 0.77. Florida, Tennessee, and Georgia are among the states that underperformed the nation as a whole for both groups, whereas states such as Pennsylvania, Minnesota, and Maryland outper-formed the national rates. A handful of states, all with relatively small Black

FIGURE 5.4

Comparison of White and Hispanic 9th- to 12th-grade progression rates

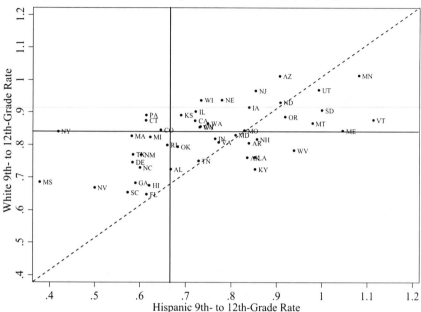

Source: Author's calculations from data drawn from NCES (2006a, 2006b).

populations—Rhode Island, Hawaii, Wyoming, Vermont, and North Dakota—had Black high school graduation rates higher than their White rates.

Figure 5.6 shows the high school graduation rates for White and Hispanic students. Some states with large Hispanic populations performed relatively well. Arizona and California, for example, outperformed the national figures for both groups. The Texas rates for both Whites and Hispanics were just about at the national rates. Hispanic students in Florida[12] performed right on the national rate, but White students lagged well behind their counterparts nationally. In contrast, White students in New York had a high school graduation rate just below that of all White students nationally, whereas the rate for Hispanic students was well below the national figure.

Figure 5.7 shows the ratio of White and Black first-time freshmen students as a proportion of high school graduates the prior spring. As noted earlier, these figures are biased somewhat upward because the denominator of the ratio includes only public high school graduates and excludes graduates of private high schools as well as GED recipients, whereas the numerator

FIGURE 5.5
Comparison of White and Black high school graduation rates

White HS Graduation Rate (y-axis)

Black HS Graduation Rate (x-axis)

Data points: DC, WI, NE, MN, IA, PA, SD, CT, ND, IL, MT, UT, AZ, OH, KS, MD, MA, CA, VA, VT, NY, MO, IN, TX, AR, OK, WY, DE, WA, OR, WV, NV, KY, NC, AK, LA, MI, AL, MS, HI, FL, TN, GA, RI

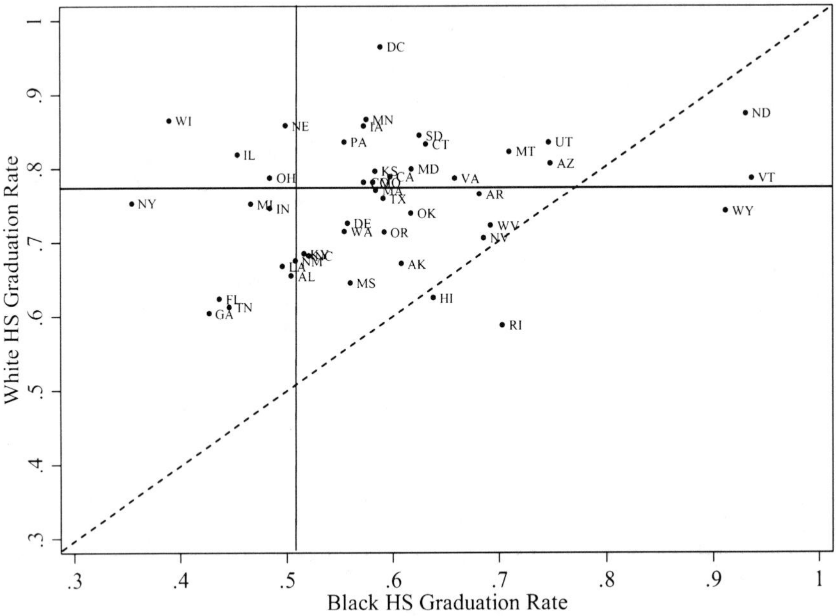

Source: Author's calculations from data drawn from NCES (2006a, 2006b).

includes students who completed secondary school with any of these credentials. The figures are also biased high because of the impact of adult students, discussed earlier.

It is also important to acknowledge the role of interstate migration. Although the majority of students attend college in the same state from which they graduated high school, some do cross state lines to continue their education at the postsecondary level. Data from NCES indicate that 20% of first-time college students attend college in a different state from that in which they graduated from high school (NCES, 2007, Table 207).[13]

In contrast to the measures of 9th- to 12th-grade transition rates and high school graduation rates, the measure of first-time enrollment in college shows more parity between White and Black students. States' placement relative to the national rates are closely related to whether they are net importers or exporters of freshmen students. For example, Massachusetts in 2004 had a freshman net import rate of 13% (calculated as net imports of students

FIGURE 5.6
Comparison of White and Hispanic high school graduation rates

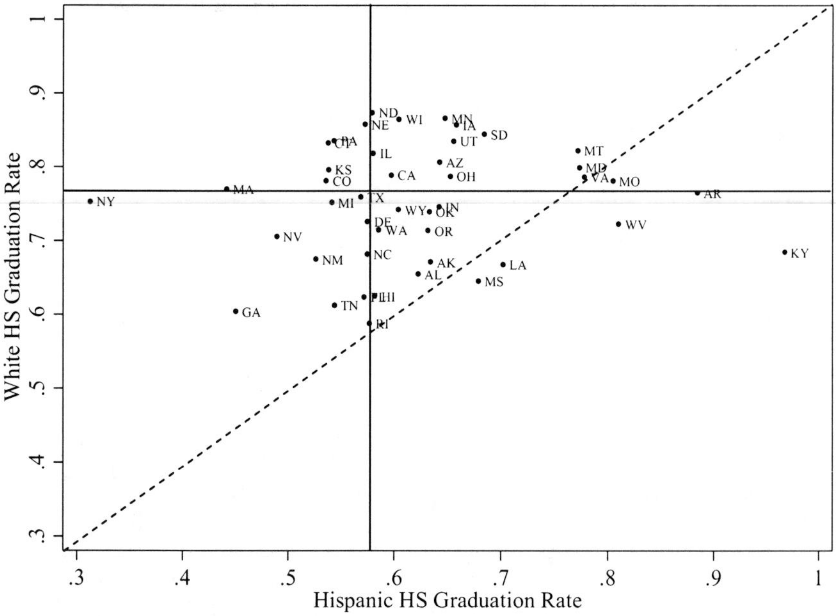

Source: Author's calculations from data drawn from NCES (2006a, 2006b).

divided by total freshmen). Massachusetts had both White and Black fresh-men enrollment rates greater than the national figures, likely driven, at least in part, by the migration of college students into the state.

In contrast, New Jersey is an exporter of freshman students; its net ex-port of students represented 47% of the total freshmen enrollment in the state. And New Jersey's freshman enrollment rate (relative to high school graduates in the state) was well below the national figure for both Black and White students. If New Jersey had been neither an importer nor exporter of students, its first-time freshmen enrollment rates for both White and Black students would have been very close to the national rates.

Figure 5.8 shows the comparison of first-time freshmen enrollment rates for White and Hispanic students in each state. Among states with large His-panic populations, there was a wide range of performance. For example, Cal-ifornia, with the nation's largest Hispanic population, had freshmen

FIGURE 5.7

Comparison of White and Black first-time freshmen college enrollment rates

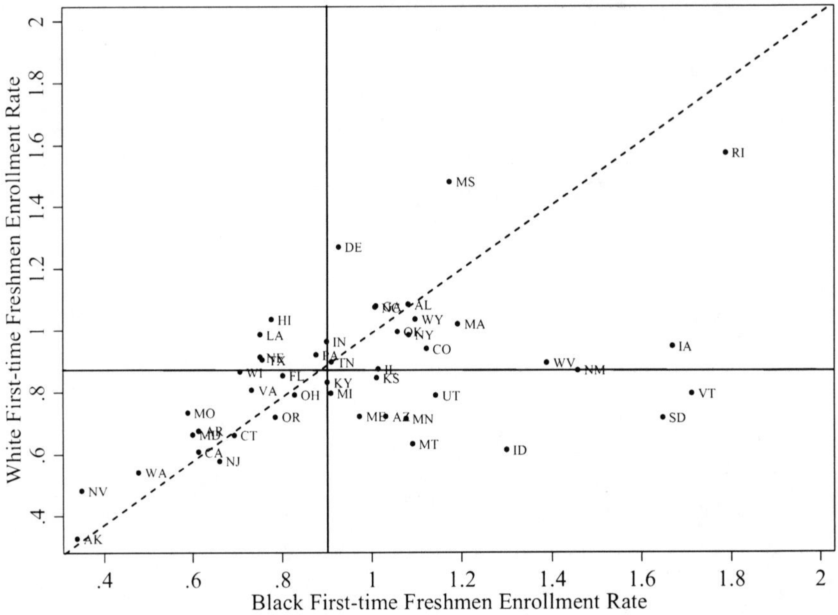

Source: Author's calculations from data drawn from NCES (2006a, 2006b).

enrollment rates well below the national figure for both Whites and Hispanics (even though its net migration of freshman students was close to zero). Texas, with the nation's second largest group of Hispanics, had freshmen enrollment rates for both Whites and Hispanics that were close to the national figures (and Texas also had net migration close to zero). In contrast to those states, both Florida and New York, with the nation's third and fourth largest Hispanic populations, had Hispanic enrollment rates well above the national level. New York's high freshmen enrollment rates (for both White and Hispanic students) were particularly impressive given that its net migration was close to zero, while Florida is a relatively large net importer of college freshmen.

The last set of comparisons is of the bachelor's degree production rates in each state. As described earlier, these figures are the ratio of the number of bachelor's degrees awarded in each state divided by the number of high school graduates 4 years earlier. As noted in table 5.1, the rate for White students nationally was 0.59, and for Black students it was 0.41. And it is

FIGURE 5.8
Comparison of White and Hispanic first-time freshmen enrollment rates

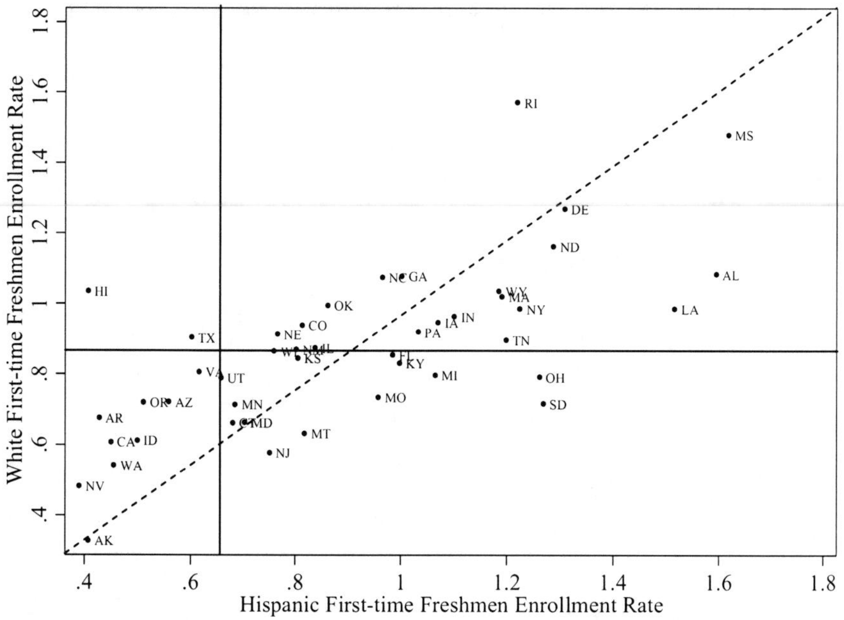

Source: Author's calculations from data drawn from NCES (2006a, 2006b).

again important to note that, as with the measures of first-time freshmen enrollment rates, these ratios across all states are all biased higher because of the impact of adult students and because the denominator of the ratio excludes graduates of private high schools as well as GED recipients. The impact of interstate migration upon enrolling in college can also affect each individual state's ratios.

Figure 5.9 shows the comparison of White and Black bachelor's degree rates in each state. As can be seen, most of the states are above and to the left of the dashed parity line, indicating that White students had higher ratios than Black students. All of the states on or to the right of the parity line—such as Maine, Iowa, North Dakota, and Idaho—have very small Black populations. Both Rhode Island and North Dakota have bachelor's degree rates in excess of 1.0 because they are both net importers of college students.

Figure 5.10 shows the same comparison for White and Hispanic students. The patterns are similar to the previous figure; most states have higher

FIGURE 5.9

Comparison of White and Black bachelor's degree rates

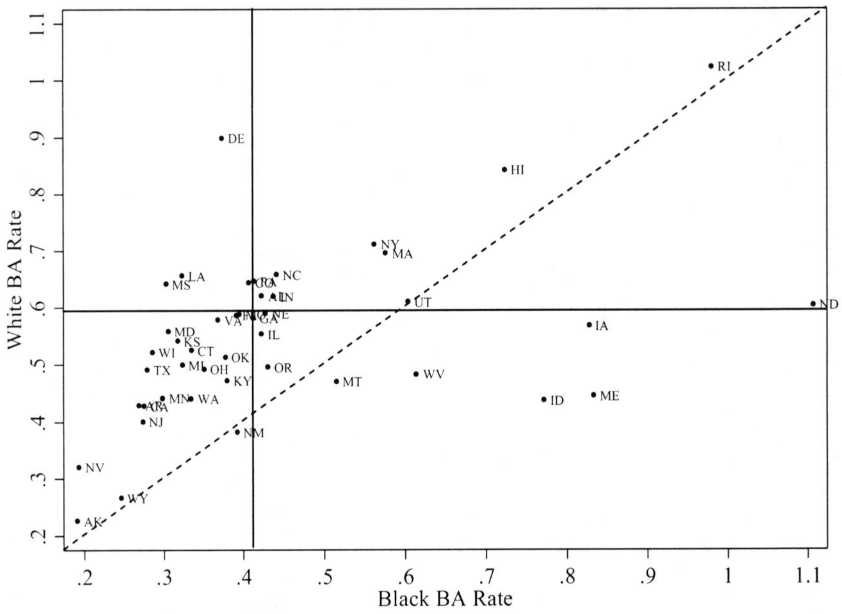

Source: Author's calculations from data drawn from NCES (2006a, 2006b).

bachelor's degree ratios for White than Hispanic students, and those states that have higher ratios for Hispanic students were those with relatively small Hispanic populations.

The data describing each step along the educational pipeline can be combined to show the progress through the entire pipeline. Figure 5.2 presented the cumulative rates of progress for each race nationally. For every 100 White ninth graders, only 45 bachelor's degrees were awarded to them 9 years later. For Black and Hispanic ninth graders, only 21 and 20 bachelor's degrees, respectively, were awarded. Thus, not only are there leakages at each step of the pipeline, but the leakage rates differ among the three racial groups.

There are also important differences in the rates at which students from each racial group navigate the pipeline in different states. Figure 5.11 shows the rates at which White, Black, and Hispanic students in the 13 largest states (in population) traversed from ninth grade to a bachelor's degree.[14] As can

FIGURE 5.10
Comparison of White and Hispanic bachelor's degree rates

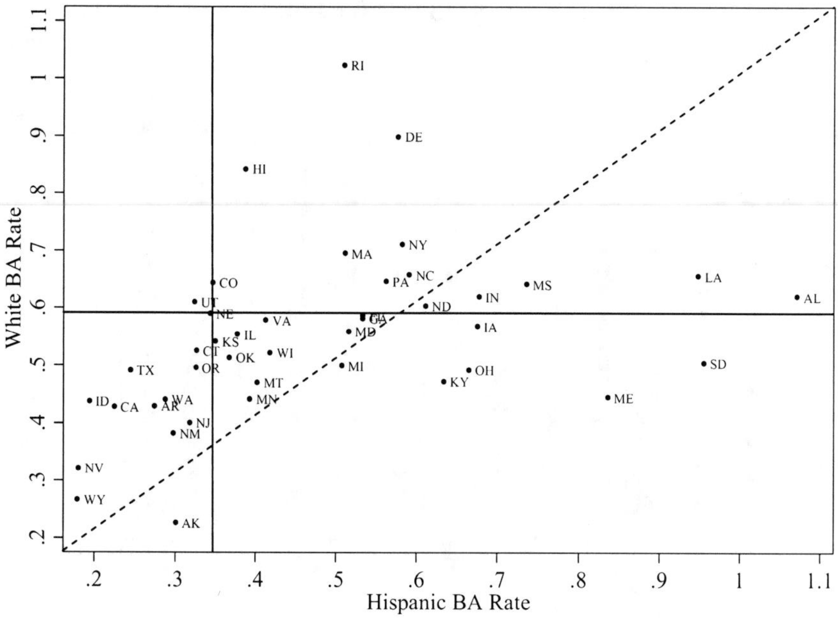

Source: Author's calculations from data drawn from NCES (2006a, 2006b).

be seen, there are large differences across the states, as well as within each state among the three groups.

The ratio for White students ranged from a low of 0.30 in Washington (meaning that for every 100 ninth graders in 1998, 30 bachelor's degrees were awarded in 2005) to 0.55 in Massachusetts.[15] Massachusetts also had the highest ratio for Black students, at 0.38, while Indiana had the highest rate for Hispanic students (0.41). Among the five states with the largest Hispanic populations (in order, California, Texas, Florida, New York, and Illinois), Florida had the highest ratio of bachelor's degree attainment at 0.28. In no state is there relative parity in the ratios among all three racial groups. Hispanic students in Ohio, for example, perform at a rate near that of White students, but Black students in that state lag behind. Black students in Massachusetts outperform Black students in all the other states, yet their performance still lags well behind that of White students in the state.

FIGURE 5.11

Ninth grade to bachelor's degree pipeline rate for White, Black, and Hispanic students, 13 largest states

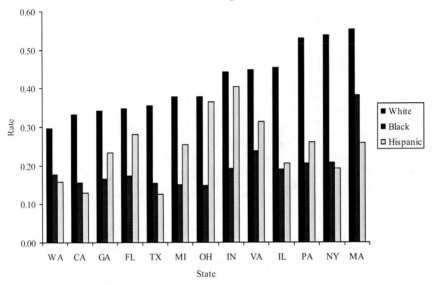

Source: Author's calculations from data drawn from NCES (2006a, 2006b).

Conclusion

As demonstrated in this chapter, and supported by earlier research, there are large differences in the rates at which White, Black, and Hispanic students navigate through the educational pipeline toward completion of a baccalaureate degree. Although the analysis in this chapter began with students in the ninth grade, we know that students' academic performance in high school is a result of their earlier preparation in middle and elementary school. So addressing inequities in the outcome at the end of this pipeline—receipt of a bachelor's degree, in this study—actually requires work at all educational levels.

The effects of leakage from the pipeline are cumulative; once a student leaves the traditional path toward attaining a college degree, it is very difficult to get back on track later in life. Longitudinal data from NCES tell us the following:

- Students who drop out of high school are less likely to achieve a secondary credential (either a high school diploma or a GED);

- Students who graduate from high school but delay enrollment in postsecondary education are less likely to attain a bachelor's degree; and
- Students who enroll in postsecondary education part time, as opposed to full time, are less likely to attain a bachelor's degree. (Ingels, Curtin, Kaufman, Alt, & Chen, 2002)

To examine these issues at the state level, it is important to understand why there are such large differences in attainment rates among the states. Educational achievement and attainment have been shown to be related to demographic and sociocultural factors, so differences in these characteristics among the population of students in the states can help drive some of these state-level discrepancies. But what goes on in schools and universities can also affect students' progress through the pipeline.

Understanding how these demographic, sociocultural, and institutional differences affect the educational attainment rates in the states is beyond the scope of this chapter. But this study provides fertile ground for researchers to continue to analyze why some states perform so well relative to others, and why some states have larger gaps among the races than do others. These researchers can further probe important questions such as these:

- What is the contribution of demographic factors—many of which are immutable, at least in the short run—such as income and parental education—to differences in educational attainment of children?
- Are there structural characteristics of schools, higher education institutions, or educational bureaucracies (at the K–12 or postsecondary levels) that contribute to these differences?

Ultimately, the evidence presented in this chapter raises doubt about whether the goal of parity in educational achievement among the races can be achieved given the current inequities in the educational system in our nation (see, also, Kurlaender & Felts and Yun & Lee, this volume, for related findings). One study that looked at trends in college participation rates over time projected how long it would be before the rates at which Blacks and Hispanics attended college would approach that of Whites (Heller, 1999).[16] Using data on enrollment trends between 1976 and 1996, this study found that the gap in the rates between Blacks and Hispanics, on the one hand,

and Whites, on the other, would slowly close over time. But even by 2021, which was as far as the study projected, gaps between the two minority groups and White students would still exist.

To make progress toward Justice O'Connor's goal of eliminating the need for affirmative action by 2028—only two decades away—much work will have to be accomplished. The work will need to focus on how to most effectively educate students of all races at the K–12 and postsecondary levels. However, this chapter suggests that addressing educational inequities will be a daunting if not impossible task if the goal of parity in educational achievement is to be achieved in such a short time. Until equity in educational attainment can be achieved, it is unlikely that Justice O'Connor's admonition can be met. Nevertheless, this goal is an important reminder of the need to emphasize the educational benefits of diversity in education as per *Bakke,* and to simultaneously address issues of educational equity.

Notes

1. The courts have historically found the use of race to remedy the present effects of past acts of discrimination legally compelling, but a strong basis in evidence has to be present that past discrimination has occurred, effects of that discrimination are present, and the two are tied together (The Civil Rights Project at Harvard University, 2002).

2. The focus of this chapter is on comparing the three largest racial groups in the country—Whites, Blacks, and Hispanics. Historically, Black and Hispanic educational achievement and attainment—in both the K–12 and postsecondary sectors—has lagged behind that of White students (see, for example, Carey, 2005; Heller, 1999; Koretz, 1990; Raudenbush, Fotiu, & Cheong, 1998). Asian American students are not included in the analysis because as a group their attainment rates tend to mirror, or in some cases exceed, those of Whites (National Center for Education Statistics, 2007, Table 12). Native American students are excluded because, in most states, their numbers are too small to make valid comparisons.

3. The study by Bensimon, Hao, and Bustillos (2003) focused on education in California and used different measures of educational achievement and attainment, but the idea of comparing rates of progress through the pipeline of students from different racial groups is adapted here from their work.

4. This measure of high school diplomas includes only those students awarded regular diplomas, and excludes those awarded any type of provisional or less than regular diploma. This measure also excludes GED recipients. The CCD does not include data on GED recipients.

5. Students who took college courses while still in high school are still considered first-time freshmen when they first enroll in a postsecondary institution.

6. These rates map very closely to those in a report by *Education Week* (2007). That study, which used a similar but slightly different methodology in calculating high school graduation rates for 2003, reported the following rates:

White:	0.76
Black:	0.52
Hispanic:	0.56
Overall:	0.70

7. If private and homeschooled students were included in the denominator when calculating this ratio, the national first-time freshmen enrollment rate for students of all races would drop from 0.89 (table 5.1) to 0.80. The National Center for Education Statistics does not collect data on private or homeschooled enrollments by race, so I was not able to calculate similarly adjusted rates for each racial group.

8. If private and homeschooled students were included in the denominator when calculating this ratio, the national bachelor's degree rate for students of all races would drop from 0.56 to 0.51.

9. Although most states report their enrollment data annually to NCES for inclusion in the CCD, some states do not. So some states will be missing from each graph. In some cases, outlying states were left off the graphs where including them would greatly expand the scale. In all cases where this was done, it was for states with very small minority populations where the ratios were likely skewed because of migration.

10. These national averages appear in table 5.1.

11. It should be noted that these are all states with relatively small Black populations. Thus, the rates can be skewed by small numbers of students in either the numerator or denominator of the ratio.

12. This plot point is on the same point as Hawaii, just above Rhode Island.

13. Unfortunately, the NCES data do not include information about the migration of students by racial groups, so it is impossible to adjust the first-time freshmen enrollment rates for such migration.

14. These are the same rates shown for the nation as a whole in Figure 5.2. They are the number of bachelor's degrees awarded in the state in 2005 divided by the number of ninth graders seven academic years earlier. I started with the 15 largest states, but North Carolina and New Jersey did not have data on ninth-grade enrollments by race.

15. Again, it is important to note that Massachusetts is a large importer of college students, so the Massachusetts figure is biased upward because of this migration.

16. This study examined college participation of *all* students, both those who graduated from high school and those who did not, so there were gaps among the racial groups driven at least in part by differences in high school graduation rates.

References

Bensimon, E. M., Hao, L., & Bustillos, L. T. (2003, October). *The state of equity in California's postsecondary education system.* Paper presented at the Conference on Expanding Opportunity in Higher Education: California and the Nation, Sacramento, CA.

Carey, K. (2005). *One step from the finish line: Higher college graduation rates are within our reach.* Washington, DC: The Education Trust.

The Civil Rights Project at Harvard University. (2002). *Overview of constitutional requirements in race-conscious affirmative action policies in education.* Cambridge, MA: Author.

Education Trust, Inc. (2006). *Education watch: Pennsylvania.* Washington, DC: Author.

Education Week. (2007). *Ready for what? Preparing students for college, careers, and life after high school.* Bethesda, MD: Author.

Ewell, P. T., Schild, P. R., & Paulson, K. (2003). *Following the mobile student: Can we develop the capacity for a comprehensive database to assess student progression?* Indianapolis, IN: Lumina Foundation for Education.

Grutter v. Bollinger, 539 U.S. 306 (2003).

Heller, D. E. (1999). Racial equity in college participation: African American students in the United States. *Review of African American Education, 1*(1), 5–29.

Horn, L., Cataldi, E. F., & Sikora, A. (2005). *Waiting to attend college: Undergraduates who delay their postsecondary enrollment* (No. NCES 2005152). Washington, DC: U.S. Department of Education, National Center for Education Statistics.

Ingels, S. J., Curtin, T. R., Kaufman, P., Alt, M. N., & Chen, X. (2002). *Coming of age in the 1990s: The eighth-grade class of 1988 12 years later* (No. NCES 2002–321). Washington, DC: U.S. Department of Education, National Center for Education Statistics.

Jacobson, J., Olsen, C., Rice, J. K., & Sweetland, S. (2001). *Educational achievement and Black-White inequality* (No. NCES 2001–061). Washington, DC: U.S. Department of Education, National Center for Education Statistics.

Koretz, D. (1990). *Trends in the postsecondary enrollment of minorities.* Santa Monica, CA: RAND.

National Center for Education Statistics. (2006a). *Common core of data.* Retrieved December 15, 2006, from http://nces.ed.gov/ccd/

National Center for Education Statistics. (2006b). *Integrated postsecondary education data system.* Retrieved December 15, 2006, from http://nces.ed.gov/ipeds/

National Center for Education Statistics. (2007). *Digest of education statistics, 2006* (No. NCES 2007017). Washington, DC: U.S. Department of Education.

Raudenbush, S. W., Fotiu, R. P., & Cheong, Y. F. (1998). Inequality of access to educational resources: A national report card for eighth-grade math. *Educational Evaluation and Policy Analysis, 20*(4), 253–267.

Regents of the University of California v. Bakke, 438 U.S. 265 (1978).

Texas Education Agency. (1995). *Report on grade level retention of Texas students, 1992–93 and 1993–94.* Austin: Author.

Wheelock, A., & Miao, J. (2005). The ninth-grade bottleneck: An enrollment bulge in a transition year that demands careful attention and action. *School Administrator, 62*(3), 36–40.

6

BAKKE BEYOND COLLEGE ACCESS

Investigating Racial/Ethnic Differences in College Completion

Michal Kurlaender and Erika Felts

I n the past century, the educational system in the United States experienced major expansion, with increasing enrollment rates of individuals
from all backgrounds at all levels of educational attainment. In 1940,
25% of the population over the age of 25 had completed at least high school.
By 2006, this figure rose to 86%. Looking at college completion, we see that
over the same time span there has been a 23-percentage point increase in the
proportion of the population older than age 25 who had completed 4 years
of college or more (5% in 1940, 28% in 2006) (U.S. Census Bureau, 1940,
2006). This was coupled with a decline in the overall high school dropout
rate from 27.2% in 1960 to 10.9% in 2000 (Kaufman, Alt, & Chapman,
2004).[1]

Although the increases in educational attainment in the United States
have been shared by all racial/ethnic and socioeconomic groups, disparities
by race and social background continue to exist. The impact of race and
social origin on years of secondary school completed has decreased over time
(Featherman & Hauser, 1978; Hout, Raftery, & Bell, 1993). However, disparities in secondary school completion among Whites and Blacks and Hispanics persist, and participation rates in postsecondary study among
minorities remain low relative to Whites. In 1975, 44.3% of Whites ages 25
to 29 had some postsecondary schooling, compared with 27.5% of Blacks

and 21.9% of Hispanics in the same age group. In 2000, 64.7% of Whites ages 25 to 29 had some postsecondary schooling, compared with only 51.9% and 32.3% of Blacks and Hispanics, respectively (National Center for Education Statistics [NCES], 2004a).[2] Rates of college going are also stratified by socioeconomic status. Among the high school class of 1992, 94% of students in the top socioeconomic quintile attended some postsecondary institution, but only 54% of those students in the bottom quintile went on to postsecondary schooling (Adelman, 2004).

The discussion around affirmative action in education for the past 30 years has been almost exclusively about ensuring access to higher education for underrepresented groups. The landmark *Regents of the University of California v. Bakke* (1978) decision, by supporting the use of race-conscious admissions policies, provided postsecondary institutions, particularly selective ones, with one tool to increase access and, therefore, the representation of minority groups on their campuses. Although the focus of the *Bakke* opinion was on the ways in which the educational setting is improved by admitting a diverse student body, the opinion also offers important commentary on the role of a diverse student body to post-college outcomes. In the majority opinion, Justice Lewis Powell discusses the relevance of diversity to the education of medical professionals and the result of such training to better prepare doctors "to render with understanding their vital service to humanity" (*Bakke,* 1978, p. 314). Studying in a diverse educational environment, therefore, is considered one necessary (but perhaps not sufficient) step in the ultimate goal of producing a diverse set of professionals prepared to serve a "heterogeneous population" (1978, p. 314). To the extent that it recognized the importance of this goal, *Bakke*'s lasting impact should be evaluated beyond the college door.

Thirty years after the historic *Bakke* decision, many more underrepresented minorities are going to college, but their rates of degree receipt are lower than that of Whites (Turner, 2004).[3] The purpose of this chapter is to investigate the racial/ethnic disparities in college participation and completion in the post-*Bakke* period. In so doing, the chapter has several goals. In the first section, we offer some context for thinking about affirmative action in higher education admissions. We describe both historical and more recent policy and legal developments that have altered access to postsecondary schooling for underrepresented minority groups. Second, we describe the trends in college participation and completion by race/ethnicity during the past 30 years.[4] Third, we explore college completion more closely, describing racial/ethnic differences in the common determinants of degree receipt. We take a critical look at the role of affirmative action, as upheld in *Bakke,* in facilitating degree receipt, by reporting the racial/ethnic differences in college participation and degree completion among the states' public 4-year flagship universities. The last section summarizes our findings and offers some next steps for researchers and policymakers.

Background and Context: Affirmative Action in Higher Education[5]

Affirmative action as a tool to increase the representation of minorities in higher education came about in the 1960s with the civil rights movement and increased focus on racial inequities in U.S. society (Bowen & Bok, 1998; Orfield, 2005). In the early days of affirmative action, there was an explicit societal goal (similar to that of school desegregation) to remedy past discrimination and expand opportunities to groups that had historically been underrepresented in higher education. Over time, however, colleges and universities applying race in admissions decisions at their own discretion faced increasing resistance from individuals and groups calling for admissions that were race-blind (Douglass, 1999; Orfield, 1998).

Legal questions surrounding affirmative action in higher education were addressed with Justice Powell's opinion in the 1978 Supreme Court decision, *Regents of the University of California v. Bakke.* The *Bakke* ruling stated that a higher education institution (using its own judgment) could consider race in admissions for the purpose of achieving a diverse student body, provided it is one among a variety of factors considered. The decision was significant because it effectively legalized a non-remedial goal of affirmative action policies—promoting diversity in higher education—and identified it as serving a compelling state interest.

How widespread was affirmative action in college admissions over the 1980s and 1990s? Bowen and Bok (1998) contend that only the most competitive colleges and universities exercised affirmative action post-*Bakke;* however, other findings suggest that a much broader range of schools engaged in affirmative action (Grodsky, 2007; Kane, 1998; Lerner & Nagai, 2001), or at least claimed to do so (Grodsky & Kalogrides, in press). Kane (1998), for example, estimates that 20% of 4-year colleges and universities engaged in race-conscious affirmative action in the 1980s, and Grodsky (2007) and Grodsky and Kalogrides (in press) find that almost half of all baccalaureate granting institutions engaged in race-conscious affirmative action or reported to do so between the 1970s and the end of the 1990s.

Despite acceptance by many that access to the university should be afforded to underrepresented groups and that diversity is beneficial for society, affirmative action policies again came under fierce legal attack in the early 1990s. Individuals and several organized groups that viewed any use of race in admissions or employment decisions as reverse discrimination started taking their complaints to the lower courts, and the diversity rationale upheld in *Bakke* was put to the test.[6] Despite conflicting lower court decisions,[7] the Supreme Court refused to review the matter in the *Hopwood v. Texas* (1996) case. As a result, the 1996 decision of the Fifth Circuit Court of Appeals effectively ended affirmative action in Texas, Louisiana, and Mississippi and raised questions about the future of race-conscious affirmative action elsewhere.[8]

During the 1990s, race-conscious admission policies were challenged in the political arena as well, and several states ultimately abandoned the practice. In 1996, California voters passed Proposition 209, which terminated consideration of race in public education, employment, and contracting. In 1998, Washington passed a similar state referendum, and several other states have considered similar initiatives (Chávez, 1998). Most recently, Ward Connerly, a well-known critic of affirmative action, has sponsored efforts in five additional states for the public to vote on a ban of "racial and ethnic preference" in admissions decisions at public colleges (Schmidt, 2007). Amid substantial legal and political uncertainty, many selective colleges and universities scaled back or abandoned their affirmative action programs (Breland, Maxey, Gernand, Cumming, & Trapani, 2002; Grodsky & Kalogrides, in press; Orfield & Miller, 2000).

In 2000, the U.S. Supreme Court agreed to hear the companion cases at the University of Michigan—*Gratz v. Bollinger* (2003) and *Grutter v. Bollinger* (2003)—that challenged race-conscious admissions policies at the undergraduate college and law school, respectively. In a 5–4 majority opinion in *Grutter,* the Supreme Court upheld the basic rationale for race-conscious admissions (promoting diversity in higher education) and established that institutions of higher education are entitled to a high degree of deference on academic decisions, including admissions, thereby reaffirming the *Bakke* ruling 25 years earlier (Ancheta, 2005).

Changes in race-conscious policies, as a result of court decisions or public referenda, have dramatically altered admissions policies in several large public higher education systems. The effects of abandoning affirmative action programs have been investigated by some researchers capitalizing on policy changes restricting affirmative action (in California and Texas, in particular) or on simulations based on small sets of elite institutions. Results from these studies suggest declines in overall enrollments of underrepresented groups at the most selective colleges and universities when race-conscious admissions programs were eliminated (Grodsky & Kurlaender, 2006; Long, 2004; Tienda, Leicht, Sullivan, Maltese, & Lloyd, 2003).

For elite institutions, the consensus is that eliminating affirmative action in college admissions would produce substantial declines in the percentage of matriculants who were African American or Hispanic. For example, at five elite colleges for which they were able to obtain complete application and admissions data (a subset of the full College and Beyond data set), Bowen and Bok (1998) found that 42% of Black applicants were accepted; in the absence of affirmative action, they predict that only 13% would have been accepted. This change in acceptance rate, assuming a constant yield, would reduce the percentage of African Americans in incoming classes from 7.1 to 3.6% (Bowen & Bok, 1998). Likewise, in their simulations of the effect of affirmative action on minority representation at three "highly selective private research universities" (p. 298), Espenshade and Chung (2005) estimate that removing the consideration of race alone would reduce the percentage of matriculants who were African American from 9.0 to 3.3%. At the same time, the percentage of first-time first-year students who were Hispanic would decline from 7.9 to 3.8%. These results rely on simulations from observational data; Texas and California offer natural experiments by which to assess the effects of eliminating affirmative action.

Looking at enrollments at selective public flagship institutions in Texas, Tienda et al. (2003) find that the percentage of admitted students who were African American at the University of Texas at Austin (UT Austin), the state's most selective public 4-year institution, declined from 4.4% before the *Hopwood* decision to 4.0% after the decision. The proportion of admitted students who were Latino dropped from 17.8 to 14.6%. At Texas A&M University (the other flagship university in Texas), Finnell (1998) finds that African American and Hispanic enrollments dropped by 19 and 20%, respectively, following *Hopwood.* After Proposition 209, the University of California (UC) system also saw overall declines in the proportion of under-represented minority students, with declines of more than a third at UC Los Angeles and almost half at UC Berkeley. The percentage of matriculants who were members of underrepresented minority students has since increased at all campuses, but not to their pre-Proposition 209 levels (University of California, 2003).

The effect of ending affirmative action is not confined to admissions decisions. Analyses of application patterns tell the same story: the proportion of African American and Hispanic students applying to top-tier institutions decline in the absence of affirmative action (Barreto & Pachon, 2003; Card & Krueger, 2004; Long, 2004). More troubling, some evidence suggests that the proportion of minority students that take a college entrance exam (required for admission to most 4-year colleges) declines in the absence of affirmative action (Dickson, 2006). If this is so, it should lead to a decline in the proportion of minority students attending baccalaureate-granting institutions overall (at least for those requiring an entrance exam), not just those attending more competitive colleges and universities.[9]

Despite some rollbacks in affirmative action, access to higher education for underrepresented groups remains an important mission of most selective public and even private postsecondary institutions (Guess, 2007). In the time since *Bakke,* all racial/ethnic groups in the U.S. have witnessed growth in educational attainment. Nevertheless, substantial disparities in educational attainment continue to persist at all levels; we describe these gaps in several ways in the following section.

Differential Rates of Postsecondary Participation and a Closer Investigation of College Completion

Before describing the trends in college participation and completion, it is important to note racial/ethnic differences in secondary school completion because high school degree receipt is a critical (although not mandatory) precursor to college participation. Blacks' high school completion rate (including GED recipients) is about 8 percentage points lower than Whites' (which is, on average, about 90%); more troubling is the Hispanic high school completion rate, which in 2004 was 20 percentage points lower than that of Whites (NCES, 2004c).[10]

Turning to postsecondary participation, figure 6.1 displays the rates of college participation (at any postsecondary institution) since 1975 for Whites, Blacks, and Hispanics. College participation during the past 30 years has generally been on the rise for all groups. However, the participation gap between Whites and Hispanics, in particular, has also been widening since the 1990s. Moreover, we notice that the rise in participation was generally much steeper post-*Bakke* and into the early 1990s when affirmative action policies were at their strongest (Grodsky & Kalogrides, in press). We also note a more subtle opposite trend starting in the mid-1990s.

We can also look at trends in educational attainment over time by turning to the national longitudinal datasets collected by the U.S. Department of Education's National Center for Education Statistics. Looking across three high school cohorts—1972, 1982, and 1992—we note several important dimensions (figure 6.2). First, college participation rates have consistently been higher for Asians and Whites relative to Blacks and Latinos. Second, postsecondary participation rates have, on average, increased for all racial/ethnic groups across these three decades. Third, we see differential rates of

FIGURE 6.1
Postsecondary participation rates among 25- to 29-year-olds, by race/ethnicity, 1975–2004

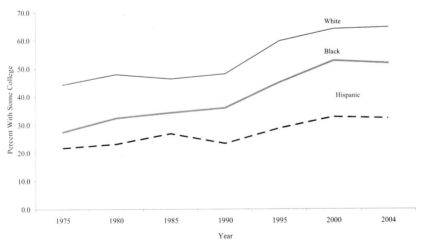

Source: NCES (2004a).

Note. Until 1990, the definition of the category "some college" was one year or more of postsecondary schooling. After 1990, the category included individuals with any amount of postsecondary schooling.

FIGURE 6.2
Postsecondary participation, by race/ethnicity, over three cohorts

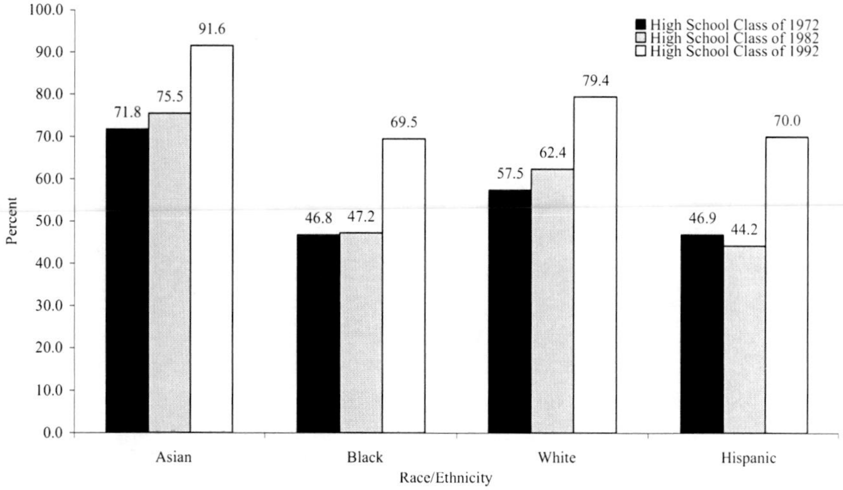

■ High School Class of 1972
☐ High School Class of 1982
☐ High School Class of 1992

Source: Adelman (2004).

growth in college participation by race/ethnicity. Specifically, we note the large gains in postsecondary participation for Blacks and Hispanics from the high school class of 1982, when 47.2% of Blacks and 44.2% of Hispanics obtained some postsecondary credits, to the high school class of 1992, when 69.5% of Blacks and 70.0% of Hispanics obtained some postsecondary credits.

Turning to college completion rates, figure 6.3 displays the rates of baccalaureate attainment among 25- to 29-year-olds since 1975 for Whites, Blacks, and Hispanics. We note that rates of baccalaureate receipt have increased for underrepresented groups, particularly Hispanics, at a much slower rate than for Whites. Moreover, we note the leveling off in BA receipt among Blacks and Hispanics in about 2000, and modest increases for Whites.

When we look at BA completion rates, conditional on enrollment (a ratio of college graduate to some college), the rates of degree receipt, despite the rise in participation, have remained stagnant for Whites and actually have declined for Blacks and Hispanics (figure 6.4). In 1975, about 50% of Whites who began postsecondary study ultimately completed a baccalaureate degree; nearly 30 years later the same is true. For Blacks, the completion rate,

FIGURE 6.3

Rates of bachelor's degree attainment (or higher) among 25- to 29-year-olds, by race/ethnicity, 1975–2004

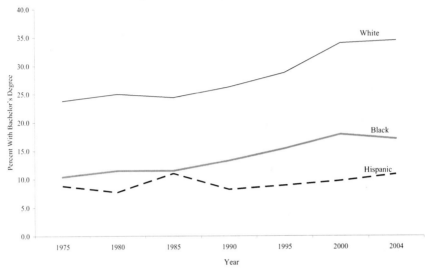

Source: NCES (2004a).

conditional on enrollment, was about 38% in 1975 and down to about 33% in 2004. Finally, for Hispanics, the completion rate in 1975 was about 40% and in 2004 is down to less than 34%.

Because "some college" remains a vague category in national dataset collections such as the Current Population Survey (CPS), it is important to look at college completion rates for undergraduates who obtained some minimum number of credits. Figure 6.5 displays baccalaureate receipt (at least 8 years after expected high school completion) for the high school classes of 1972, 1982, and 1992, by race/ethnicity, for individuals who obtained more than 10 postsecondary credits. Although there was clearly an upward trend, on average, in BA receipt for all groups across the three cohorts, we note first that, compared with the 1972 cohort, degree receipt declined, or at least remained stable in the 1980s, relative to college enrollment. Second, despite overall increases in baccalaureate receipt by the 1990s, important racial/ethnic disparities in college completion persist. For the class of 1972, the White-Black gap in BA receipt was 16.1 percentage points, and the White-Hispanic gap

FIGURE 6.4

Rates of bachelor's degree attainment (or higher), conditional on enrollment, among 25- to 29-year-olds, by race/ethnicity, 1975–2004

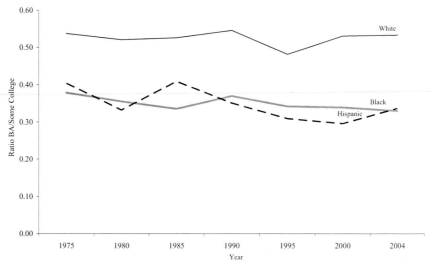

Source: NCES (2004a).

was 24.5 percentage points. For the class of 1982, the White-Black gap in BA receipt actually widened to 23.0 percentage points, and the White-Hispanic gap was 21.5 percentage points. For the class of 1992, which, for these calculations, would have completed their college degree by about 2000, the White-Black gap in BA receipt decreased, but only to near the 1972 level at 15.2 percentage points; the White-Hispanic gap returned to the 1972 level at 24.5 percentage points.

There are many possible explanations for low college completion rates. First, and perhaps most obvious, is that not all students desire a college degree. With widespread expansion of higher education, particularly at the sub-baccalaureate level, students' ability to experiment with college is more feasible. Moreover, a dominant college-for-all policy rhetoric (Grodsky & Felts, 2007; Rosenbaum, 2001) has many students pressed to at least attempt some postsecondary schooling, but not necessarily complete it. Students make decisions to enroll and subsequently complete a college degree based on an interaction of their tastes, abilities, and resources. Students weigh benefits,

FIGURE 6.5

Percentage of students who earned at least a bachelor's degree, among those who obtained more than 10 postsecondary credits, by race/ethnicity, over three cohorts

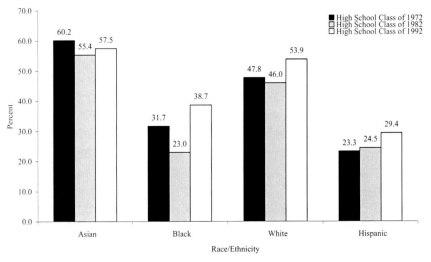

Source: Adelman (2004).

such as higher earnings or the collegiate experience, against costs, such as tuition and foregone earnings. Thus, many students who do not know if college is for them engage in an experiment by enrolling (Manski, 1989). During this experiment, they gain new information about what they like and do not like. Students' decisions about whether to remain in college are normally based on more information than their decisions about whether to enter college. They usually know more about what they can learn, and whether it seems likely to be valuable. In some cases, they also know more about costs and about the amount of help they can get from various sources. As a result, the decision-making process about completing college may be quite different from that which determines entering.

Other explanations for existing college completion patterns include changes in the composition of postsecondary participation, continued financial constraints experienced by undergraduates, a lack of academic preparation, and a lack of institutional effort to facilitate student persistence. We discuss each in turn, noting, in particular, important racial/ethnic differences along each of these dimensions.

Changes in the Composition of Postsecondary Participation

Colleges in recent years have encountered an increasingly diverse student body. Thirty years ago, Whites made up 81% of U.S. undergraduates; by 1990, they were 77.5%, and today they are just 65% of the total undergraduate population (NCES, 2006a). Although increases in Black enrollment contribute some to these compositional changes (about three percentage points overall), steady growth in the Hispanic undergraduate enrollment—largely as a function of more widespread demographic trends—has been much more pronounced (about eight percentage points overall). Asian undergraduate enrollment has also experienced a steady increase during this time period (about five percentage points overall).

Colleges in recent years have also faced an increasingly more complicated student body. Today's college student is less likely to be attending a 4-year institution and more likely to be of a nontraditional college age, to have delayed postsecondary entry, to be working part-time, to have interrupted her or his college education, and to have attended multiple institutions in the quest for a college degree (Kurlaender & Horn, 2007). Racial/ethnic minorities are also more likely to enroll in college part-time than are their White counterparts (NCES, 2004b). In particular, the increase in Hispanic representation in postsecondary study has been disproportionately at the 2-year college. Moreover, Black and Hispanic growth in postsecondary enrollment has been particularly pronounced at private 2-year institutions, a more recent trend in postsecondary enrollment (NCES, 2006a; Stephan & Rosenbaum, 2007). These sub-baccalaureate institutions are an increasingly important aspect of higher education expansion, offering a more diverse set of training and degree options. These may be particularly attractive for students who face considerable barriers, such as time, academic preparation, or financial resources.

Financial Constraints

Lower-income students are at greater risk of dropping out of higher education than are students from higher income backgrounds. Looking at financial constraints by race/ethnicity, more than 40% of Black and Hispanic and more than 30% of Asian undergraduates are from low-income families relative to 20% of White undergraduates (Choy, 2000).[11] Underrepresented minorities are also more likely to receive aid, regardless of the source. Among undergraduates in 2003–2004, 89.2% of Black, 80.7% of Hispanic, and 74% of White undergraduates received some financial aid (KewalRamani, Gilbertson, Fox, & Provasnik, 2007). Moreover, we cannot explain the strong association between income and college completion with differences in college entry. Income disparities persist even when only considering those already through the college door. Although the association between income and college completion is a bit weaker when just evaluating students who begin college at 4-year institutions, they still persist with a nearly 25 percentage point difference in college completion rates between students from the lowest family income quartile and students from the highest family income quartile (Choy, 2000).

There is more direct evidence of the causal impacts of college costs and financial aid on college enrollment and completion. Several studies have demonstrated that reducing college costs increases college attendance (Dynarski, 2003; Kane, 1994; Turner, 2004). Less is known about the impact of cost on college completion, but some evidence indicates that tuition reduction can increase college retention. Dynarski (in press) finds that state merit aid programs introduced in Georgia and Arkansas (and followed by many additional states) increase the college completion rates, on average, by about three percentage points. Bettinger (2004) finds that need-based aid provided by Pell grants can help reduce the college dropout rate. Yet, even when scholarship or aid programs effectively eliminate the cost of schooling, many students continue to drop out of college.

The effects of financial aid also vary across racial/ethnic groups. Linsenmeier, Rosen, and Rouse (2006) find that at one institution, changing aid packages consisting of loans, grants, and campus work into predominately grants has an especially strong, positive effect on low-income minority students' matriculation. Dynarski (in press) also finds that a tuition subsidy program is most beneficial for non-White women in both college entry and completion. Additional evidence shows that minority students' graduation is more sensitive to the amount of aid received than is that of nonminority students (Alon, 2007).

Academic Preparedness

Today, about 30% of freshmen are enrolled in some remedial course. Although most of these students are at 2-year institutions, the rate of remedial course taking at many 4-year public institutions is greater than 20%. Underrepresented students are more likely to enroll in remedial coursework.

Among the high school class of 1992, only 38.3% of Blacks and 36.8% of Hispanics did not enroll in any remedial courses, compared with 64.4% of Whites and 62.0% of Asians who did not enroll in any remedial coursework (Adelman, 2004). The disparities in remediation are largely in remedial reading, whereas the rates of remedial mathematics are much more similar across race/ethnicity (Adelman, 2004).

In recent years, many states have been questioning the role of remedial courses in their postsecondary institutions. Although some believe that these courses serve an important bridge between poor K–12 schooling and college readiness, there is considerable debate about their presence in 4-year degree-granting institutions. Moreover, there is very little evidence regarding the effect of remedial courses on college completion. In one study of students attending Ohio 4-year colleges, Bettinger and Long (2005) find that students placed in remediation courses were more likely to drop out or transfer to a lower-level college than were similar students not placed in such classes. However, among those who do complete the remedial course of study, the results are mixed, suggesting that these courses may help facilitate degree completion, albeit through a longer route of study.

Academic skills and preparation in high school influence college completion rates. Yet, the role of academic preparation in explaining college completion is more complex. A majority of high school students report intent to attend college, regardless of their academic performance in school (Rosenbaum, 2001). Moreover, the choice of institution first entered may directly affect college completion. Students sort themselves into different types of postsecondary institutions, resulting in some "mismatch" between academic preparation and college choice. The evidence on the impact of this mismatch on college completion is not conclusive. Light and Strayer (2000) find that a mismatch between student ability and institutional selectivity can impede college completion. However, evidence also indicates that attending a more selective institution is associated with higher graduation rates (Alon & Tienda, 2005; Kane, 1998). Specifically, minority students' likelihood of graduation rises as selectivity of the institution attended rises (Alon & Tienda, 2005).

Institutional Practices

There is great variation in college completion across U.S. postsecondary institutions. Yet, the institutional role in facilitating degree receipt has received much less scholarly attention than has individual determinants. The average

4-year completion rate at degree-granting institutions is approximately 35%. However, considerable variation exists, with many schools graduating fewer than 15% of students in 4 years and other institutions graduating 85% of their students in 4 years (NCES, 2005a). On average, private schools have higher completion rates than do public institutions, as do smaller versus larger institutions. This is not surprising, though, given that, on average, students who enroll in private institutions have greater resources and are more prepared for postsecondary work. Graduation rates also tend to increase the longer students have to complete school (NCES, 2005a).

There is also a body of research on the institutional practices that lead to college persistence, including student interaction with faculty, student peers and sense of community, active engagement with the institution, and mentoring.[12] Of course, these studies cannot control for all the differences between students who select different kinds of colleges, so we cannot conclude how, absent particular policies, structures, or institutional culture, colleges can improve their graduation rates. To the extent that the collegiate experience of minority groups is distinct from that of the dominant group, this is an important area of further exploration in the quest to better understand college departure. Recent reports by the American Association of State Colleges and Universities (2006) and The Education Trust (Carey, 2004, 2005a, 2005b) examine the reasons why some public 4-year colleges and universities do a good job retaining students. In particular, the Education Trust report (Carey, 2005a) and accompanying website (www.CollegeResults.org) focus on comparing graduation rates at similar institutions (in terms of size, sector, prestige, and other characteristics) and highlight institutions that stand out among their "peers" as having high 6-year graduation rates, high graduation rates for minority students in particular, or that have demonstrated improvement in graduation rates since 1997.[13] All of these reports suggest that campus leadership on the retention issue may influence graduation outcomes, but more direct evidence of how specific institutional policies would lead to increased college completion is warranted.

The Role of State Flagships

To more fully explore the institutional role in facilitating both access and degree receipt for different racial/ethnic groups, we conduct a descriptive analysis looking at each state's primary flagship institution.[14] As a publicly funded institution intended to provide postsecondary schooling to its population, a state's flagship plays an important role in facilitating opportunities in educational attainment. Therefore, it is reasonable to evaluate how closely the racial/ethnic makeup of each flagship institution mirrors that of the state's racial/ethnic composition. Specifically, we compare each state's proportion of Black and Hispanic high school completers with the proportion of Black and Hispanic enrollees at the state's public flagship institution. Doing so provides us with a snapshot of how well racial and ethnic minorities are represented in enrollment at the states' flagship institutions. This indicator does not perfectly measure representation because some students leave their home state and attend college in another state. These data do not allow us to examine the extent of out- and in-migration for each state so our estimates assume an equal number of entrants and leavers. In reality, choosing to leave one's home state for college depends on a variety of factors such as cost, school quality, availability of financial aid out-of-state, proximity, and characteristics of the student (Abbott & Schmid, 1975; Kyung, 1996). After examining representation in terms of access, we provide graduation rates disaggregated by race/ethnicity for each of these institutions to evaluate the variation in completion across racial/ethnic groups.

College Access

Figure 6.6 shows the difference (in percentage points) between the percentage of each state's high school graduates who are Black and the percentage of the state's flagship institution's enrollees who are Black in 2005. Schools are sorted along the y-axis by the percentage of their high school graduates who are Black, and these numbers are shown in parentheses. We can draw three broad conclusions about the condition of representation at these institutions. First, we see that very few schools are actually at parity with the state's proportion of Black high school graduates. For example, in Mississippi, 46.5% of high school graduates are Black. Yet at Mississippi's flagship institution, Black students make up only 13.8% of the 2005 enrollees. The difference between these two values is shown in figure 6.6 (a 33.3 percentage point difference). In fact, only six states (New Mexico, South Dakota, North Dakota, Wyoming, Idaho, and Montana) have a proportion of Black enrollees at their flagship institution that is equal to or above the proportion of Black high school graduates in their state. Second, the higher the percentage

FIGURE 6.6
Representation of Black students at state flagship institutions, 2005

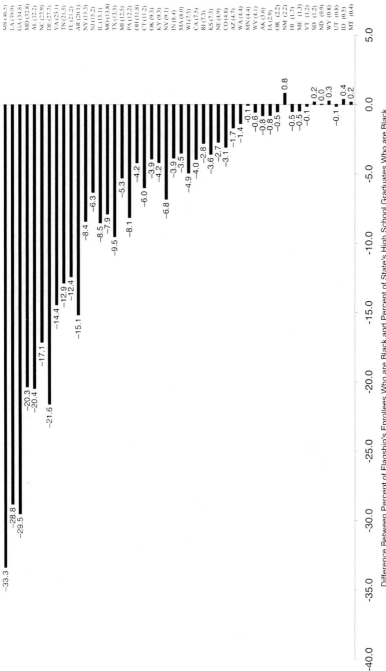

Difference Between Percent of Flagship's Enrollees Who are Black and Percent of State's High School Graduates Who are Black

Source: NCES (2005a, 2005b, 2006b).

Note. High school graduate calculations are based on an average of 2004 and 2005 figures to account for possible college delayers. CCD 2004 high school completers include GED holders.

of Black high school graduates in the state, the greater the gap between institutions' percentage of Black and the state's percentage of Black high school graduates. Although much of this is certainly due to sample size, we can examine representation ratios as well, which essentially tell us how well the state is representing Black students conditional on the size of its Black population.

Table 6.1 presents these as ratios computed by dividing the percentage of Black enrollees at each respective flagship institution by the percentage of Black high school graduates in each respective state. A value of 1.0 would represent equal representation. Values less than 1.0 reflect underrepresentation and values over 1.0 show how much that racial group is overrepresented at the flagship institution. These ratios show that the states with the biggest percentage point difference in representation also have some of the lowest enrollee to high-school-graduate ratios. These two results are consistent with the finding that states with larger proportions of Black high school graduates fare worse in their ability to equally represent Black students at the flagship institution. A third and especially interesting point is the significant amount of variation that exists across institutions. Looking at the ratios in table 6.1, we see that 6 states have ratios below 0.3 (more severe underrepresentation), 16 states have a ratio between 0.3 and 0.5, 12 states have a ratio between 0.5 and 0.7, 8 states have a ratio between 0.7 and 1.0 (close to parity), and 6 states have a ratio above 1.0 (admitting a higher percentage of African American students than their state's overall Black high school graduation rate).[15]

Figure 6.7 displays the same information but for Hispanic students in 2005. Again we see that flagship institutions in only 12 states (Maryland, Michigan, Alaska, Missouri, Louisiana, Tennessee, Ohio, Alabama, Vermont, Maine, Mississippi, and West Virginia) are at or above parity with the state's proportion of Hispanic high school graduates. We also see that, on average, states with larger shares of Hispanics have a harder time producing equal representation at their flagship institution. Looking at table 6.1, we see that the states with the 10 largest proportions of Hispanic high school graduates all have a ratio of Hispanic enrollees at the flagship to Hispanic high school graduates below 0.6, with the exception of Florida (0.67) and New Mexico (0.75), which stand out as having slightly more equitable representation at their flagship institutions than comparable institutions in other states. However, again we see considerable variation among states. Although only 2 states have a ratio below 0.3, 8 have a ratio between 0.3 and 0.5, 13 states have

TABLE 6.1
Black and Hispanic Representation at Public Flagship Institutions, 2005

Institution	State	Black	Hispanic
		Ratios	
University of Alaska, Fairbanks	AK	0.78	1.06
University of Alabama	AL	0.37	1.38
University of Arkansas	AR	0.25	0.65
University of Arizona	AZ	0.64	0.51
University of California, Berkeley	CA	0.47	0.29
University of Colorado, Boulder	CO	0.36	0.38
University of Connecticut	CT	0.46	0.45
University of Delaware	DE	0.22	0.88
University of Florida	FL	0.41	0.67
University of Georgia	GA	0.15	0.52
University of Hawaii, Manoa	HI	0.70	0.50
University of Iowa	IA	0.73	0.85
University of Idaho	ID	1.68	0.51
University of Illinois, Urbana–Champaign	IL	0.44	0.53
Indiana University, Bloomington	IN	0.54	0.71
University of Kansas	KS	0.51	0.56
University of Kentucky	KY	0.55	0.75
Louisiana State University	LA	0.28	1.80
University of Massachusetts, Amherst	MA	0.56	0.41
University of Maryland, College Park	MD	0.38	1.27
University of Maine	ME	0.66	0.97
University of Michigan, Ann Arbor	MI	0.58	1.86
University of Minnesota, Twin Cities	MN	0.99	0.94
University of Missouri, Columbia	MO	0.43	0.99
University of Mississippi	MS	0.28	1.24
University of Montana	MT	1.44	0.83
University of North Carolina, Chapel Hill	NC	0.39	0.92
University of North Dakota	ND	1.03	0.90
University of Nebraska at Lincoln	NE	0.45	0.48
University of New Hampshire	NH	—	—
Rutgers University	NJ	0.59	0.59
University of New Mexico	NM	1.37	0.75
University of Nevada, Reno	NV	0.25	0.37
State University of New York, Buffalo	NY	0.45	0.28
Ohio State University	OH	0.65	1.75
University of Oklahoma, Norman	OK	0.58	0.77
University of Oregon	OR	0.77	0.37

(continues)

TABLE 6.1 (Continued)

Institution	State	Ratios Black	Ratios Hispanic
Pennsylvania State University	PA	0.33	0.90
University of Rhode Island	RI	0.62	0.40
University of South Carolina, Columbia	SC	—	—
University of South Dakota	SD	1.16	0.86
University of Tennessee	TN	0.40	0.97
University of Texas, Austin	TX	0.30	0.46
University of Utah	UT	0.84	0.67
University of Virginia	VA	0.38	0.78
University of Vermont	VT	0.89	1.60
University of Washington, Seattle	WA	0.69	0.55
University of Wisconsin–Madison	WI	0.34	0.63
West Virginia University	WV	0.86	2.81
University of Wyoming	WY	1.34	0.60

Source: Author calculations from NCES (2005a, 2005b, 2006b).

Note. Representation is presented as the ratio of the racial group's percentage of enrollees at the flagship institution to the racial group's percentage of HS graduates in that state. States are listed alphabetically by abbreviation. New Hampshire and South Carolina are missing because of missing state-level data in the CCD. High school graduate calculations are based on an average of 2004 and 2005 figures to account for possible college delayers. CCD 2004 high school completers include GED holders.

a ratio between 0.5 and 0.7, 16 states have a ratio between 0.7 and 1.0, and 9 states exceed parity with the state's proportion of Hispanic high school graduates.

College Completion[16]

Table 6.2 presents the graduation rates by race/ethnicity for each flagship institution.[17] Perhaps most notable is the difference between the graduation rates for Whites and Blacks and for Whites and Hispanics. In 2005, the flagship institutions in Oregon, Kansas, New York, Indiana, and Nebraska showed the largest Black-White graduation rate gap. No state had a Black graduation rate that exceeded the rate of White students. Averaged across all states, the Black flagship campus graduation rate was approximately 15 percentage points less than the White graduation rate. For Hispanics, the states with the largest White-Hispanic gaps in flagship campus graduation

FIGURE 6.7
Representation of Hispanic students at state flagship institutions, 2005

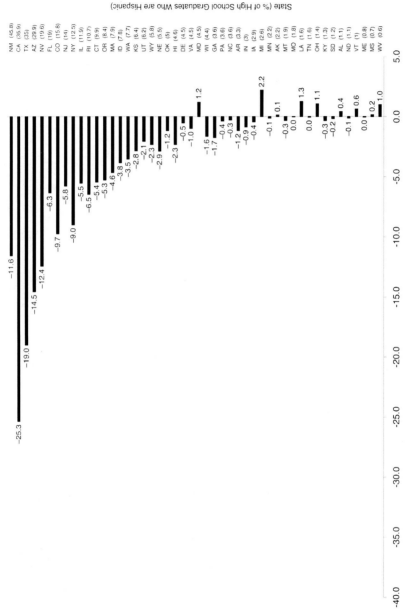

State (% of High School Graduates Who are Hispanic)

Difference Between Percent of Flagship's Enrollees Who are Hispanic and Percent of State's High School Graduates Who are Hispanic

Source: NCES (2005a, 2005b, 2006b).

Note. High school graduates calculations are based on an average of 2004 and 2005 figures to account for possible college delayers. CCD 2004 high school completers include GED holders.

TABLE 6.2
College Graduation Rates, by Race/Ethnicity, 2005

Institution	State	White	Black	Hispanic	Black-White	Hispanic-White
Univ. of Alaska, Fairbanks	AK	25	—	—	—	—
Univ. of Alabama	AL	64	59	—	− 5	—
Univ. of Arkansas	AR	58	47	55	− 11	− 3
Univ. of Arizona	AZ	61	42	51	− 19	− 10
Univ. of California, Berkeley	CA	87	70	76	− 17	− 11
Univ. of Colorado, Boulder	CO	67	59	59	− 8	− 8
Univ. of Connecticut	CT	73	57	71	− 16	− 2
Univ. of Delaware	DE	77	60	76	− 17	− 1
Univ. of Florida	FL	81	67	78	− 14	− 3
Univ. of Georgia	GA	74	69	71	− 5	− 3
Univ. of Hawaii, Manoa	HI	28	—	—	—	—
Univ. of Iowa	IA	67	51	53	− 16	− 14
Univ. of Idaho	ID	58	—	47	—	− 11
Univ. of Illinois, Urbana-Champaign	IL	86	65	67	− 21	− 19
Indiana Univ., Bloomington	IN	73	50	64	− 23	− 9
Univ. of Kansas	KS	61	34	64	− 2	73
Univ. of Kentucky	KY	61	46	—	− 15	—
Louisiana State Univ.	LA	58	51	59	− 7	1
Univ. of Massachusetts, Amherst	MA	67	56	60	− 11	− 7
Univ. of Maryland, College Park	MD	80	68	67	− 12	− 13
Univ. of Maine	ME	54	—	—	—	—
Univ. of Michigan, Ann Arbor	MI	92	72	81	− 20	− 11
Univ. of Minnesota, Twin Cities	MN	64	44	47	− 20	− 17
Univ. of Missouri, Columbia	MO	67	57	61	− 10	− 6
Univ. of Mississippi	MS	58	44	—	− 14	—
Univ. of Montana	MT	44	—	—	—	—
Univ. of North Carolina, Chapel Hill	NC	85	76	83	− 9	− 2
Univ. of North Dakota	ND	57	—	—	—	—
Univ. of Nebraska at Lincoln	NE	65	42	42	− 23	− 23
Univ. of New Hampshire	NH	74	—	—	—	—
Rutgers Univ.	NJ	72	63	62	− 9	− 10
Univ. of New Mexico	NM	44	26	39	− 18	− 5

(continues)

TABLE 6.2 (Continued)

Institution	State	White	Black	Hispanic	Black-White	Hispanic-White
Univ. of Nevada, Reno	NV	52	31	51	−21	−1
SUNY Buffalo	NY	62	37	52	−25	−10
Ohio State Univ.	OH	69	55	62	−14	−7
Univ. of Oklahoma, Norman	OK	57	43	56	−14	−1
Univ. of Oregon	OR	64	35	54	−29	−10
Pennsylvania State Univ.	PA	86	66	73	−20	−13
Univ. of Rhode Island	RI	58	42	43	−16	−15
Univ. of South Carolina, Columbia	SC	67	58	66	−9	−1
Univ. of South Dakota	SD	49	—	—	—	—
Univ. of Tennessee	TN	58	54	67	−4	9
Univ. of Texas, Austin	TX	76	70	66	−6	−10
Univ. of Utah	UT	41	—	30	—	−11
Univ. of Virginia	VA	94	86	88	−8	−6
Univ. of Vermont	VT	65	—	—	—	—
Univ. of Washington, Seattle	WA	75	52	69	−23	−6
Univ. of Wisconsin, Madison	WI	79	57	60	−22	−19
West Virginia Univ.	WV	56	36	40	−20	−16
Univ. of Wyoming	WY	59	—	—	—	—

Source: NCES (2005a).

Note. States are listed alphabetically by abbreviation. Graduation rates are calculated as the total number of students completing a bachelor's degree or equivalent within six years (150% of normal time) divided by the number of full-time, first-time students seeking a bachelor's or equivalent degree. Where insufficient data are available (less than 30 enrolled), cells are left empty.

rates were Nebraska, Wisconsin, Illinois, Minnesota, and West Virginia. Three states (Louisiana, Kansas, and Tennessee) had Hispanic graduation rates that exceeded the White students' graduation rate. On average, the Hispanic graduation rate was approximately eight percentage points less than the White graduation rate.

These numbers, perhaps more than any others reported in this chapter, speak to the importance of extending the discussion of access and opportunity in higher education beyond entrance. Most of our nation's flagship institutions continue to have substantial disparities in baccalaureate degree completion of Black and Hispanic students, relative to Whites. Moreover, enrollment figures reveal that 30 years after *Bakke* successfully preserved the generalized right of selective institutions to use race/ethnicity as one factor in admissions for the purpose of increasing diversity, state flagship institutions, on average, continue to be much less diverse relative to their population of high school completers.

Conclusion

Three decades ago, the *Bakke* decision gave colleges and universities the ability to use race-conscious admissions policies to create a diverse student body. This effort, although not without its challenges (politically and legally), has been, to some degree, successful. Today, the composition of our nation's colleges and universities is much more racially and ethnically diverse than it was 30 years ago. Despite these overarching gains in postsecondary participation, however, racial/ethnic disparities in college enrollment persist. Additionally, the rates of degree receipt have not kept up and are particularly lagging for Blacks and Latinos. Taking a closer look at state flagship public higher education institutions, they are, on average, underserving the state's Black and Latino high school completers. Among those enrolled at the state flagship institutions, we witness substantial disparities in completion rates between racial/ethnic groups.

An important argument outlined in *Bakke* was the need to diversify our professions and the critical role colleges and universities (particularly professional schools) can play in that effort. This premise was supported in the 2003 *Grutter* case in which the Supreme Court upheld the diversity rationale of *Bakke* and highlighted the importance of diverse schooling environments for enhanced preparation for our society and the workforce (Ancheta, 2005). This pressing need for a diverse and highly educated workforce demands new attention on college completion and degree receipt (Brief of the General Motors Corporation, 2003; Brief of the Retired Military Officers, 2003).

Why are students not completing college? In reality, the explanations suggested in this chapter are not discrete. Minority students are more likely to face financial barriers to postsecondary study than White students are (Heller, 2005). Black and Hispanic students are, on average, more likely to be academically underprepared when they arrive in college, given their limited access to quality K–12 schooling (Hauser, Simmons & Pager, 2004; Swanson, 2004a; Yun & Moreno, 2006). Secondary schooling experiences continue to be chief predictors of educational success in college (Adelman, 1999). Minority students are also more likely to attend less selective public institutions that may be under-resourced both in direct aid and in the types of mentorship and postsecondary experiences previously identified to facilitate degree completion (Carey, 2005a). Each of these areas must be examined further and corresponding policy solutions implemented.

This chapter provides a descriptive picture of a relatively understudied area in affirmative action—college completion. It turns out we know much more about how to get students (of all backgrounds) to enter college than how to keep them there. To the extent that *Bakke* sought to preserve the ability of colleges and universities to diversify their student bodies for both short- and long-term benefits, its lasting impact must be evaluated beyond the college door.

Notes

1. Note that these figures include GED recipients as high school graduates. We present these estimates yet acknowledge that recent work has shown that estimates from the Current Population Survey (CPS) may not present the most accurate or useful measure of dropout. More recently, some researchers find dropout rates that are considerably higher than the CPS rates (Orfield, 2004; Swanson, 2004b; Warren, 2005). See Yun and Lee (this volume) and Heller (this volume) for additional discussion on high school graduates.

2. We use the terms *Hispanics* and *Latinos* interchangeably.

3. For the purposes of this chapter, underrepresented minorities are defined as Black/African American students and Hispanic/Latino students.

4. Whenever possible, we display figures for four racial/ethnic groups—Whites, Blacks, Hispanics, and Asians. However, some of our analyses we restrict to Whites, Blacks, and Hispanics as a result of data availability or sample sizes.

5. This section is based, in part, on an unpublished paper by Grodsky and Kurlaender (2006).

6. Such groups challenging affirmative action policies include the Center for Equal Opportunity and the Center for Individual Rights.

7. See, for example: *Smith v. University of Washington Law School* (2004/2005) where the Ninth Circuit Court upheld the law school's use of race as one of several factors in the admissions process.

8. In *Hopwood v. Texas* (1996) the Court asserted that, contrary to Justice Powell's opinion in *Bakke,* diversity does not provide a compelling interest for race-conscious decisions in student admissions. This was overturned by the Supreme Court's *Grutter v. Bollinger* opinion in 2003.

9. It is difficult to estimate the direct effect of the termination of affirmative action because several state systems that ended race-conscious admissions replaced them with race-neutral policies to attempt to account for the inequities in K–12 schooling and the socioeconomic inequities that result in racial disparities in higher education admission.

10. Again, we note that estimates of high school completers from the CPS may be inflated (see Orfield, 2004; Swanson, 2004b; Warren, 2005).

11. Choy (2000) defines low-income students as those whose family income was below 125% of the federally established poverty level for their family size.

12. For reviews of this body of literature, see Astin (1993), Braxton (2000), and Tinto (1993).

13. Using the National Center for Education Statistics' Integrated Postsecondary Data System (IPEDS), the Education Trust report incorporates the following 11 variables (based on a regression analysis) to determine an institutional peer group to compare graduation rates: median SAT, Barron's *Profiles of American Colleges* admissions selectivity, Carnegie classification, sector, size, whether the institution self-identifies as a commuter campus, per full-time undergraduate student expenditures, percentage of students receiving Pell grants, percentage of undergraduate students age 25 or older, percentage of part-time undergraduates, and whether the institution is a Historically Black College or University.

14. Although not all 50 states designate one institution as their flagship institution, we present one flagship from each state. A similar method has been used in previous work. Our choices are identical with those in Gerald and Haycock (2006).

15. New Hampshire and South Carolina are missing from these counts because of missing state-level data in the Common Core of Data for the relevant years.

16. The approach we take to understanding completion rates by race/ethnicity at flagship campuses has several important limitations. First, despite their flagship status, some states' top institutions were not permitted to use race-conscious affirmative action during the period considered (e.g., Washington and California). Second, selectivity across flagship campuses varies, in some cases dramatically. Despite these limitations, however, taking this analytical approach is an important one in providing an understanding of college completion rates.

17. Graduation rates are not presented for states that had less than 30 students in the denominator.

References

Abbott, W. F., & Schmid, C. F. (1975). University prestige and first-time undergraduate migration in the United States. *Sociology of Education, 48*(2), 168–185.

Adelman, C. (1999). *Answers in the tool box: Academic intensity, attendance patterns, and bachelor's degree attainment.* Washington, DC: U.S. Department of Education.

Adelman, C. (2004). *Principle indicators of student academic histories in postsecondary education: 1972–2000.* Washington, DC: U.S. Department of Education.

Alon, S. (2007). The influence of financial aid in leveling group differences in graduating from elite institutions. *Economics of Education Review, 26*(3), 296–311.

Alon, S., & Tienda, M. (2005). Assessing the "mismatch" hypothesis: Differentials in college graduation rates by institutional selectivity. *Sociology of Education, 78*(4), 294–315.

American Association of State Colleges and Universities. (2006). *Graduation rates and student success: Squaring means and ends.* Washington, DC: Author. Retrieved November 4, 2007, from http://www.aascu.org/pdf/06b_perspectives.pdf

Ancheta, A. N. (2005). After *Grutter* and *Gratz*: Higher education, race, and the law. In G. Orfield, P. Marin, & C. L. Horn (Eds.), *Higher education and the color line: College access, racial equity, and social change* (pp. 175–196). Cambridge, MA: Harvard Education Press.

Astin, A. W. (1993). *What matters in college? Four critical years revisited.* San Francisco: Jossey-Bass.

Barreto, M. A., & Pachon, H. P. (2003). *The reality of race neutral admissions for minority students at the University of California: Turning the tide or turning them away?* Retrieved November 4, 2007, from http://www.trpi.org/PDFs/uc_admissions04.pdf

Bettinger, E. (2004). How financial aid affects persistence. In C. M. Hoxby (Ed.), *College choices: The economics of where to go, when to go, and how to pay for it* (pp. 207–237). Chicago: University of Chicago Press.

Bettinger, E., & Long, B. T. (2005). *Addressing the needs of under-prepared college students: Does college remediation work?* Cambridge, MA: National Bureau of Economic Research.

Bowen, W. G., & Bok, D. (1998). *The shape of the river: Long-term consequences of considering race in college and university admissions.* Princeton, NJ: Princeton University Press.

Braxton, J. (2000). Reinvigorating theory and research on the departure puzzle. In J. Braxton (Ed.), *Reworking the student departure puzzle* (pp. 257–274). Nashville: Vanderbilt University Press.

Breland, H., Maxey, J., Gernand, R., Cumming, T., & Trapani, C. (2002). *Trends in college admissions 2000: A report of a survey of undergraduate admissions policies, practices, and procedures.* New York: The College Board.

Brief of the General Motors Corporation as *amicus curiae* in support of respondents, *Grutter v. Bollinger,* 539 U.S. 306 (2003) and *Gratz v. Bollinger,* 539 U.S. 244 (2003).

Brief of the Retired Military Officers as *amici curiae* in support of respondents, *Grutter v. Bollinger,* 539 U.S. 306 (2003) and *Gratz v. Bollinger,* 539 U.S. 244 (2003).

Card, D., & Krueger, A. B. (2004). Would the elimination of affirmative action affect highly qualified minority applicants? Evidence from California and Texas. *Industrial and Labor Relations Review, 58*(3), 416–434.

Carey, K. (2004). *A matter of degrees: Improving graduation rates in four-year colleges and universities.* Retrieved November 4, 2007, from http://www2.edtrust.org/NR/rdonlyres/11B4283F-104E-4511-B0CA-1D3023231157/0/highered.pdf

Carey, K. (2005a). *Choosing to improve: Voices from colleges and universities with better graduation rates.* Retrieved November 4, 2007, from http://www2.edtrust.org/NR/rdonlyres/40EEF8D0-1257-48C2-8622-10AEB8988727/0/Choosing_to_improve.pdf

Carey, K. (2005b). *One step from the finish line: Higher college graduation rates are within our reach.* Retrieved November 4, 2007, from http://www2.edtrust.org/NR/rdonlyres/5ED8CD8A-E910-4E51-AEDB-6526FFED9F05/0/one_step_from.pdf

Chávez, L. (1998). *The color bind: California's battle to end affirmative action.* Berkeley: University of California Press.

Choy, S. P. (2000). *Low-income students: Who they are and how they pay for their education* (No. NCES 2000–169). Washington, DC: U.S. Department of Education, National Center for Education Statistics.

Dickson, L. M. (2006). Does ending affirmative action in college admissions lower the percent of minority students applying to college? *Economics of Education Review, 25*(1), 109–119.

Douglass, J. A. (1999). *The evolution of a social contract: The University of California before and in the aftermath of affirmative action.* Berkeley, CA: Center for Studies in Higher Education.

Dynarski, S. (2003). Does aid matter? Measuring the effect of student aid on college attendance and completion. *The American Economic Review, 93*(1), 279–288.

Dynarski, S. (in press). Building the stock of college-educated labor. *Journal of Human Resources.*

Espenshade, T. J., & Chung, C. Y. (2005). The opportunity cost of admission preferences at elite universities. *Social Science Quarterly, 86*(2), 293–305.

Featherman, D. L., & Hauser, R. M. (1978). *Opportunity and change.* New York: Academic Press.

Finnell, S. (1998). The *Hopwood* chill: How the court derailed diversity efforts at Texas A&M. In G. Orfield & E. Miller (Eds.), *Chilling admissions: The affirmative action crisis and the search for alternatives* (pp. 71–82). Cambridge, MA: Harvard Education Press.

Gerald, D., & Haycock, K. (2006). Engines of inequality: Diminishing equity in the nation's premier public universities. Washington, DC: The Education Trust.

Gratz v. Bollinger, 539 U.S. 244 (2003).

Grodsky, E. (2007). Compensatory sponsorship in higher education. *American Journal of Sociology, 112*(6), 1662–1712.

Grodsky, E., & Felts, E. (2007). *Social stratification in higher education.* Paper presented at the meeting of the American Educational Research Association, Chicago, IL.

Grodsky, E., & Kalogrides, D. (in press). The declining significance of race in college admission decision. *American Journal of Education.*

Grodsky, E., & Kurlaender, M. (2006). *The demography of higher education in the wake of affirmative action.* Paper presented at the meeting Equal Opportunity in Higher Education: The Past and Future of Proposition 209, Berkeley, CA.

Grutter v. Bollinger, 539 U.S. 306 (2003).

Guess, A. (2007, October 24). *Race-based aid, after a statewide ban.* Retrieved October 24, 2007, from http://www.insidehighered.com/news/2007/10/24/michigan

Hauser, R. M., Simmons, S. J., & Pager, D. I. (2004). High school dropout, race/ethnicity, and social background from the 1970s to the 1990s, In G. Orfield (Ed.), *Dropouts in America: Confronting the graduation rate crisis* (pp. 85–106). Cambridge, MA: Harvard Education Press.

Heller, D. E. (2005). Can minority students afford college in an era of skyrocketing tuition? In G. Orfield, P. Marin, & C. L. Horn (Eds.), *Higher education and the color line: College access, racial equity, and social change* (pp. 83–106). Cambridge, MA: Harvard Education Press.

Hopwood v. Texas, 78 F.3d 932 (5th Cir.), *cert. denied,* 518 U.S. 1033 (1996).

Hout, M., Raftery, A. E., & Bell, E. O. (1993). Making the grade: Educational stratification in the United States, 1925–1989. In Y. Shavit & H. P. Blossfeld (Eds.), *Persistent inequality: Changing educational attainment in thirteen countries* (pp. 25–49). Boulder, CO: Westview Press.

Kane, T. J. (1994). College entry by Blacks since 1970: The role of college costs, family background, and the returns to education. *Journal of Political Economy, 102*(5), 878–911.

Kane, T. J. (1998). Racial and ethnic preferences in college admissions. In C. Jencks & M. Phillips (Eds.), *The Black-White test score gap* (pp. 431–456). Washington, DC: Brookings Institution Press.

Kaufman, P., Alt, M. N., & Chapman, C. (2004). *Dropout rates in the United States: 2001* (No. NCES 2005–046). Washington, DC: U.S. Department of Education. National Center for Education Statistics.

KewalRamani, A., Gilbertson, L., Fox, M., & Provasnik, S. (2007). *Status and trends in the education of racial and ethnic minorities* (NCES 2007–039). Washington, DC: National Center for Education Statistics, Institute of Education Sciences, U.S. Department of Education. Retrieved November 4, 2007, from http://nces.ed.gov/pubs2007/2007039.pdf

Kurlaender, M., & Horn, C. L. (2007). *College exit: An investigation of the timing decisions of college leavers.* Paper presented at the meeting of the American Educational Research Association, Chicago, IL.

Kyung, W. (1996). In-migration of college students to the state of New York. *The Journal of Higher Education, 67*(3), 349–358.

Lerner, R., & Nagai, A. K. (2001). *Pervasive preferences: Racial and ethnic discrimination in undergraduate admissions across the nation.* Washington, DC: Center for Equal Opportunity.

Light, A., & Strayer, W. (2000). Determinants of college completion: School quality or student ability? *Journal of Human Resources, 35*(2), 299–332.

Linsenmeier, D. M., Rosen, H. S., & Rouse, C. E. (2006). Financial aid packages and college enrollment decisions: An econometric case study. *Review of Economics and Statistics, 88*(1), 126–145.

Long, B. T. (2004). How have college decisions changed over time? An application of the conditional logistic choice model. *Journal of Econometrics, 121*, 271–296.

Manski, C. F. (1989). Schooling as experimentation: A reappraisal of the postsecondary dropout phenomenon. *Economics of Education Review, 8*(4), 305–397.

National Center for Education Statistics. (2004a). *Digest of education statistics.* Washington, DC: U.S. Department of Education.

National Center for Education Statistics. (2004b). *National postsecondary student aid study.* Washington, DC: U.S. Department of Education.

National Center for Education Statistics. (2004c). *Status completion rates, and number and distribution of completers ages 18–24 not currently enrolled in high school or below, by selected background characteristics.* Washington, DC: U.S. Department of Education. Retrieved October 16, 2007, from http://nces.ed.gov/pubs2007/dropout/Table2.asp?table = 9

National Center for Education Statistics. (2005a). *Integrated postsecondary education data system.* Washington, DC: U.S. Department of Education.

National Center for Education Statistics. (2005b). *State nonfiscal survey of public elementary/secondary education.* Washington, DC: U.S. Department of Education. Retrieved December 2, 2007, from http://nces.ed.gov/ccd/stNfis.asp

National Center for Education Statistics. (2006a). *Digest of education statistics.* Washington, DC: U.S. Department of Education.

National Center for Education Statistics. (2006b). *State nonfiscal survey of public elementary/secondary education.* Washington, DC: U.S. Department of Education. Retrieved December 2, 2007, from http://nces.ed.gov/ccd/stNfis.asp

Orfield, G. (1998). Campus resegregation and its alternatives. In G. Orfield & E. Miller (Eds.), *Chilling admissions: The affirmative action crisis and the search for alternatives* (pp. 1–16). Cambridge, MA: Harvard Education Press.

Orfield, G. (Ed.). (2004). *Dropouts in America: Confronting the graduation rate crisis.* Cambridge, MA: Harvard Education Press.

Orfield, G. (2005). Higher education and the color line: Introduction. In G. Orfield, P. Marin, & C. L. Horn (Eds.), *Higher education and the color line: College access, racial equity, and social change* (pp. 1–10). Cambridge, MA: Harvard Education Press.

Orfield, G., & Miller, E. (2000). *Chilling admissions: The affirmative action crisis and the search for alternatives.* Cambridge, MA: Harvard Education Press.

Regents of the University of California v. Bakke, 438 U.S. 265 (1978).

Rosenbaum, J. E. (2001). *Beyond college for all: Career paths for the forgotten half.* New York: Russell Sage Foundation.

Schmidt, P. (2007, October 19). 5 more states may curtail affirmative action. *The Chronicle of Higher Education,* pp. A1, A19–20.

Smith v. University of Washington Law School, 392 F.3d 367 (9th Cir. 2004) *cert. denied,* 546 U.S. 813 (2005).

Stephan, J. L., & Rosenbaum, J. E. (2007). *How do college type and high school grades interact to affect degree completion?* Paper presented at the meeting of the American Educational Research Association, Chicago, IL.

Swanson, C. B. (2004a). Sketching a portrait of public high school graduation: Who graduates? Who doesn't? In G. Orfield (Ed.), *Dropouts in America: Confronting the graduation rate crisis* (pp. 13–40). Cambridge, MA: Harvard Education Press.

Swanson, C. B. (2004b). *Who graduates? Who doesn't? A statistical portrait of public high school graduation, class of 2001.* Washington, DC: Urban Institute.

Tienda, M., Leicht, K. T., Sullivan, T., Maltese, M., & Lloyd, K. (2003). *Closing the gap? Admissions and enrollments at the Texas public flagships before and after affirmative action.* Princeton, NJ: Office of Population Research.

Tinto, V. (1993). *Leaving college: Rethinking the causes and cures of student attrition.* Chicago: University of Chicago Press.

Turner, S. E. (2004). Going to college and finishing college: Explaining different education outcomes. In C. Hoxby (Ed.), *College choices: The economics of where to go, when to go, and how to pay for it* (pp. 13–62). Chicago: University of Chicago Press.

U.S. Census Bureau. (1940). *Educational attainment.* Retrieved November 4, 2007, from http://www.census.gov/population/www/socdemo/educ-attn.html

U.S. Census Bureau. (2006). *Annual social and economic supplement.* Washington, DC: U.S. Department of Commerce, Bureau of the Census. Retrieved November 4, 2007, from http://www.census.gov/population/www/socdemo/educ-attn.html

University of California. (2003). *Undergraduate access to the University of California:*

After the elimination of race-conscious policies. Retrieved November 4, 2007, from http://ucop.edu/outreach/aa_finalcx%202.pdf

Warren, J. R. (2005). State-level high school completion rates: Concepts, measures, and trends. *Education Policy Analysis Archives, 13*(51), 1–38

Yun, J. T., & Moreno, J. F. (2006). College access, K–12 concentrated disadvantage, and the next 25 years of education research. *Educational Researcher, 35*(1), 12–19.

PART THREE

POLICY AND PRACTICE

$$7$$

IS 1500 THE NEW 1280?

The SAT and Admissions Since *Bakke*

Catherine L. Horn and John T. Yun

T he *Regents of the University of California v. Bakke* (1978) opinion affirmed the right of colleges and universities to consider race/ethnicity in college admissions decisions. In affirming *Bakke*, the 2003 *Grutter v. Bollinger* decision ruled as legal the University of Michigan's law school admissions practice of reviewing an array of student information (e.g., a personal statement, letters of recommendation, an essay describing how the applicant will contribute to Law School life and diversity, undergraduate grade point average, and Law School Admissions Test [LSAT] score) to make admissions offers (*Grutter*, 2003). Such practices, the University successfully argued, were necessary to reap the educational benefits of diversity.

In their dissenting opinion in *Grutter*,[1] Justices Clarence Thomas and Antonin Scalia write,

> No one would argue that a university could set up a lower general admission standard and then impose heightened requirements only on Black applicants. Similarly, a university may not maintain a high admission standard and grant exemptions to favored races. The Law School, of its own choosing, and for its own purposes, maintains an exclusionary admissions system that it knows produces racially disproportionate results. Racial discrimination is not a permissible solution to the self-inflicted wounds of this elitist admissions policy . . .

We would like to thank Laila DiGuilio and Eric M. Olsen for their research assistance on this chapter, as well as John Wiley of the College Board for providing SAT data for our analysis.

One must also consider the Law School's refusal to entertain changes to its current admissions system that might produce the same educational benefits. The Law School adamantly disclaims any race-neutral alternative that would reduce "academic selectivity," which would in turn "require the Law School to become a very different institution, and to sacrifice a core part of its educational mission." . . . In other words, the Law School seeks to improve marginally the education it offers without sacrificing too much of its exclusivity and elite status. (*Grutter,* 2003, pp. 350, 355–356)

Thomas and Scalia's argument that universities may be unnecessarily relying on affirmative action to offset an institutional unwillingness to forego other potentially racially/ethnically discriminatory admissions criteria is not a new one. Thirty years previous, Justice Lewis Powell, in *Bakke,* wrote,

Racial classifications in admissions conceivably could serve a fifth purpose, one which petitioner does not articulate: fair appraisal of each individual's academic promise in the light of some cultural bias in grading or testing procedures. To the extent that race and ethnic background were considered only to the extent of curing established inaccuracies in predicting academic performance, it might be argued that there is no "preference" at all. (*Bakke,* 1978, p. 306)

This similar acknowledgement of the potential bias inherent in the tests used in admission decisions between strong opponents of race-conscious decision making (i.e., Justices Thomas and Scalia) on the one hand and advocates of such an approach (i.e., Justice Powell) on the other highlight the need to understand in greater detail the extent to which colleges and universities are self-selectively using "race-neutral"[2] tools that may actually be working contrary to the stated desire of admitting racially and ethnically diverse classes to reap their educational benefits.

Although a plethora of such race-neutral admissions criteria might be considered, this chapter focuses specifically on the use of the SAT in admissions decisions. In 1978, the year of the landmark *Bakke* decision, standardized tests were already a ubiquitous factor in college admissions (Lemann, 1999; Manski, 1983). In its conception, large-scale standardized testing was intended to be a meritocratic indicator of academic potential (Lemann, 1999). But as intimated by the previous admonitions, such testing in general, and the SAT in particular, has not had such a pristine history. This chapter analyzes the changing significance of standardized testing policies on the enrollment characteristics at elite colleges[3] since *Bakke* by addressing two main research questions. Who is going to college and how has that changed during the last 30 years with respect to key admission criteria indicators (e.g., SAT scores) by race and ethnicity? To what extent have institutional admissions policies contributed to elite institutions' insistence that race-conscious policies are necessary to maintain diversity?

The chapter begins with a more detailed discussion of Justices Thomas and Scalia's arguments and is followed by a brief review of the literature on the evolving and expanding role, at both the individual and institutional levels, of standardized testing (specifically the SAT) in college admissions. It then turns to a descriptive discussion of who is going to college and how that group has changed over the last 30 years, looking specifically at the ways in which performance on the SAT has shifted. The chapter next looks at the question of whether institutions are "creating their own problems" with respect to admitting racially/ethnically diverse classes by analyzing the proportions of incoming freshmen scoring at the highest levels on the math and verbal SAT exams over time at the country's most selective institutions. Finally, the chapter concludes with considerations of the ways in which colleges and universities operationalize prestige and how that might be shifted to reap the benefits of a diverse student body that *Bakke* describes and institutions have fought to defend. The goal of this analysis is to begin to address the critiques leveled at elite colleges by Justices Scalia and Thomas who suggest that institutions are looking to race-conscious policies to address a lack of diversity resulting from their own admissions policies. We intend to examine the extent to which these critiques are valid and explore ways that institutions can address what we argue is a false dichotomy between diversity and academic excellence.

The Thomas and Scalia Argument

In disagreeing with the majority opinion in *Grutter,* Justice Thomas, joined by Justice Scalia, argued that elite institutions were essentially creating their own need to rely on affirmative action by maintaining admissions standards that would work against the creation of a racially/ethnically diverse student body. Specifically, the justices note,

No modern law school can claim ignorance of the poor performance of Blacks, relatively speaking, on the Law School Admissions Test (LSAT). Nevertheless, law schools continue to use the test and then attempt to "correct" for Black underperformance by using racial discrimination in admissions so as to obtain their aesthetic student body. The Law School's continued adherence to measures it knows produce racially skewed results is not entitled to deference by this Court. The Law School itself admits that the test is imperfect, as it must, given that it regularly admits students who score at or below 150 (the national median) on the test. . . . And the Law School's *amici* cannot seem to agree on the fundamental question whether the test itself is useful.

Having decided to use the LSAT, the Law School must accept the constitutional burdens that come with this decision. The Law School may freely continue to employ the LSAT and other allegedly merit-based standards in whatever fashion it likes. What the Equal Protection Clause forbids, but the Court today allows, is the use of these standards hand-in-hand with racial discrimination. An infinite variety of admissions methods are available to the Law School. Considering all of the radical thinking that has historically occurred at this country's universities, the Law School's intractable approach toward admissions is striking. (*Grutter,* 2003, pp. 369–370)

Similar to the University of Michigan law school admissions practice described by the justices, elite colleges and universities across the country have historically made use of the SAT in deciding whether to accept applicants as freshmen (Bowen & Bok, 1998). What lies at the heart of this concern about "allegedly merit-based standards" is the continued reliance on measures on which much research has documented disparate performance between Whites and Asians on one hand and Blacks and Latinos on the other.[4] To this end, the chapter now turns to a brief review of the literature on the role of the SAT in college admissions, the persistent racial gap in performance, and possible explanations for that gap.

The Evolving and Expanding Role of the SAT in College Admissions

The SAT had an auspicious beginning tied to the development and vogue of intelligence testing, particularly the Army Alpha exam, that preceded it during the late 1800s and early 1900s (Crouse & Trusheim, 1988). First administered in 1926 by the Educational Testing Service (ETS), the SAT was intended to measure "future promise independent of past opportunity" (Crouse & Trusheim, 1988, p. 24), to say that regardless of courses offered within and between high schools, a student's aptitude for postsecondary work would be captured. As a rationale, ETS argued,

> The individual's entitlement to college is fair because the test that measures whether he or she will succeed is not biased by the quality of the person's past schooling. The individual's place in a college is efficient because any allocation other than by predicted success is a waste of potential talent. For example, to accept unqualified students who failed would not only produce unnecessary psychological damage but would also deny places to qualified students and cripple the efficiency of the educational and occupational system. (Crouse & Trusheim, 1988, pp. 24–25)

Such egalitarian rhetoric carried the day as sound reason to include SAT scores in admission decision making because scores represented latent possibilities rather than necessarily manifest talent. In years subsequent to the 1920s, the SAT has taken on an increasingly prominent presence in the process of admitting students to college (Lemann, 1999).

Longitudinal work by the College Board documents that between 1979 and 2000, testing requirements as part of admissions increased from 91 to 96% of public 4-year institutions and from 91 to 92% in private 4-year colleges (Milewski & Camara, 2002). For college applicants, then, the SAT has at least some bearing on the outcomes of college decision making. Additionally, much research has documented that the most selective postsecondary institutions also have admitted students among the highest SAT scorers (e.g., Bowen & Bok, 1998; Carnevale & Rose, 2003; Pascarella et al., 2006). This chapter attends to the institutional implications of this fact in turn but, suffice it to say, because the SAT matters so much for admission to elite schools, the individual applicant may have a substantial value added in top performance on the test. This value added comes in the form of a payoff for students who attend a selective college, including a greater likelihood of graduating, greater access to graduate school, and a wage premium in the labor market (Berg Dale & Krueger, 2002; Carnevale & Rose, 2003; Loury & Garman, 1995). Although the admission process for such institutions is a complex one, often based on many factors (Bowen & Bok, 1998), with few exceptions the SAT has remained an important component among those in general and at selective institutions in particular (Milewski & Camara, 2002).

The SAT and the Individual Performance Gap

A substantial body of research has documented differential performance on the SAT by race/ethnicity, gender, and socioeconomic status. Carnevale and Rose (2003), for example, note that nearly two out of every three test-takers who scores above 1300 on the SAT are in the top socioeconomic income quartile. Jencks (1998) provides an interesting lens through which to understand disparate performance. He argues that "bias" as it relates to standardized testing takes several forms: labeling, content, methodological, prediction, and selection system. Labeling bias occurs when a test claims to measure one thing but, in fact, measures something else. With respect to the SAT, Jencks notes,

> Intelligence and aptitude tests are claiming to measure something innate. Yet almost all psychologists now agree that while an individual's score depends partly on his or her genetic makeup, it also reflects a multitude of environmental influences . . . Intelligence and aptitude tests are therefore racially biased estimates of innate traits that many nonpsychologists think such tests are claiming to measure. (1998, p. 82)

Accordingly, then, the SAT may not be measuring a test-taker's aptitude in math or verbal reasoning; it may instead be assessing the effects, for instance, of that person's opportunities to learn. For example, "Blacks and Hispanics make up a higher proportion of those who attend high schools with the lowest rates of college attendance, the most widespread incidence of subsidized school lunches, and the least 'social capital'" (Carnevale & Rose, 2003, p. 36). Therefore, the SAT might be considered a biased estimate of that individual's ability.[5]

Continuing his discussion, Jencks argues that content bias—when a test fails to measure something that could otherwise be assessed in an unbiased manner—does not seem to be plausible with respect to explaining the Black-White SAT test score gap. Much research has been done to suggest that disparate performance cannot be accounted for by the test makers' use of culturally biased questions. Although the existence of such questions has certainly been an issue, especially in the early development of the SAT, the gap in performance "does not depend in any simple, predictable way on the nominal content of the test" (Jencks, 1998, p. 69). Methodological bias, however, may have some influence on test-taker performance. Although the research supporting that argument is limited, Steele's work (1998), for example, has provided evidence showing that able Black students will get lower scores on difficult tests if they are told that the exam is one of "ability" rather than one of achievement. If minority students do poorly on a test more because of the method of assessment rather than because of differences in skills, methodological bias may be, at least partly, to blame for test score differences.

With respect to predictive bias (when Blacks and Whites with the same score perform differently in their first years of college), Jencks writes that SAT scores do not evidence strong prejudice against minorities. "Test scores have a moderate correlation with performance, . . . the gap between Blacks and Whites grows wider as their test scores rise, . . . and in neither case, do these facts tell us whether using tests to select students is 'fair' " (1998, p. 76). Jenck's final point about the fairness of the SAT, however, is crucial and directly tied to the last form of bias: selection system. In the reliance on a paper-and-pencil test to select among college applicants, many more Blacks and Hispanics will be excluded. Where a performance-based system that includes additional characteristics of applicants not captured by the SAT might incorporate more minorities in the eligible pool, the heavy or exclusive use of SAT scores will continue to bias a Black or Hispanic student's chances for admission.

In their dissent, Justices Thomas and Scalia argue the performance gap on standardized test scores (in this case the LSAT), may be perpetuated by the use of affirmative action:

> An applicant's LSAT score can improve dramatically with preparation, but such preparation is a cost, and there must be sufficient benefits attached to an improved score to justify additional study. . . . It is far from certain that the LSAT test-taker's behavior is responsive to the Law School's admissions policies. Nevertheless, the possibility remains that this racial discrimination will help fulfill the bigot's prophecy about Black underperformance. . . . (*Grutter*, 2003, p. 377)

The implicit suggestion by the justices, then, is that simple shifts in motivational structure—that is, clear and unbending articulation of an expected standard on par with other applicants—may alone shrink the standardized test performance gap between Whites and Asians on the one hand and

Blacks and Latinos on the other. In his conclusion, however, Jencks takes a position counter to that of the justices:

> It seems fair to say that the invention of standardized tests has harmed blacks as a group, both because of labeling bias and because of selection system bias. This does not mean that the tests themselves are flawed. The skill differences that the tests measure are real, and these skills have real consequences both at school and at work. But inability to measure the other predictors of performance, on which blacks seem to be far less disadvantaged, poses a huge social problem. (1998, p. 84)

Jenck's final point must be taken seriously. Regardless of the reliability of the measure, the SAT's inability to assess additional predictors of success (e.g., tenacity, motivation, or untested knowledge/skills) is of primary concern, especially as we see an increasing reliance on SAT scores in a race-neutral admissions setting (see Lederman, 1999). The notion, then, that the SAT functions as a completely unbiased individualized measure of post-secondary potential seems untenable. In addition, individual SAT performance is now being considered at the aggregate institutional level in ways that may exacerbate performance gaps and is the issue to which this chapter now turns.

SAT, the Rankings Game, and the Institutional Performance Gap

Although ranking colleges is not a new undertaking (Meredith, 2004), the contemporary use, exemplified by the *U.S. News and World Report*'s annual college ratings issue, burgeoned in the 1980s (Meredith, 2004). The specific combination and weighting of factors has changed over time and by analytical agency, but, in general, rankings typically consider information across four broad categories: faculty quality, institutional resources, student retention, and student selectivity (Sanoff, 2007). The latter, in particular, might include data such as acceptance rates, the mean SAT score of the entering freshman class, and high school rank information. McDonough, Antonio, Walpole, and Perez (1998) describe the appeal of the ranking system as two-fold. First, from the consumer perspective, rankings provide an accessible, succinct representation of value defined by a certain set of considerations.[6] Second, from the organizational side, ratings offer quantification to a set of intangible conditions. "Choosing a college is an intangible, expensive purchase perceived to be fraught with risks . . . The more uncertain the decision, the greater the likelihood that consumers consult ratings information in an attempt to lower their risks" (McDonough et al., 1998, pp. 515–516). To the extent that colleges and universities can leverage rankings as a mechanism for representing their "commodity," they potentially benefit.

Gaming the System and Who It Hurts

Even though rankings have a simplistic appeal couched in an objective façade as described earlier, many scholars have identified the troubling unintended consequences of the college rating process. As Clarke encapsulates,

> Rankings contribute to [the] increasing stratification of the U.S. higher education system by creating incentives for schools to recruit students who will be "assets" in terms of maintaining or enhancing their position in the rankings. These incentives seem directly related to the student-selectivity indicators used in *U.S. News* and other rankings, including test scores for entering students, the proportion of entering students who graduated in the top ten percent of their high school class, and the percentage of applicants accepted. (2007, p. 37)

The potentially perverse incentive structure has led to institutions gaming the system, for example, by excluding scores of certain groups from submitted data, admitting weak students during a period not included in the requested data (e.g., spring semester), and manipulating graduation data (Sanoff, 2007).

Additionally, opposite the perceived democratization of information the rankings are perceived to provide, several studies suggest that organizational engagement with the rankings process may exacerbate disparities between traditionally underserved and dominant student populations in needed college information and admissions considerations (*Journal of Blacks in Higher Education,* 2002; McDonough et al., 1998). More subtly, the rankings also operationalize merit in a way that may limit or marginalize institutions that seek to define their own identities in ways that deviate from the metrics used to calculate the rankings. Given the increasingly powerful influence of rankings such as those produced by *U.S. News and World Report* on the college choice process (Pike, 2004), such marginalization may lead to reductions in school desirability defined by status on the ranking system and limit institutional opportunities in a way that may be unacceptable to most institutional leaders.

This construction of merit and how it interacts with the autonomy of institutions is at the core of the Thomas and Scalia argument, which seems to suggest that you can have either quality and selectivity as defined by high test scores or diversity, but not necessarily both. We argue that this dichotomy is a false one and move toward a reconceptualization of merit. To this end, we now examine some of the demographic realities faced by institutions as they undertake the admissions process, and then move toward understanding how test scores have changed in the years since *Bakke*. We end by studying how elite institutions have responded to the increasing numbers of students taking the SAT and applying to college from different racial/ethnic groups.

Who Is Going to College and How Has That Changed?

The proportion of students applying to and attending college has changed quite a bit since the time of *Bakke* (see, also, Kurlaender & Felts, this volume, for a discussion of college access changes). According to the Digest of Education Statistics (National Center for Education Statistics [NCES], 2006a), in 1978, approximately 1.58 million students ages 16 to 24 enrolled in 4-year institutions within 12 months of completing high school, representing a postsecondary enrollment rate of approximately 50%. By 2005, that number had increased to approximately 1.83 million, for a postsecondary enrollment rate of about 69%. Therefore, although only about 300,000 more students were attending 2- or 4-year colleges within a year of high school graduation between 1978 and 2004, the number of high school graduates had fallen during that same interval thus leading to the increased yield. As a proportion of students eligible, then, postsecondary participation has increased substantially since *Bakke*.

Examining higher education enrollments by race/ethnicity, we see that in 1978 approximately 160,000 Black, 56,000 Hispanic, and 1.3 million White students enrolled within a year of high school graduation. By 2004, those numbers had changed to about 250,000, 180,000, and 1.3 million Black, Hispanic, and White students, respectively (NCES, 2006b). Although these increases in raw numbers are large for both Black and Hispanic students (an approximately 50% increase for Black students and 200% increase for Hispanic students), they represent an even larger change in the enrollment rate of high school graduates, with an increase from 46 to 63% for

Black students, from 42 to 62% for Hispanic students, and from 51 to 69% for White students. These changes are important because they represent an increase in access to postsecondary education for all three racial groups. But they also represent that the gaps in enrollment share persist between White high school graduates on the one hand and Black and Hispanic graduates on the other, with White graduates enrolling at 6 to 7 percentage points higher than their Black and Hispanic peers.

As important as this increase is, many of the students who are likely to benefit from this new access to postsecondary education are not going to be attending the highly selective schools that are using race as a component of their admissions system. In fact, a study conducted using the National Education Longitudinal Study of 1988 (NELS:88) found that only 5.9% of college-bound seniors met the criteria for admissions to highly selective institutions (Owings, McMillien, Burkett, & Pinkerton, 1995). The patterns were even more stark when these qualifications were disaggregated by race. The authors of the NELS:88 study found that 8.8% of Asian, 2.5% of Hispanic, 0.4% of Black, and 6.5% of White students met all five selectivity criteria[7] (Owings et al., 1995). Findings like these suggest that there is likely to be a significant shortfall of "qualified" Black and Hispanic candidates to these highly selective institutions because such a small percentage of them met all the conditions necessary for entry. Given these 1995 findings, we might expect that the percentage of minority students attending highly selective colleges would be low. However, the percentages of Black students attending highly selective and Ivy League schools increased from 4 to 6.3% from 1967 to 1977 (Blackwell, 1987; Bowen & Bok, 1998). Krueger, Rothstein, and Turner (2005) note that for census cohorts (which correspond to the 1967 to 1977 time span), the BA attainment ratio between Black and White men did not change but, at the same time, the ratio of those who attained some college increased. Krueger et al. (2005) suggest that this implies the increases in attainment for Black students in these selective institutions are not indicative of an overall improvement in access to 4-year institutions but instead indicate a redistribution of Black students toward more selective institutions during the pre-*Bakke* period. This contention is supported by the fact that Hispanic and Black students who attend national universities are represented at elite institutions in similar (or higher) proportions to their White peers (Owings et al., 1995).[8]

In addition, the College Board found that between 1996 and 2006, diversity in the pool of college-bound seniors who took the SAT in the year before college entry changed, with the share of English-only speakers falling from 83 to 77%, and the share of White students falling from 69 to 62%, with approximate one percentage point increases in the share of Mexican, other Latino, Asian, and other students making up the difference (College Board, 2006). These compositional changes during the past decade, combined with increases in the raw numbers of students taking the examination (1.08 million in 1996 and 1.5 million in 2006), generate much larger numbers of minority students taking the SAT with the number of Asian, African American, and Latino students increasing by approximately 56,000, 53,000, and 86,000, respectively (table 7.1).

Regardless of how these students are performing, given these large increases in the numbers of minority student taking the SAT and presumably attending college, as well as the relatively limited numbers of spaces available at the elite colleges, at no other time in history has the potential applicant pool been more diverse or held more opportunity for selective institutions interested in creating diverse learning environments. The quality of that pool

TABLE 7.1
Number, Change, and Percent Change in College-Bound Seniors Taking the SAT Reasoning Examination During Their High School Careers, 1996 and 2006

Race/Ethnicity	1996	2006	Change	% Change
American Indian	8,737	9,897	1,160	13
Asian/Pacific Islander	84,319	140,794	56,475	67
African American	106,573	159,849	53,276	50
Hispanic/Latino				
Mexican	36,689	61,240	24,551	67
Puerto Rican	13,103	19,778	6,675	51
Other Latino	32,193	87,526	55,333	172
White	681,053	828,038	146,985	22
Other	28,099	53,901	25,802	92
No Response	93,959	133,508	39,549	42
Total	1,084,725	1,494,531	496,365	43

Source: College Board (1996, 2006).
Note. The SAT reasoning test is the encompassing name for the math and verbal sections typically used in undergraduate college admissions decisions.

(with respect to test scores) and how performance on the SAT has changed by race/ethnicity will be examined next.

How Has SAT Performance by Race/Ethnicity Changed?

In contextualizing the increased access to college, it is important to look concurrently at the changes in SAT performance. Figure 7.1 presents mean scores on both the critical reading[9] and math sections of the SAT from 1967 to 2007. Several trends are noteworthy. The mean score on the critical reading SAT witnessed a fairly substantial decline during the early- to mid-1970s followed by a sustained period of stagnant performance (vacillating between mean scores of 499 and 509 from 1976 to 2007). On the contrary, although math scores saw a similar but less precipitous drop during the same period of the 1970s, the scores have very slowly but steadily increased during the subsequent decades (from 497 in 1976 to its peak in 2005 of 520).

Looking at similar trends by race/ethnicity, we see that several patterns emerge (figures 7.2 and 7.3). Regardless of racial/ethnic group, mean performance on the SAT verbal section has remained relatively flat from 1987 to 2006. Equally important to note, however, is that the gap in performance has also persisted. Specifically, while White students have SAT verbal scores, on

FIGURE 7.1
Mean SAT scores of incoming college students, 1967–2007

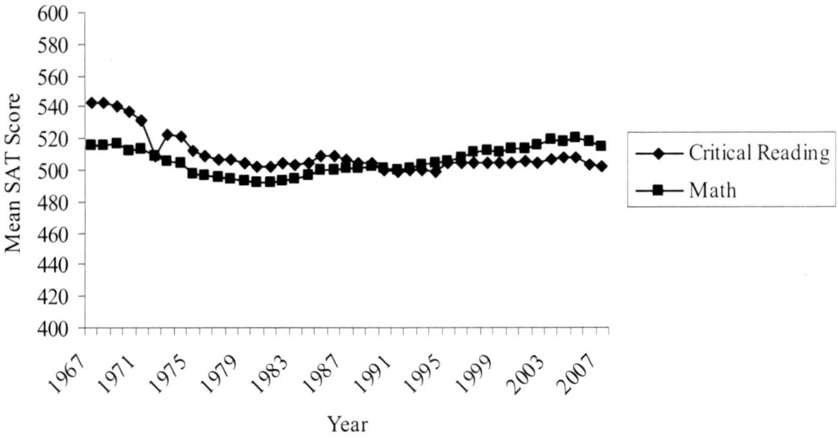

Source: College Board (2007).
Note. All scores reflect a shared scale based on the 1995 recentering of scores.

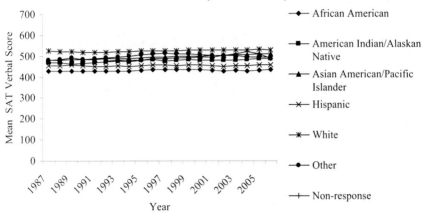

FIGURE 7.2

Mean SAT verbal scores, by race/ethnicity, 1987–2006

Source: Korbin, Sathy, and Shaw (2007).

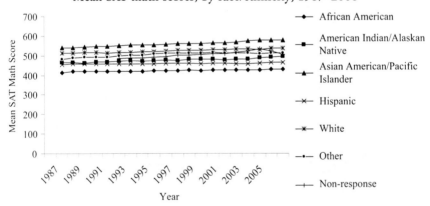

FIGURE 7.3

Mean SAT math scores, by race/ethnicity, 1987–2006

Source: Korbin, Sathy, and Shaw (2007).

average, around 520, African Americans and Hispanics have had mean scores between 427 and 434 and 453 and 458, respectively. Asian students have seen the greatest increase in scores (from a mean of 479 in 1987 to 510 in 2006).

The trends in mean SAT math scores by race/ethnicity diverge slightly from those seen in verbal SAT performance. Over the 20-year period for which data are available, mean math SAT scores have risen across all racial/ethnic groups. For example, for African Americans, mean scores rose from 411 in 1987 to 429 in 2006. Similarly, Hispanic mean scores rose during that same period from 453 to 463. By comparison, White mean math SAT scores also increased from 514 in 1987 to 536 in 2006. Again, however, note that the performance gap between Whites and traditionally underserved students continues throughout the period and actually grows over time. In combination, then, these data tell us that overall SAT performance nationally has not shifted much in the last 30 years and, perhaps more troubling, the racial/ethnic disparities in performance have not dissipated.

Given these testing realities, Krueger et al. (2005) use simulations based on a series of assumptions about college admissions, the reduction in test score gaps, and increases in schooling quality to model the viability of the 25 year goal put forward by Justice Sandra Day O'Conner in her majority opinion in the *Grutter* decision.[10] They conclude that even when somewhat optimistic estimates are placed on the narrowing of the test-score gap between Black and White students, combined with reductions in Black-White poverty differentials and overall increases in school quality, there remain substantial negative differentials in Black enrollments in selective schools compared with current levels obtained with race-conscious admissions policies. Although the results of this simulation are important and provide some insight into the plausibility of achieving race-neutral outcomes within 25 years, it is important to examine the logic of the entire approach. Krueger et al. (2005) as well as Justices O'Conner and Ruth Bader Ginsberg seem to be placing the burden of eliminating the need for race-conscious policies on the primary and secondary schools as well as on individuals, not necessarily on the postsecondary institutions that are setting the criteria for admission to college, or on the conception of merit that forms the context for institutional action.

Are Elite Institutions Creating Their Own Problems?[11]

The previous two sections show that more students are applying to college and taking the SAT, with important positive changes occurring among the numbers of Asian, Black, and Hispanic students taking the SAT exam. Among these students, even if the average SAT score stayed constant, there are likely to be increases in the number of students scoring at the extremes of the distributions (i.e., the lower and upper limits of the 200 to 800 scale-score continuum), providing many of the elite schools greater access to more higher-scoring minority students. Given this greater access, then, schools have a choice with respect to the use of test scores in admission considerations. They can weigh SAT scores in their decision making such that, given current test score distributions, the process may perhaps allow for a larger pool from which to choose and create a more diverse class. Or they may simply accept more students at the upper ends of the distribution, resulting in both higher mean SAT scores and greater proportions of their classes at the upper end of the test score distribution, a decision that might have a complex set of implications both for the individual students admitted as well as for the institution in its ranking standings.

Elite schools showing similar test score distributions at the beginning and end of the period since *Bakke* would be consistent with these institutions making important enrollment decisions that weigh the level of test score achievement relatively less than did schools that created admissions environments privileging entry to those scoring highest. The latter decision would manifest as an increasing share of the entering class scoring at the upper end of the testing distribution. The more extreme the change in share of students with exceptionally high SAT scores, the greater the suggested preference for accepting students at the upper end of the testing spectrum. Of course, institutions must have access to these high-scoring students via their applicant pool to consider admitting them. Our data do not allow us to determine which institutional pools were heavy or light with students scoring in the upper tail of the testing distribution, but we can suggest that schools that show the largest changes in high-scoring student enrollment most likely fall into three categories: (1) they always had a supply of high-scoring students and changed their preference for high SAT scores, (2) they had a large increase in high-scoring applicants who were accepted at the typical rates, or (3) they had a large increase in high-scoring applicants who were accepted at very high rates. We would expect category one schools to be those that have always had elite status (e.g., Yale, Harvard, Princeton, etc.) and a ready supply of applicants at the higher ends of the distribution. Thus, changes in these schools would be largely the result of changes in acceptance preference.

Further, we would expect category two schools to be those with historically low to moderate shares of high-scoring students and would expect increases in shares of high-scoring students to be moderate. Finally, we would expect category three schools to be those that were aggressively targeting and accepting students with high test scores. We would also expect schools that successfully reached this goal to show very large changes in the shares of its entering classes with extreme test scores. Given the relatively low supply of these high-scoring students (in 2006, for example, approximately 74,000 students scored at or above 700 on the SAT verbal section), these category three schools likely have the highest preference for these high scorers, potentially limiting institutional access to underrepresented minority students who are few in number at these high-scoring levels.[12]

Given this framework for understanding how admission preferences may affect the distribution of high-scoring students in college entering classes, we examine the patterns of incoming freshmen scoring above 500, 600, and 700 on the SAT math exam from 1969 to 2007 for the 30 highest ranked colleges in the 2007 *U.S. News and World Report* (tables 7.2 and 7.3). The rows in tables 7.2 and 7.3 are the top 30 schools in the 2007 *U.S. News and World Report*'s college rankings, in rank order. The columns are divided into three sections that represent the percentage of the freshmen class, over time, whose SAT scores were greater than 500[13], 600, and 700 from 1969 to 2007. When examining the tables, note several important findings. First, even in 1969, for schools for which data are available, all but five of these colleges had greater than 90% of their enrolled freshman classes with verbal scores of 500 or greater. Since the mean score[14] on the SAT is normed to be 500, this suggests that the population of students in these schools is well above average on these metrics (as we would expect for elite schools).

Second, we see that in 2007 all but four of the schools for which data are available had more than 30% of their freshmen class scoring 700 or greater on the SAT verbal and half of these colleges have more than 50% of their freshmen classes with greater than a 700 on their SAT verbal test (table 7.2). Although one can argue that this is to be expected at the top schools in the country, remember that only approximately 74,000 students nationwide in 2006 scored above 700 on their SAT verbal exam, and these 30 schools (of more than 2,000 public and private 4-year institutions [*Chronicle of Higher Education,* 2007]) enrolled approximately 25,000 of them.[15] By comparison, in 1989, more a decade after *Bakke,* only one of the 30 institutions had more

TABLE 7.2
Percentage of Incoming Freshmen Scoring Above 500, 600, and 700 on the SAT Verbal Exam for the 30 Highest Ranked Colleges in the 2007 U.S. News and World Report, 1969–2007

Colleges	% Above 500* Verbal					% Above 600 Verbal					% Above 700 Verbal				
	1969	1979	1989	1999	2007	1969	1979	1989	1999	2007	1969	1979	1989	1999	2007
Princeton	93	93	648a	100	100	70	63	—	—	96	21	20	—	—	73
Harvard	700*	—	660a	—	100	—	—	—	—	—	—	—	—	—	—
Yale	99	96	96	—	100	90	78	79	—	97	50	32	33	—	78
Stanford	654c	94	96	99	99	90	63	74	—	94	50	15	24	—	67
University of Pennsylvania	99	600a	91	99	100	74	78	57	—	94	19	—	9	—	54
Cal Tech	99	94	95	100	—	92	78	79	—	—	42	30	29	—	—
MIT	99	95	91	99	99	91	74	65	—	95	54	23	17	—	68
Duke	630a	88	618a	98	99	—	53	—	—	94	—	9	—	—	63
Columbia	97	91	620a	—	100	82	68	—	—	93	49	23	—	—	67
University of Chicago	99	617a	96	99	100	84	—	73	—	96	34	23	18	—	68
Dartmouth	98	620b	630a	100	100	78	—	—	—	93	25	—	—	—	69
Washington University	90	78	84	93	100	47	40	37	—	97	9	10	5	—	59
Cornell	93	86	90	97	99	66	50	54	—	86	20	8	10	—	41
Brown	98	86	93	98	100	76	55	64	—	92	25	14	17	—	64
Northwestern	89	85	79	99	100	51	51	36	—	92	10	9	4	—	53
Johns Hopkins	97	93	91	99	98	70	65	60	—	88	22	15	10	—	46
Rice	100	91	631a	98	98	88	72	73	—	91	37	20	19	—	57
Emory	91	544a	83	98	99	46	—	33	—	87	8	—	4	—	32
Vanderbilt	95	565a	84	98	99	60	—	32	—	89	12	—	4	—	41
University of Notre Dame	580a	83	85	97	100	—	35	39	—	88	—	4	4	—	47
UC Berkeley	569a	67	72	92	93	—	33	40	—	73	—	6	7	—	33
Carnegie Mellon	620a	74	78	94	98	—	25	35	—	81	—	2	4	—	33
University of Virginia	93	90	83	95	96	49	48	33	—	77	9	7	8	—	32
Georgetown	97	79	92	97	99	69	45	64	—	88	17	91	5	—	53
UCLA	—	48	62	91	93	41	15	22	—	66	—	2	2	—	21
University of Michigan	83	65	77	91	95	41	23	32	—	69	9	3	4	—	20
USC	75	443a	482a	90	99	29	—	—	—	86	—	—	—	—	35
UNC Chapel Hill	74	511a	550a	93	96	31	—	—	—	73	—	—	—	—	23
Tufts	97	79	92	97	100	66	32	50	—	91	—	3	6	—	52
Wake Forest University	75	72	67	98	98	28	22	30	—	85	—	3	2	—	29

Source: Cass and Birnbaum (1969, 1979, 1989); Peterson's (1998); Thomson Peterson (2006).
Note. An empty cell means data was unavailable for that year and that institution.
*In 1996, the College Board recentered the SAT.
aSome institutions only reported mean scores for a given year.
bSome institutions only reported median scores for a given year.

TABLE 7.3

Percentage of Incoming Freshmen Scoring Above 500, 600, and 700 on the SAT Math Exam for the 30 Highest Ranked Colleges in the 2007 U.S. News and World Report, 1969–2007

Colleges	% Above 500* Math					% Above 600 Math					% Above 700 Math				
	1969	1979	1989	1999	2007	1969	1979	1989	1999	2007	1969	1979	1989	1999	2007
Princeton	99	97	699[a]	100	100	82	77	—	—	98	40	40	—	—	74
Harvard	713[a]	—	700[a]	—	—	—	—	—	—	—	55	45	54	—	78
Yale	99	97	99	—	100	91	83	91	—	98	55	37	55	—	74
Stanford	671[b]	96	99	99	100	—	77	90	—	97	—	—	41	—	69
University of Pennsylvania	98	660[a]	99	100	100	82	—	87	—	97	31	—	—	—	—
Cal Tech	100	100	100	100	100	100	100	100	—	100	94	96	96	—	92
MIT	100	100	99	100	100	99	98	96	—	95	94	82	74	—	68
Duke	660[a]	95	676[a]	99	99	—	76	—	—	95	44	31	—	—	60
Columbia	98	92	655[a]	—	100	88	72	—	—	95	33	34	18	—	60
University of Chicago	98	644[a]	96	99	100	80	—	73	—	94	47	—	—	—	64
Dartmouth	99	665[b]	690[a]	100	100	91	—	—	—	99	—	26	26	—	70
Washington University	92	89	97	100	100	65	61	77	—	94	40	33	40	—	73
Cornell	99	96	97	99	100	83	77	85	—	95	45	29	37	—	60
Brown	99	93	98	99	100	84	70	82	—	94	18	25	20	—	66
Northwestern	90	92	88	100	99	60	65	66	—	94	40	43	41	—	63
Johns Hopkins	99	97	97	100	99	88	84	87	—	93	59	50	56	—	61
Rice	100	98	690[a]	99	100	97	88	92	—	87	11	—	15	—	63
Emory	98	590[a]	95	100	100	66	—	66	—	93	18	22	16	—	45
Vanderbilt	97	608[a]	97	99	99	74	—	71	—	94	—	20	26	—	52
University of Notre Dame	600[a]	96	94	99	100	—	74	75	—	83	—	30	33	—	57
UC Berkeley	603[a]	86	86	95	96	—	57	68	—	97	—	63	31	—	50
Carnegie Mellon	704[a]	97	92	100	100	—	84	73	—	84	17	11	27	—	71
University of Virginia	98	93	93	97	98	68	93	73	—	90	16	8	61	—	39
Georgetown	98	79	98	98	99	74	49	80	—	77	—	15	18	—	51
UCLA	—	70	80	95	96	—	35	57	—	84	19	—	26	—	39
University of Michigan	90	86	93	95	97	60	51	72	—	93	—	—	—	—	40
USC	78	548[a]	537[a]	95	100	44	—	—	—	78	—	—	—	—	50
UNC Chapel Hill	89	552[a]	550	93	98	45	—	—	—	93	—	—	—	—	27
Tufts	99	92	97	99	100	78	69	80	—	96	—	—	26	—	64
Wake Forest University	89	89	91	97	98	46	47	60	—	88	—	9	11	—	38

Source: Cass and Birnbaum (1969, 1979, 1989); Peterson's (1998); Thomson Peterson (2006).
Note: An empty cell means data was unavailable for that year and that institution.
*In 1996, the College Board recentered the SAT.
[a] Some institutions only reported mean scores for a given year.
[b] Some institutions only reported median scores for a given year.

than 30% of their freshmen classes with a verbal score greater than 700. Although many data points are missing (simply because institutions did not report this number, or possibly because some of the non-reports are actually zeros), the differences between the data before 1989 and the 2007 data are extreme, suggesting a real shift in admissions toward very high-scoring individuals as they increasingly populated the available applicant pool with increased college-going and greater participation in the SAT program. In addition, there is much more homogeneity in the scores in 2007 than there was before 1989. Even among the top 5 or 10 schools that have always been perceived to be of high quality, the percentage of students scoring 700 or above on the SAT verbal in 1969, for example, shows considerable variation with values of 21% at Princeton and 54% at MIT. However, these institutions report 73 and 68% of students scoring similarly in their 2007 freshman classes. The story is similar for math SAT score distributions (table 7.3). One would be hard-pressed to make the argument that Princeton or MIT was an inferior institution in the late 1960s, or, in fact, that now they are wholly superior because of the greater proportion of students scoring at such high levels on the SAT in their entering classes today. Instead, it is possible that by focusing so completely on these high-scoring students they are simply "pricing" themselves out of the "market" for a more diverse learning environment. With these institutions in particular, it is difficult to see that if the testing distributions of the early 1970s and 1980s were reestablished, providing more access for minority students, that the "quality" of the institutions would suffer appreciably.

Returning to the framework described earlier, category one schools, then, clearly have the most to lose in terms of the diversity of their environments and the least to lose in terms of their reputations and applicant pools. Other schools like the University of Michigan, UCLA, and Wake Forest seem to fit into the category three pattern with sharp increases in populations at the upper end of their testing distribution. None of them, for example, enrolled greater than 4% of their first-year classes scoring 700 or above on the SAT verbal in 1979 or 1989, but, as of 2007, all of these schools have 20% or more of their classes scoring over 700. This pattern is more stark for these schools in the 600 verbal range. In 1979 and 1989, no more than 32% of the enrolled classes in these institutions had scores of 600 or greater on the SAT verbal. By 2007, none of the schools on the list that reported data enrolled *fewer* than 66% of their students with scores over 600 on the SAT verbal.

This shift in the over 600-score range simply increases competition for the proportionally lower number of minority students scoring over 600, and excludes the large number of minority students scoring in the 500 or higher range, a range that these elite schools are virtually ignoring despite their past experiences and successes with these students.

Conclusion

As Lemann (1999) notes, "The conflict between testing and Black progress hadn't gone away. Decisions like *Bakke* only heightened it, by making clear that the structure of opportunity was now the supreme question in contemporary American life" (p. 211). The alignment of argument between such disparate thinkers as Justices Thomas and Scalia on the one hand and Justice Powell on the other ought to give the reader pause when considering the role of testing and elite college admissions decisions. As this chapter has demonstrated, elite colleges and universities have not always defined high SAT scores as a primary component to successful entry. In fact, during the first half of the 40-year time span examined in this chapter, elite colleges and universities had far fewer top-SAT students relative to the total similar population.

Although we do not concur with Justices Thomas and Scalia's conclusion that the race-conscious admissions process upheld in the *Grutter* decision is a "practice that can only weaken the principle of equality embodied in the Declaration of Independence and the Equal Protection Clause" (2003, p. 378), the analysis in this chapter does highlight the complex role of testing in the creation of elite and diverse campuses. Our work suggests that this dichotomy between high academic standards and the creation of a campus that reaps the educational benefits of diversity is a false one and that these institutions need to move toward (or perhaps, more accurately, return to) a reconceptualization of merit. To the extent that elite colleges and universities are willing to move away from the *U.S. News and World Report* framework that rewards postsecondary institutions for attending to such admissions considerations as test scores that are relatively easy to operationalize (rather than the often richer but more difficult to quantify), the closer they may come to realizing *Bakke*'s legacy that elite colleges fought to defend in *Grutter*.

Notes

1. Dissenting opinions disagree with the decision of a court case and often provide a detailed legal rationale for that disagreement. Even though they are not binding in any way, they may have influence on future decisions.

2. Although they may be facially race-neutral, certain admissions criteria may effectively discriminate against non-White applicants because of inherent racial/ethnic biases in the measures themselves. Please see subsequent sections of this chapter for a more detailed discussion.

3. Kane (1998) has demonstrated that race-conscious affirmative action admission policies are situated in elite institutions, thus defining the colleges and universities considered in this study.

4. Throughout the chapter, the terms *Black* and *African American* and *Latino* and *Hispanic* are used interchangeably.

5. Although, as Jencks indicates, most researchers now agree that environment plays a significant role in how a test-taker scores, a vocal dissenting group still argues that the SAT is an accurate measure of *ability,* and that genetics remains the primary determinant of performance. Some researchers (e.g., Herrnstein & Murray, 1994; Jenson, 1991) go so far as to state that because tests such as the SAT are equally valid predictors of ability for Whites, Asians, and Blacks, the gap in performance indicates the existence of a "g" or general intelligence factor that is present to a larger degree in Whites and Asians than in Blacks. No compensation or alteration to the test can fairly be made because innate ability cannot be altered regardless of the test.

6. It is important to note that a range of ranking systems exist across a diverse set of criteria. For example, *Playboy* ranks the best party schools, Hispaniconline rates the best colleges for Hispanics, and so forth.

7. The criteria used for the study were a GPA of 3.5 or greater, an SAT combined score of 1100 or greater, high level course taking patterns (four credits of English; three credits each of math, science, and social studies; and two foreign language credits), positive teacher comments, and participation in two or more extracurricular activities.

8. Owings et al. (1995) found, using NELS:88 data and college rankings based on the *U.S. News and World Report* criteria, that of students who attended "national" universities, 29% of Hispanic, 20% of Black, and 21% of White students attended the top tier schools. Asians were the exception here with 50% attending top tier universities.

9. "Critical reading" was formally known as the verbal section of the SAT (College Board, 2007).

10. In her majority opinion, O'Connor issued an admonition that if progress in the educational pipeline continues, affirmative action in college admissions would not be needed 25 years hence.

11. In tables presented in this section, where data are missing, cells have been left blank.

12. For instance, according to John Wiley (personal communication, December 5, 2007) at the College Board, there were only 1,176 Black and 2,673 Hispanic students who scored above 700 on the SAT verbal section in 2007.

13. In 1995, the College Board recentered the SAT to take into account the modern test-taking population. On the verbal exam, for example, 500 pre-1995 is equivalent to a 580 post-1995; 600 pre-1995 is approximately equal to 680 post-1995; and 700 pre-1995 is approximately equal to a 760 post-1995. Mathematics scores remained virtually unchanged by the recentering (e.g., 700 pre-1995 is equivalent to 690 post-1995; 500 pre-1995 is equivalent to 520 post-1995; and 750 pre-1995 is equivalent to 760 post-1995). This resulted in the need for us to find an equivalency between the pre- and post-1995 SAT scores. We choose to ignore the recentering in our analysis even though the differences are substantial for the verbal scores because, while although the actual percentages of entering classes scoring above 600 on the verbal test pre-1995 would be equivalent to post-1995 classes' score of 680, we have no clear way of making those percentages equivalent. Further, the gross patterns of results are unlikely to differ since the changes we are seeing are extremely large.

14. This mean score value would be the result of the normal distribution of the SAT median score, as well, because in normal distributions the mean and median have the same value.

15. These are based on authors' tabulations from a dataset created with data from *Peterson's four-year colleges 2007* (Thomson Peterson, 2006) for the top 30 institutions.

References

Berg Dale, S., & Krueger, A. B. (2002). *Estimating the payoff to attending a more selective college: An application of selection on observables and unobservables.* Working Paper Number 7322, National Bureau of Economic Statistics. Retrieved December 3, 2007, from http://www.nber.org/papers/w7322

Blackwell, J. (1987). *Mainstreaming outsiders: The production of Black professionals* (2nd ed.). Dix Hills, NY: General Hall.

Bowen, W. G., & Bok, D. (1998). *The shape of the river: Long term consequences of considering race in college and university admissions.* Princeton, NJ: Princeton University Press.

Carnevale, A. P., & Rose, S. J. (2003). *Socioeconomic status, race/ethnicity, and selective college admissions.* New York: The Century Foundation.

Cass, J., & Birnbaum, M. (1969). *The comparative guide to American colleges* (4th ed.). New York: Harper & Row.

Cass, J., & Birnbaum, M. (1979). *The comparative guide to American colleges* (9th ed.). New York: Harper & Row.

Cass, J., & Birnbaum, M. (1989). *The comparative guide to American colleges* (14th ed.). New York: Harper & Row.

Chronicle of Higher Education. (2007). Colleges enjoy more state money, but some fight spending caps. *The 2006–07 Almanac, 53*(1), 3. Retrieved November 30, 2007, from http://chronicle.com/weekly/almanac/2006/nation/nation.htm

Clarke, M. (2007). The impact of higher education rankings on student access, choice, and opportunity. In Institute for Higher Education Policy (Ed.), *College and university ranking systems: Global perspectives and American challenges* (pp. 35–48). Washington, DC: Institute for Higher Education Policy.

College Board. (1996). *1996 college-bound seniors: A profile of SAT program takers.* Retrieved November 13, 2007, from http://professionals.collegeboard.com/prof-download/CBS%2096%20National.PDF

College Board. (2006). *Table 1: How have college-bound seniors changed in 10 years.* Retrieved December 4, 2007, from http://www.collegeboard.com/prod_down loads/about/news_info/cbsenior/yr2006/table1-college-bound-students.pdf

College Board. (2007). *2007 college-bound seniors tables and related items.* Retrieved November 13, 2007, from http://www.collegeboard.com/about/news_info/cbsen ior/yr2007/links.html

Crouse, J., & Trusheim, D. (1988). *The case against the SAT.* Chicago: University of Chicago Press.

Grutter v. Bollinger, 539 U.S. 306 (2003).

Herrnstein, R., & Murray, C. (1994). *The bell curve: Intelligence and class structure in American life.* New York: Free Press.

Jencks, C. (1998). Racial bias in testing. In C. Jencks & M. Phillips (Eds.), *The Black-White test score gap* (pp. 55–85). Washington, DC: Brookings Institution Press.

Jenson, A. (1991). Spearman's g and the problem of educational equality. *Oxford Review of Education, 17*(2), 169–187.

Journal of Blacks in Higher Education. (2002). How some colleges improve their *U.S. News* rankings by backpedaling on recruiting Black students. *Journal of Blacks in Higher Education, 35,* 20–21.

Kane, T. J. (1998). Misconceptions in the debate over affirmative action in higher education. In G. Orfield & E. Miller (Eds.), *Chilling admissions: The affirmative action crisis and the search for alternatives* (pp. 17–31). Cambridge, MA: Harvard Education Publishing Group.

Korbin, J. L., Sathy, V., & Shaw, E. J. (2007). *A historical view of subgroup perfor-mance differences on the SAT reasoning test.* New York: College Board.

Krueger, A., Rothstein, J., & Turner, S. (2005). *Race, income and college in 25 years: The continuing legacy of segregation and discrimination.* Working Paper 11445, Na-tional Bureau of Economic Research. Retrieved October 30, 2007, from http://www.nber.org/papers/w11445

Lederman, D. (1999, October 30). Persistent racial gaps in SAT scores fuels affirma-tive-action debate. *The Chronicle of Higher Education,* pp. A36–A37.

Lemann, N. (1999). *The big test: The secret history of the American meritocracy.* New York: Farrar, Straus, and Giroux.

Loury, L. D., & Garman, D. (1995). College selectivity and earnings. *Journal of Labor Economics, 13*(2), 289–308.

Manksi, C. F. (1983). *College choice in America.* Cambridge, MA: Harvard University Press.

McDonough, P. M., Antonio, A. L., Walpole, M. & Perez, L. X. (1998). College rankings: Democratized college knowledge for whom? *Research in Higher Education, 39*(5), 513–537.

Meredith, M. (2004). Why do universities compete in the ratings game? An empirical analysis of the effects of the *U.S. News and World Report* college rankings. *Research in Higher Education, 45*(5), 443–461.

Milewski, G. B., & Camara, W. J. (2002). *Colleges and universities that do not require the SAT or ACT scores.* New York: College Entrance Examination Board.

National Center for Education Statistics. (2006a). *The digest of education statistics.* Washington, DC: U.S. Department of Education. Retrieved December 3, 2007, from http://nces.ed.gov/programs/digest/do6/tables/dto6_186.asp?referrer = list

National Center for Education Statistics. (2006b). *The digest of education statistics.* Washington, DC: U.S. Department of Education. Retrieved December 3, 2007, from http://nces.ed.gov/programs/digest/do6/tables/dto6_187.asp?referrer = list

Owings, J., McMillien, M., Burkett, J., & Pinkerton, B. (1995, April). *Making the cut: Who meets highly selective college entrance criteria* (NCES Brief 95–732). Washington, DC: National Center for Education Statistics.

Pascarella, E. T., Cruce, T., Umbach, P. T., Wolniak, G. C., Kuh, G. D., Carini, R. M., et al. (2006). Institutional selectivity and good practices in undergraduate education: How strong is the link? *Journal of Higher Education, 77*(2), 251–285.

Peterson's. (1998). *Peterson's 4 year colleges, 1999* (29th ed.). Princeton, NJ: Peterson's Guides.

Pike, G. R. (2004). Measuring quality: A comparison of the *U.S. News* rankings and the NSSE benchmarks. *Research in Higher Education, 45*(2), 193–208.

Regents of the University of California v. Bakke, 438 U.S. 265 (1978).

Sanoff, A. P. (2007). *The U.S. News* college rankings: A view from inside. In Institute for Higher Education Policy (Ed.), *College and university ranking systems: Global perspectives and American challenges* (pp. 23–34). Washington, DC: Institute for Higher Education Policy.

Steele, C. M. (1998). A threat in the air: How stereotypes shape intellectual identity and performance. In J. Eberhardt & S. Fiske (Eds.), *Confronting racism: The problem and the response* (pp. 202–233). Thousand Oaks, CA: Sage.

Thomson Peterson. (2006). *Peterson's four-year colleges 2007* (37th ed.). Lawrenceville, NJ: Thomson/Peterson's.

8

BAKKE AT 30

A History of Affirmative Action in U.S. Law Schools

William C. Kidder

I n *Regents of the University of California v. Bakke* (1978), Justice Lewis Powell provided the crucial swing vote for two divergent majority holdings. The conservative members of the U.S. Supreme Court and Powell struck down the affirmative action program at the University of California (UC), Davis, medical school, ruling that having a dual track admissions plan with a predetermined number of places reserved for minorities violated the Equal Protection Clause of the Fourteenth Amendment. The more liberal members of the Court and Powell held that race could be used as a "plus factor" in higher education admissions decisions. Before the 2003 *Grutter v. Bollinger* case, federal courts were quite divided about the question of whether a key portion of Justice Powell's opinion—in which he wrote that racially diverse learning environments can enhance all students' educational experiences and, therefore, provide universities with a compelling interest in adopting race-conscious admissions—was to be interpreted as part of the holding of the case.

Even though the legal challenge was against a medical school's admissions plan, at the 1976 annual meetings of the Association of American Law Schools (AALS) the *Bakke* case, as it was moving through the appellate court system, was described as a "cause celebre in the higher education world" (AALS, 1977, p. 161). When the case was appealed to the U.S. Supreme Court, the record number of briefs filed (Kearney & Merrill, 2000) actually included as much, if not more, discussion of law school admissions as medical school admissions (Selmi, 1999; Slocum, 1978). In fact, a large share of the major higher education affirmative action cases over the years has involved challenges to law school admission policies, including *DeFunis v. Odegaard* (1974), *Hopwood v. Texas* (1996), *Smith v. University of Washington Law School* (2000), and, most recently, *Grutter v. Bollinger* (2003).

Affirmative action at law schools is important for social scientists and policymakers for a simple reason. There is a larger concentration of African Americans and Latinos[1]—generally the groups most consistently included in race-conscious affirmative action programs—among law degree recipients than among other professional school programs. Law has the greatest concentration of Latinos and American Indians of any of the 10 professions tracked in the federal Integrated Postsecondary Education Data System (IPEDS) data system, and for African Americans, law trails only the much smaller programs in pharmacy and theology among the same 10 professional school programs (Law School Admission Council [LSAC], 2002; Wilder, 2003). Likewise, the concentration of African Americans, Latinos, and American Indians in the pool of LSAT test-takers exceeds these groups' relative shares of new bachelor's degree recipients, and these three groups are also relatively more likely than Whites and Asian Americans to take the LSAT than the GRE or GMAT (Wilder, 2003). This suggests that when African American, American Indian, and Latino college graduates are weighing options about the value of professional or graduate school degrees (e.g., return on investment and perceived intrinsic value versus loan indebtedness, career satisfaction, or time out of the labor market), they have consistently demonstrated great interest in legal education (Olivas, 2005).[2] Thus, to the extent affirmative action matters in creating opportunities in a postbaccalaureate context, it matters more in American law schools than for other graduate and professional schools.

In looking back at the 30-year impact of *Bakke* on law school admissions, a helpful indicator is Ramsey's 1979 survey of 100 law schools, with a 95% response rate. He found that 72% of American law schools reportedly had affirmative action programs immediately after *Bakke,* with the South lagging significantly behind the rest of the U.S. (Ramsey, 1980). A second important work highlighting the impact of *Bakke* on law schools is Welch and Gruhl's book (1998a) on affirmative action in law and medical schools. On the 20-year anniversary of *Bakke,* Welch and Gruhl concluded that the *Bakke* ruling had the ultimate effect of institutionalizing preestablished affirmative action admission practices, rather than leading to a significant increase or decrease in opportunities for African Americans and Latinos between the 1970s and the late 1980s (Welch & Gruhl, 1998a). Welch and Gruhl reported, however, that post-*Bakke,* many schools did report broadening the groups to receive a plus factor on the basis of race/ethnicity, consistent with Justice Powell's opinion (*Bakke,* 1978).

This chapter seeks to describe a collection of important issues all related to the role of affirmative action and law school student demographics. First, building in part on the work of Welch and Gruhl (1998a), the chapter describes the racial/ethnic transformation of the legal education landscape during the last three decades[3] and then considers the role of affirmative action at America's most selective law schools. It next looks historically and through empirical simulations at the likely effects of ending affirmative action in law school admissions. Finally, this chapter briefly reviews the often misunderstood position of Asian Americans and Pacific Islanders (AAPIs) in affirmative action discourse. The chapter ends recognizing the challenges law schools would face in the absence of affirmative action.

The Rapid Transformation of Legal Education Pre-*Bakke*[4]

Although today African Americans, Latinos, and American Indians may have relatively strong application and enrollment levels at U.S. law schools, only a decade before *Bakke* law schools were extraordinarily lacking in racial and ethnic diversity. Understanding the unprecedented demographic transformation that swept through legal education between the late-1960s and the Court's historic ruling in *Bakke* is essential if one is to make sense of claims (e.g., Welch & Gruhl, 1998a, 1998b) that the *Bakke* ruling merely led to a continuation of the status quo with respect to affirmative action. That is, the status quo compared with what?

What, for example, did law schools look like in 1963, the year of the famous civil rights march in Washington, D.C., and a decade before Allan Bakke applied to UC Davis? At that time, there were zero African Americans at the law schools of UC Berkeley (Boalt Hall) and UCLA and only three at Harvard (table 8.1). Similarly, at the University of Michigan and University of Texas law schools, there were between zero and two African Americans in the entering classes before the late 1960s (Edwards, 1971; Jones, 1969). Though the three law schools in table 8.1 are among the most highly

TABLE 8.1
Number of Entering Black Law Students at Three Highly Selective Law Schools: Berkeley (Boalt Hall), Harvard, and UCLA, 1963–1980

Year	Boalt Hall	Harvard	UCLA
1963	0	3	0
1964	0	12	0
1965	2	15	1
1966	3	21	0
1967	3	22	13
1968	14	33	15
1969	10	40	26
1970	33	45	28
1971	37	65	31
1972	31	51	28
1973	24	56	28
1974	26	48	29
1975	29	53	31
1976	30	45	31
1977	39	48	29
1978	22	61	39
1979	28	40	25
1980	24	43	47

Source: Karabel (1999); Kidder (2003); Wilkins, Chambliss, Jones, and Adamson (2002).
Note. Karabel's (1999) pre-1970 data for the UC Berkeley School of Law are for enrolled Black students who *subsequently graduated*, rather than all who may have enrolled. The latter data were not originally recorded in the 1960s, and Karabel had to reconstruct such data from archival files decades after the fact.

selective,[5] this pattern of *de facto* segregation was similar across legal education generally. Although data are rather spotty for Blacks during this period (and unavailable for other minority groups), an AALS committee estimated that there were 701 African American law students in 1964–1965, with 267 of these at six predominantly Black law schools (Kidder, 2003).[6] All told, African Americans were about 1.3% of national law school enrollments and, when excluding these six historically Black law schools, less than 1.0% of enrollments. And law schools were hardly unique in this respect; when the UC Davis medical school opened its doors in 1968, for example, merely 5 years before Bakke applied for admission, the school enrolled zero African Americans or Latinos (Selmi, 1999).

Increasing Demand for and Selectivity of Law Schools in a Changing Demographic Context

To situate the *Bakke* era in historical perspective, law school affirmative action programs were in their infancy in the late 1960s precisely when other demographic trends (which I describe momentarily) were pushing the selectivity of legal education to new heights. At UC Berkeley's Boalt Hall, for instance, applications rose from 1,500 in 1966 to about 5,000 in 1972 (Boalt Hall School of Law, 1977). LSAT administrations increased by 244% between 1964 and 1973, whereas first-year enrollments at ABA law schools increased at a much more modest rate of 63% (figure 8.1).[7] In other words, demand for legal education skyrocketed even relative to increased supply. Consequently, in 1961, the median LSAT score at 81% of U.S. law schools was below 485 (on the previous 200 to 800 scale), but by 1975, *none* of the 128 ABA-accredited law schools had LSAT means below 510, and 70% had LSAT class means between 572 and 693 (Nairn, 1981).

Although the number of African American and Latino applications and enrollments to U.S. law schools increased significantly between the 1960s and the 1970s, because their numbers were relatively small, this only played a modest part in increasing the selectivity of law school admissions in the *Bakke* era. Far more important, numerically speaking, was that the baby boom generation was graduating from college and doing so in an era when federal and state policies supported the availability of higher education for a larger segment of society (Kidder, 2003; Sander & Williams, 1989).

FIGURE 8.1
LSAT administrations and entering law school enrollments, 1964–1977

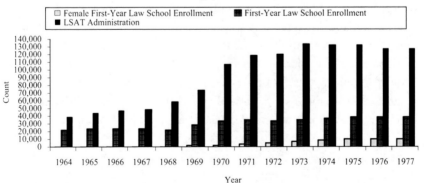

Source: Abel (1989); Kidder (2003).

Another major contributor to the increased demand for legal education in the 1970s was the sharp rise in the number of women entering law school. As the social norms keeping women out of postbaccalaureate education eroded between the 1960s and the *Bakke* era, a higher proportion of women enrolled in law school than in medicine or other professions (Sander & Williams, 1989).[8] In particular, upper-class and upper-middle class White women were often in the best position educationally and economically to take advantage of greater opportunities to go to law school as the feminist movement and other social forces pushed open doors in nontraditional fields for women (Nelson, 1994). Since the 1970s, in sheer numbers, the increased proportion of women, rather than the increased presence of underrepresented minority students, was the single most significant demographic shift in American legal education (Kay, 2000; Nelson, 1994). All told, in 1967–1968 women were 4.9% of enrollments at ABA law schools, compared with 30.0% in 1977–1978 when Justice Powell issued his landmark opinion in *Bakke,* and 49.4% by 2000–2001 (American Bar Association & Law School Admission Council, 2007).[9]

A corollary of all these demographic transformations (which apply to law school specifically but also patterns in higher education more generally) was that misdirected anxiety in a heightened atmosphere of competition fueled some of the negative attention on affirmative action in the 1970s and the "reverse discrimination" suits such as *DeFunis* and *Bakke.*[10] Although critics in the 1970s decried that affirmative action meant that law schools were admitting "unqualified" students (Graglia, 1970), admission standards were relatively more relaxed during the 1950s and early 1960s when White men maintained virtually total control over access to legal (and medical) education. An example Edwards (1972) noted was that the students of color in the entering class of 1971 at the highly selective University of Michigan Law School had equivalent LSAT/undergraduate GPA index scores to Michigan's White male-dominated class of 1957. A second example is that in ABA law schools in 1976, 23% of African Americans with 500 to 550 LSAT scores were denied admission at all the law schools to which they applied (Evans, 1977) though, as noted previously, in the early 1960s four-fifths of ABA law schools had median LSAT scores below 485.

Another example is that of Allan Bakke, who was a 33-year-old White aerospace engineer with solid MCAT scores and grades when he first applied to the UC Davis medical school. More harmful to Bakke's admission prospects than affirmative action was that many medical schools in the 1970s penalized older applicants, based on the notion that they would have shorter periods of service in the medical profession. After all, Bakke applied to 14 medical schools in 1973 and 1974 and was denied admission at every single medical school to which he applied, and at least two medical schools informed Bakke that age was a factor working against him, with other schools hinting as much (Dreyfus & Lawrence, 1979).[11] The first time Bakke applied to Davis, he was hurt by applying late in the cycle, after many seats in the entering class were already filled. The second time he applied, Bakke fared relatively poorly in his committee interview with UC Davis faculty and staff, which occurred after he had already complained about the school's special admissions program (Schwartz, 1988). Yet despite these and other factors, Bakke blamed "racial quotas" for keeping him out of medical school. Generally speaking, then, the broad and rapid transformation of the educational landscape for law schools led to a unique opportunity structure, in which the *Bakke* opinion was applied moving forward and to which the chapter now turns.

The Opportunity Structure of U.S. Law Schools, 1976–2006

In preparation for its *Bakke amicus curiae* brief before the U.S. Supreme Court, the LSAC conducted an extensive simulation analysis of admission outcomes for the 1976 entering class at ABA-approved law schools (Evans, 1977). The 1976 cycle marks the beginning of when systematic national admission data became available and, therefore, serves as the anchor for descriptive statistics about law school admissions during the past 30 years. Figure 8.2 displays the percentage of African Americans in the national applicant and admission pools to U.S. law schools, displaying the years between 1976 and 2006, except the early 1980s when data were not available.[12] The most notable feature of the LSAC data is that in every year African Americans constituted a lower proportion of the admission pool than of the applicant pool, whereas the converse is true of Whites (e.g., in the 1978 cycle Whites were 87.9% of applicants and 90.3% of admits). In other words, despite affirmative action, in the period stretching back to *Bakke,* African Americans have significantly lower cumulative admission rates than Whites (here admission is defined as getting at least one admission offer from a law school where the candidate applied).

FIGURE 8.2

African Americans as a percentage of the national applicant/admit pools, ABA law schools, 1976–2006

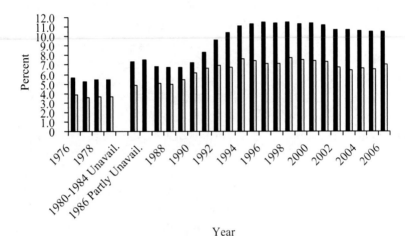

Source: Author's calculations based on Evans (1977); LSAC (1981, 1987, 1988–2007).
Note. The scale on the y-axis only goes to 12% to allow the reader to see small changes over time clearly.

The same data in figure 8.2 can be used to calculate the ratio of the Black admission rate with the White admission rate (not shown in figure 8.2)—data that Welch and Gruhl (1998a) had for medical schools but not for law schools. At medical schools, the Black-White admission ratio was about 1.05 in 1976, and then settled to a range of 0.80 to 0.85 during the late 1970s and the 1980s (Welch & Gruhl, 1998a). By contrast, at ABA law schools, the Black-White admission ratio stayed at about 0.67 in the years immediately before and after *Bakke* (1976–1979) and increased only marginally to 0.70 by 1985.

Equally important, whereas Welch and Gruhl's study of law and medical schools ended with the 1989 cohort, figure 8.2 indicates the late 1980s and the 1990s were a period of significant change for African American admission prospects. The gap between Blacks' proportion in the applicant and admit pools narrowed from 1989 to 1991 (in 1990, the Black-White admission ratio was 0.86, an all-time high since *Bakke*).

Figure 8.3 shows a similar pattern for Chicanos, with the 1990 admissions cycle also indicating a 30-year high for the Chicano-White admission ratio (1.00). Although the Chicano category in figure 8.3 is not entirely comparable to Welch and Gruhl's data on Latinos, a review of these data sources still suggests that Chicanos applying to law school fared relatively worse off relative to Whites than did those applying to medical school. At American medical schools, the Latino-White acceptance ratios ranged from 1.2 to 1.05 from 1975 to 1985. By contrast, the Chicano-White acceptance ratios for ABA law schools climbed from 0.80 in 1976 to 0.89 in 1979, and were at 0.85 in 1985.[13]

What is notable about figure 8.3 is that in 1979, immediately after the *Bakke* ruling, Chicanos constituted 1.37% of all students admitted to ABA-accredited law schools. The proportion of Chicanos admitted at U.S. law schools slowly climbed to 2.0% by 1998, but by 2006, it had dropped below *Bakke* levels (to 1.28%).

One cannot consider these law school data without simultaneously understanding the context within which these changes were occurring. The diversity movement in legal education was probably at its strongest in the early

FIGURE 8.3

Chicanos/Mexican Americans as a percentage of the national applicant/admit pools, ABA law schools, 1976–2006

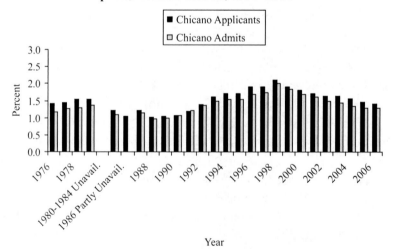

Source: Author's calculations based on Evans (1977); LSAC (1981, 1987, 1988–2007).

Note. The scale on the y-axis only goes to 3% to allow the reader to see small changes over time clearly.

1990s. There was a successfully coordinated "Nationwide Law Student Strike for Diversity" in April 1989, with students from at least 30 schools boycotting class and conducting teach-ins (Cho & Westley, 2000). Cho and Westley (2000) document how the student strike was associated with a substantial, though temporary, increase in the hiring of law faculty of color nationwide: from 1980 to 1987 less than two Latinos per year were hired as full-time law teachers, compared with an average of 12 from 1989 to 1993.

There was a quick reversal of fortune, however, by about 1993. In the early 1990s, the Office for Civil Rights in the U.S. Department of Education launched investigations into the admission practices at selective public professional and graduate school programs (Moran, 2006). The *Hopwood* case was filed in 1992, and resulted in a highly controversial 1996 Fifth Circuit opinion that rejected Justice Powell's *Bakke* opinion that racial/ethnic diversity in the student body is a compelling governmental interest.[14] Though the repudiation of the diversity rationale in *Hopwood* would later be overruled by the Supreme Court's 2003 *Grutter* decision, *Hopwood* effectively banned affirmative action at both public and private law schools in Texas, Louisiana, and Mississippi for the 1997 to 2003 admission cycles.

Other affirmative action bans soon followed, including resolutions by the University of California Regents in 1995, California's Proposition 209 in 1996, Washington's I-200 in 1998, an executive order by the governor of Florida in 1999, and an adverse district court ruling in *Johnson v. Board of Regents of the University System of Georgia* against the University of Georgia in 2000 that was later affirmed by the Eleventh Circuit (2001). Consequently, it appears that *Hopwood*, Proposition 209, and the threat of litigation had a chilling effect on the extent to which affirmative action was practiced at U.S. law schools by the mid- to late-1990s. This parallels empirical analysis of undergraduate admissions since the 1980s (Grodsky & Kalogrides, 2007).

Affirmative Action at America's Most Selective Law Schools

Although understanding the national picture of racial/ethnic representation in the law school applicant and admissions pools is important, it is perhaps most informative to understand those trends with respect to the country's most selective law schools. Justice Powell's *Bakke* opinion and Justice Sandra Day O'Connor's majority opinion in *Grutter* both cite *Sweatt v. Painter* (1950) for the proposition that law schools "cannot be effective in isolation from the individuals and institutions with which the law interacts" (*Bakke,* 1978, p. 314). *Grutter* (extending language in *Sweatt*) states that the pattern of law schools training a large share of America's leaders "is even more striking when it comes to highly selective law schools" (2003, p. 332). Yet, Michigan voters passed a ballot initiative in November 2006 (Proposal 2) prohibiting the University of Michigan Law School and other public institutions from considering race in admissions, and California voters passed a similar initiative a decade ago (Proposition 209). Access at highly selective law schools since *Bakke* is also an interesting labor market issue because total J.D. enrollments in ABA law schools grew by 25% from 1976 to 2006 (from 112,401 to 141,031), but at the top 20 law schools listed in *U.S. News & World Report,* J.D. enrollments actually declined by 6% during this span (from 21,251 to 19,975), despite high demand from applicants (American Bar Association, 1977, 2007).[15]

In recent years, African Americans hovered around 7.6% of enrollments at the top 20 ranked law schools, and Latinos around 6.5% (Kidder, 2005). Wightman's logistic regression analysis of candidates who applied in 2001 to the top tier schools (which includes 18 law schools) indicates that if admissions were based solely on LSAT scores and grades, African American offers would decline by 84%, Latinos (all groups combined) would decline by 58%, and American Indian admissions would decline by 42% (2003). Because these law schools now have deeper applicant pools than they did in 2001, the effects could be expected to be more severe today. Sander similarly concedes that ending affirmative action at elite law schools would reduce African American enrollment to about 1 to 2% of the class (2004).

Indeed, one does not necessarily need empirical models to corroborate this basic point because real-world experience from California confirms it as well. Figure 8.4 displays African American and Latino entering enrollments during the past four decades at the UC Berkeley and UCLA law schools.[16] To display the "big picture" in an economic manner, the data are broken down by decade (1967–1976, 1977–1986, 1987–1996, and 1997–2006, with the last decade corresponding to an affirmative action ban in California). In the pre-*Bakke* decade (1967–1976), an average of 23.7 African Americans entered Berkeley each year (out of a class of about 270) and 26.0 entered UCLA (out of a class of about 300). In the post-affirmative action decade (1997–2006), annual enrollments for Blacks dropped to an average of 10.4 at Berkeley and 10.1 at UCLA. Combined, this represents a 59% decline in Black

FIGURE 8.4

Number of entering African American and Latino law students at UC Berkeley and UCLA, by decade, 1967–2006

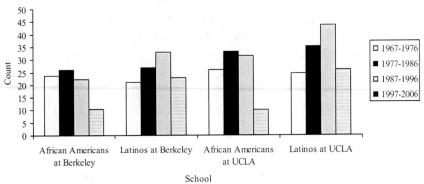

Source: Karabel (1999); University of California, Berkeley School of Law (1993); University of California Office of the President (2007).

Note. Annual averages are listed within each decade; an affirmative action ban was in effect from 1997 to 2006.

enrollments relative to 30 years ago at Berkeley and UCLA (all the more remarkable considering changes in the national applicant pool over that span), and a combined 62% decline compared with the last decade with affirmative action (1987–1996).

Adding to these data, the UC system issued a report on professional schools during the pendency of *Bakke*. Combining data from the law schools at Berkeley, Davis, and UCLA, African Americans, Latinos, and American Indians were 18.1% of entering UC law students in 1976 (University of California, 1977). By comparison, in 2006 at the same three UC law schools, African Americans, Latinos, and American Indians were (combined) 12.3% of the entering class, which is a decline of about one-third despite the gains in the size and strength of the student of color applicant pools during the past 30 years.

The contributions of elite law schools have been significant. An analysis of all of the 600 or so African American law professors in the *AALS Directory of Law Teachers* found that 60.1% graduated from top-20 law schools, as had about 40% of African American federal judges (Chambers, Clydesdale, Kidder, & Lempert, 2005). Further, 77% of Black partners at corporate law firms graduated from elite law schools (Wilkins, 2005). Likewise, about half of Latino federal judges graduated from top-20 law schools and affirmative action no doubt played a role in increasing the ranks of Latino law professors in the United States from a handful in the early 1970s to about 250 by 2005 (Kidder, 2005). In assessing the impact of eliminating affirmative action at highly selective law schools, then, it is important to look at long-term career and civic benefits as well. Further, eliminating affirmative action implicates broader societal harms because, as the Court recognized in *Grutter,* "In order to cultivate a set of leaders with legitimacy in the eyes of the citizenry, it is necessary that the path to leadership be visibly open to talented and qualified individuals of every race and ethnicity" (p. 332).

Actual and Simulated Impacts of Eliminating Affirmative Action, 1976–2006

A key question addressed in the 1977 LSAC study by Evans and in many of the *Bakke amicus curiae* briefs is what the likely impact of ending affirmative action would have been, particularly for African Americans. The question is no less relevant today. On the legal front, Justice O'Connor's majority opinion in *Grutter* raises the specter of sunsetting (ending) affirmative action by 2028,[17] and President George W. Bush's two subsequent nominees made the Supreme Court even more solidly conservative. Second, substantial scholarly and media attention has recently focused on research by Sander in the *Stanford Law Review* and elsewhere. In particular, both conservative opinionmakers and columnists (e.g., Heriot, 2007; Taylor, 2007) as well as social science criticism (e.g., Ayres & Brooks, 2005; Barnes, 2007; Chambers et al., 2005; Ho, 2005; Rothstein & Yoon, in press) have focused on Sander's provocative forecast that the "number of Black lawyers produced by American law schools each year and subsequently passing the bar would probably increase if those schools collectively stopped using racial preferences" (2004, p. 474). Sander's race-blind simulations for the 2001 law school admission cycle (combined with bar examination data from the 1991 entering class) indicate a net increase of 7.9% in new Black lawyers if affirmative action were eliminated. His rationale for this projected 7.9% increase is his expectation that ending affirmative action would only curtail African American admissions and enrollments at ABA law schools by 14% (relying on 2001 data derived from Wightman, 2003). Sander's estimate is also rooted in his assertion that race-conscious admission policies "mismatch" students of color at law schools where their admission credentials are not competitive, causing them to learn (and earn) less than they would at less selective law schools (Sander, 2004).

Both Evans' race-blind simulation for the 1976 admission cycle and Sander's claim using 2001 estimates are based on one of two general approaches to estimating the national impact of ending affirmative action: the so-called "grid model." Essentially, the grid model collapses admission decisions from individual law schools into a single national pool and then, within roughly 90 LSAT and undergraduate grade-point average (UGPA) cells on a grid (e.g., a cell for students with 150 to 154 LSATs and 3.0 to 3.24 UGPAs, another cell for those with 150 to 154 LSATs and 3.25 to 3.49 UGPAs, and so on), applies the White admission rate (for getting into at least one law school) to African Americans and other minority groups in those same LSAT/UGPA ranges. The second approach is to use logistic regression to determine what proportion of students of color could still get into the law schools to which they actually applied based upon LSAT scores and UGPAs (Wightman, 1997, 2003).

The range of empirical results of race-blind simulations vary considerably based on (1) one's choice about which race-blind model is most appropriate, and (2) what inferences and conclusions are justifiable from the results of such a simulation. For instance, Evans' grid model results for 1976 showed a 58% decline in African American admission offers (from 1,697 to 710) and a 41% decline in Chicano admission offers (from 510 to 300). However, Evans was careful to point out that these estimates of the number of minority students who would still have been admitted without affirmative action are "probably overestimated" partly because of the questionable assumption that "minority candidates would apply to and be willing and able to attend any [ABA] law school regardless of its location or cost" (1977, p. 612).

Years later, when Wightman (then a vice president at LSAC) approached the same empirical issue, she conducted both grid model and logistic regression model simulations on the 1991 law school admissions pool, partly because she concluded that her data and analyses counter the grid model's less realistic assumptions (Wightman, 1997). Wightman, like Evans, found it was questionable to assume that students of color would necessarily apply and enroll at less selective law schools in equivalent numbers regardless of tuition cost, geographic location, and other factors.

Actually, several factors suggest that the grid model overestimates the number of Black law students who would apply to and enroll at U.S. law schools absent affirmative action, including these: (1) African Americans tend to apply later in the admission cycle (which decreases one's chances of acceptance in an environment where admission decisions are made on a rolling basis), (2) there were relative application declines at public law schools in states that banned affirmative action in the late 1990s (see next section), and (3) enrolling at lower-tier law schools does not diminish law school indebtedness relative to more selective schools, though it tends to be associated with lower earning potential, suggesting that price-sensitive students of color mindful of return on investment considerations would not regard legal education as equally attractive in a post-affirmative action world (Chambers et al., 2005).

To be clear, the logistic regression model is not ideal either, for *some* minority candidates could be expected to apply to lower-ranked schools absent affirmative action, and certainly admission is not solely determined by test scores and grades. However, overall the logistic regression model is more realistic insofar as it is anchored to applicants' real-world choices. In 2006, the average candidate applied to six law schools (Handwerk, 2007),[18] and because most candidates already apply to a range of schools (i.e., including one or two "back-up" schools), such a range of outcomes is already incorporated in logistic regression estimates (Wightman, 1997). Although logistic regression estimates are preferable, they also require pooling individual-level data from the applicant–admit pools at all (or virtually all) of the U.S. law schools—there were 192 in 2006—and these data have not been publicly available.

Thus, in this chapter, figure 8.5 displays grid-model estimates of ending affirmative action during the past 15 years, but this is with the explicit caution that a grid-model estimate should be regarded as approximating a *lower-bound limit* regarding the projected impact. In addition, where logistic regression estimates are available (1991 and 2001 only), these figures are noted for context. By contrast, Sander (2004) argues unpersuasively that the logistic regression model is "nonsensical" (Sander, 2004), and he assumes that in a post-affirmative action world, African Americans would adjust by applying to less selective law schools without any net drop-off in interest at either the application or matriculation (yield) stages.[19]

FIGURE 8.5

African Americans applying to ABA law schools, 1991–2005: Number of actual admission offers versus "grid model" estimated numbers if affirmative action ended

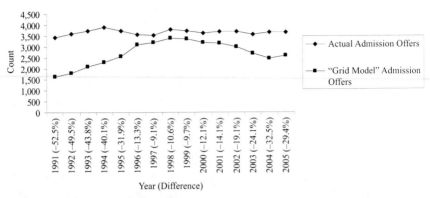

Year (Difference)

Source: Author's calculations based on data from the LSAC (1992–2006), except for 1991 and 2001, which are from Wightman's published estimates using the identical methodology (Wightman, 1997, 2003). Most of these data were first reported in Chambers, Clydesdale, Kidder, and Lempert (2005, p. 1861, Table 1).
Note. Percentage differences are indicated in parentheses, next to the year.

The grid-model estimates in figure 8.5 also point to another problem with Sander's claim that if affirmative action ended today, it is reasonable to expect only a 14.1% difference in African American admission offers. That is, the extent to which grid-model estimates of race-blind admission curtail African American admissions varies considerably from year to year. This variation is largely a function of fluctuations in selectivity caused by changes in the size of the national applicant pool. During admission cycles when total applicant volume was roughly 85,000+ (1991–1995 and 2002–2005), the grid-model results were much worse for African Americans (differences of 19 to 53%). During admission cycles when total applicant volume was less than 80,000 across ABA law schools, the grid model predicts much less substantial differences (9 to 14% differences in 1996–2001). Grid-model estimates for 2004 indicate a difference in African American admission offers of 32.5% and a difference of 22.6% for all Latinos combined, including a difference of 55.7% for Puerto Rican candidates (Kidder, 2005); again, grid model simulations tend to understate the impact of eliminating affirmative action.

Figure 8.5 also provides sobering data relevant to Justice O'Connor's aspiration (or declaration) in *Grutter* about ending affirmative action by 2028.

For example, in 1985 the grid model indicated a difference in African American admission offers of 32.9% (author's calculations). Yet two decades later, the difference in African American admission offers without affirmative action would be very similar (32.5% in 2004, 29.4% in 2005). And these results are obtained despite two related trends: admitted African American students had stronger LSAT/UGPA index scores in 2004 than in the 1990s (or even 2001), and law schools, like undergraduate institutions (Grodsky & Kalogrides, 2007), appear to be using race as less of a plus factor in 2004–2005 than they did in the 1980s and early 1990s (a change that, other things being equal, would tend to bring actual admissions and race-blind grid-model estimates closer together).

The issue of whether the "mismatch" hypothesis is adequately established as an empirical matter is quite complicated and beyond the scope of this chapter. Suffice it to say that several social science critiques have concluded that Sander's evidence of law school mismatch does not hold up to close examination (Ayres & Brooks, 2005; Barnes, 2007; Chambers et al., 2005; Ho, 2005; Lempert, Kidder, Clydesdale, & Chambers, 2006; Rothstein & Yoon, in press). Barnes recently concluded, "To date, I have been unable to find a published article or working paper in an academic venue that defends Sander's work, other than his own" (Barnes, 2007, p. 1765). However, with the exception of my coauthors and I—Chambers et al. (2005); Lempert et al. (2006)—most of the empirical critics of Sander have thus far more or less adopted his tenets about law school admissions, at least for purposes of independent reanalysis and evaluating potential effects of "mismatch" within the same dataset used by Sander.

Thus, in this chapter, it is perhaps more productive to emphasize how large an impact Sander's unwarranted assumptions about post-affirmative action admissions have on his conclusion, "The balance of evidence suggests an increase [in Black lawyers] is more likely" if affirmative action ended today (Sander, 2004, p. 477). To that end, note that Sander's post-affirmative action graduation and bar passage estimates incorporate a significant, but overlooked departure from the Evans/Wightman grid model. Under the grid model, many of the admitted students of color who would be denied admission under race-neutral policies are actually in the middle- and lower-middle part of the curve of LSAT/UGPA index scores. Yet, Sander estimates the effect of ending affirmative action by eliminating the 14.1% of African Americans in the LSAC's 1991 Bar Passage Study who had the lowest index scores and keeping all the Black law students with higher index scores.

How much does this error skew his post-affirmative action bar passage estimates for African Americans? Deriving estimates from "real" grid model data rather than Sander's "cut out the bottom" version of the grid model—in combination with using more recent data for 2003 to 2005 in light of the earlier discussion about how fluctuations in selectivity influence grid model results—cast strong doubt on his claim that a windfall of ending affirmative action will be an increase in African American attorneys. Even when following Sander's other questionable methodological steps related to academic "mismatch," these two changes alone produce an estimated net decrease in Black lawyers of 11% in 2003, 21% in 2004, and 18% in 2005 (author's calculations based upon LSAC, 2004–2006). In summary, there are good reasons that Sander's prediction—that ending affirmative action will increase the number of Black lawyers—sounds too good to be true. This claim simply has not been empirically validated by the academic community, nor does it deserve the substantial media attention it has received. His results, therefore, should not be used to support the end of affirmative action.

Questionable Claims and Political Games: Asian Americans/Pacific Islanders and Affirmative Action in U.S. Law Schools[20]

Although there has been much discussion about the impact of affirmative action on African Americans and Latinos, less is said regarding Asian Americans and Pacific Islanders (AAPIs). Going back to the *Bakke* era, AAPIs have often been mischaracterized in the affirmative action debate (Asian American Law Students' Association, 1978). A telling recent example was in *Grutter v. Bollinger* (2003) and *Gratz v. Bollinger* (2003), where the individual plaintiffs were all White, but their legal counsel at the Center for Individual Rights (CIR) successfully obtained class action status with AAPIs included among individuals alleged to have suffered racial discrimination. In their Supreme Court brief, CIR argued that affirmative action harms not only Whites but "especially Asian Americans" (Brief for the Petitioner in *Grutter,* 2003). In response, the National Asian Pacific American Legal Consortium (NAPALC), now the Asian American Justice Center, and 27 other public interest and civil rights organizations in the AAPI community filed a brief in *Grutter* defending the benefits of affirmative action generally and for AAPIs specifically (NAPALC, 2003).

I have criticized both supporters and opponents of affirmative action for marginalizing AAPIs from the policy debate, which can result, for example,

in politically charged but empirically exaggerated claims about AAPIs benefiting enormously from the elimination of affirmative action in legal education (Kidder, 2000, 2006). The larger problem is that such marginalization
can foster a divisive public discourse in which AAPIs are falsely portrayed as
natural adversaries of affirmative action and of the interests of African Americans and Latinos in particular.

The dynamics of marginalization and misleading data claims about
AAPIs were evident soon after affirmative action was banned at the UC law
schools in 1997. Harvard historian and affirmative action critic Stephan
Thernstrom claimed at that time that at the UC Berkeley, UC Davis, and
UCLA law schools, the elimination of affirmative action "has already bene-
fited Asian Americans, who have won 41% more places in the first-year law-
school classes than they did the year before" (Thernstrom, 1998, p. 49).[21]
Affirmative action supporters, in turn, took at face value Thernstrom's factual claim and then wrestled with the notion that affirmative action chiefly
amounted to "displacement" of one racial minority by another (Jacobs,
1998). More recently, Princeton researchers Espenshade and Chung concluded that if affirmative action ended at elite universities, 80% of the offers
taken away from Blacks and Latinos would go to AAPIs. The authors review
data from affirmative action bans in California and Washington, including
the law schools at UC Berkeley, UCLA, and UC Davis in concluding, "Our
simulation results are in very good agreement with the California experience" (Espenshade & Chung, 2005, p. 303).

Do such claims hold up to close scrutiny? Table 8.2 displays pre- and
post-affirmative action enrollment percentages for AAPIs at five highly selective law schools between 1993 and 2005: UCLA, UC Berkeley, UC Davis,
University of Washington, and the University of Texas. Since the timing of
the affirmative action ban in Washington was a couple years after California
and Texas, and since *Grutter* recently afforded the University of Texas the
opportunity to restart affirmative action, the post-affirmative action cells are
italicized. Contrary to expectations based on the aforementioned claims, average AAPI enrollments actually declined at UCLA (from 19.4 to 18.1%) and
at Washington (from 17.8 to 15.21%). Average AAPI enrollments increased
somewhat at UC Berkeley (from 15.5 to 17.9%) and UC Davis (from 17.1 to
20.6%) and increased marginally at the University of Texas (from 5.7 to
6.3%). Table 8.2 indicates that for the five public law schools combined,
AAPIs were, on average, 12.9% of entering law students with affirmative action and 14.3% without affirmative action.

TABLE 8.2

Asian American and Pacific Islander Enrollment Percentages at Five Selective Public Law Schools With and *Without* Affirmative Action, 1993–2005

	UCLA	UC Berkeley	UC Davis	U. of Washington	U. of Texas
1993	18.5%	18.5%	19.4%	20.9%	4.6%
1994	20.9%	14.9%	15.7%	24.1%	5.7%
1995	22.8%	13.5%	19.1%	11.2%	6.2%
1996	15.6%	17.5%	14.5%	13.4%	5.8%
1997	*21.5%*	*17.5%*	*14.0%*	17.5%	*8.8%*
1998	*17.7%*	*17.8%*	*16.4%*	19.7%	*6.8%*
1999	*22.8%*	*13.0%*	*14.9%*	*13.9%*	*5.6%*
2000	*17.4%*	*18.9%*	*20.2%*	*14.7%*	*5.0%*
2001	*17.1%*	*16.1%*	*24.3%*	*16.3%*	*6.1%*
2002	*17.7%*	*19.9%*	*20.5%*	*20.1%*	*6.4%*
2003	*13.8%*	*20.6%*	*26.9%*	*11.5%*	*5.8%*
2004	*17.5%*	*19.3%*	*23.7%*	*14.3%*	*6.0%*
2005	*16.9%*	*17.8%*	*21.6%*	*15.6%*	*6.5%*
Average With & *Without* Affirmative Action	19.4%	15.5%	17.1%	17.8%	5.7%
	18.1%	*17.9%*	*20.6%*	*15.2%*	*6.3%*

Cumulative Average (all 5) With Affirmative Action: 12.9%	*Cumulative Average (all 5) Without Affirmative Action: 14.3%*

Source: Kidder (2006).
Note. AAPI n = 840 with affirmative action and n = 1720 without affirmative action.

The table 8.2 data span more than a dozen years, so one might expect some increase in AAPI enrollments because of larger demographic trends in higher education rather than because of affirmative action bans. At a national level, AAPIs in 1993 were 5.50% of applicants (and 5.47% of enrollments) at ABA-accredited law schools, whereas in 2005, AAPIs were 8.29% of applicants (and 8.21% of enrollments) at ABA schools. Thus, the proportion of AAPIs in the applicant pool and first-year class at ABA law schools increased by 50% between 1993 and 2005 with most American law schools practicing affirmative action to some extent during this entire period. In California, AAPIs' proportion of the applicant pool at UC law schools was already gradually increasing before the ban on affirmative action, and it kept increasing at the same rate after the ban, so it is not surprising there was some increase in UC enrollment percentages, as that would have been expected with or without Proposition 209. Likewise, during a time with affirmative action, AAPI enrollments at Texas increased from 1% from 1986 to 1989 to 5.5% from 1993 to 1996, so AAPIs' additional gains under *Hopwood* (to 6.3% in 1997–2004) are relatively meager. In sum, for AAPIs, the cumulative effect of affirmative action bans at the University of California, Washington, and Texas Law Schools appears to be more or less a wash. Moreover, Wightman's logistic regression model of race-blind admissions at the top 30 U.S. law schools reports declines for AAPIs (Wightman, 2003). These data reveal the importance, then, of keeping AAPIs in the discussion of affirmative action and law school admission.

Conclusion

Lawrence (1997) has described affirmative action as having both a backward-looking purpose (remedying prior discrimination) as well as a forward-looking purpose (facilitating the possibility that students may learn more in racially diverse institutions and become better equipped to contribute to a multiracial democracy). Looking back at the history of law school affirmative action leading up to *Bakke* and the three subsequent decades illuminates how important, yet fragile, the forward-looking gains of affirmative action, as provided by *Bakke,* have been. In 1970, there were roughly 6,200 African American and Latino lawyers and judges, but by 2005, this figure rose to about 80,000, a thirteenfold increase (Kidder, 2005). Without affirmative action, and without law schools' reliance on Justice Powell's swing-vote opinion in *Bakke,* the American bar would be significantly less integrated today.

As evidenced throughout this chapter, the history of affirmative action in law school admission has been a complicated one. *Bakke*'s influence must be understood in the context of the changing demand and supply for a law school education and in relation to an evolving social, political, and legal environment. For instance, despite students of color making inroads to closing the U.S. higher education opportunity gap in some respects, simulations of the impact of ending affirmative action suggest the adverse impact on African Americans would be about the same in 1985 and 2005 (i.e., declines in admission offers of about 30% nationally when applying optimistic assumptions). Moreover, despite affirmative action, African Americans, Latinos, and American Indians continue to have significantly lower cumulative admission rates than Whites, and AAPIs have somewhat lower rates than Whites. This chapter's historical review of law school admissions, then, suggests that it would be very difficult for Justice O'Connor's admonition about sunsetting race-conscious admissions by 2028 to become a reality in legal education without significantly restricting opportunities for underrepresented minorities, particularly at highly selective law schools.

Notes

1. In this chapter, I use the terms *African American* and *Black* interchangeably. Further, I discuss Latinos as a single category, except where data limitations prevent this and require a more specific focus (e.g., Chicanos/Mexican Americans).

2. Although African American interest at both application and enrollment stages is relatively strong at the law school level, this interest in legal education is fragile in ways that matter for purposes of race-blind admission simulations. Affirmative action bans can dampen application volume in affected jurisdictions (discussed in this chapter) and many African Americans tend to apply later in the admission cycle than Whites do (Handwerk, 2007).

3. Welch and Gruhl had better data on medical schools than law schools; for law schools, they included national enrollments, cross-sectional information on individual schools, and a 1989 survey of admissions officers. In addition, Welch and Gruhl's data on law school enrollments were also limited because they combined Blacks and Latinos into a single category (Welch & Gruhl, 1998a, 1998b).

4. Elements of this section are adapted from Kidder (2003).

5. For convenience and consistency, I am defining the top 20 law schools based on the 2008 *U.S. News* rankings, using the same list for 1976 and 2006. Although a school's individual position may shift from year to year, sometimes based on how statistically meaningless tie-breakers shake out, the rankings of law school prestige tend to be quite durable overall (Schmalbeck, 1998).

6. Comprehensive data on African American law school enrollment are difficult to come by for much of the 1960s. The American Bar Association and other national organizations did not collect data on Latino, American Indian, and Asian American/Pacific Islander students until 1969. In 1965, the AALS Committee on Minority Groups, in the most comprehensive effort up to that point, surveyed ABA-accredited law schools about minority enrollment figures. The AALS Committee found that most law schools could not provide information on Latino students for two reasons: (1) There was confusion among deans regarding what these terms meant; and (2) most schools simply had no idea of the past or present enrollment levels of these groups. Even after reluctantly restricting the focus of their study to African Americans, the AALS Committee had to rely on help from faculty members, students, and personal visits to law schools because some uncooperative deans would not provide the requisite data.

7. National application data were not available until the mid-1970s (when there was better centralization under LSAC's Law School Data Assembly Service), but LSAT administration trends are a good proxy for application trends even though some take the LSAT and do not apply to law school.

8. "Social norms" is putting it gently with respect to many law schools in the pre-*Bakke* period because some schools either explicitly barred women or had predetermined enrollment caps (Kidder, 2003).

9. The proportion of women dropped somewhat by 2006, to 46.2%, but this had more to do with resurgent interest among men applying to law school in an era where the labor market opportunities for recent college graduates are perhaps not as promising as they were in the late 1990s. The number of women in law school increased from 21,499 in 2000–2001 to 22,615 in 2006–2007 (American Bar Association, 2007).

10. *DeFunis* was a challenge to affirmative action at the University of Washington Law School. The U.S. Supreme Court granted review, and this would have been "the" affirmative action case of the 1970s except that the plaintiff was allowed to enroll during the appellate process and a majority of the Court ruled that the case was, therefore, moot.

11. At UC Davis, the faculty member who initially interviewed Bakke in 1973 wrote in his file, "This applicant is a well-qualified candidate for admission whose main hardship is the unavoidable fact that he is now 33 . . ." (White, 1977, p. 7).

12. There are several data memoranda and articles analyzing the law school applicant pools of the early 1980s. Unfortunately, none that I could find provide comparable information necessary for Figures 8.2 and 8.3. For example, LSAC provides tantalizing detailed but fragmented minority data for the 1981–1985 admission cycles (LSAC, 1987) and Simien meshes applicant data from LSAC with enrollment data from the ABA for 1980 to 1984 to roughly estimate "acceptance rates" because LSAC admission data were apparently unavailable (1987). Likewise, Vernon and Zimmer (1987) extensively analyze the national applicant pool of the early 1980s but do not report race/ethnicity in a useful way for present purposes.

13. Although Welch and Gruhl's data are for all Latinos, my data are for Chicanos specifically because of the absence of available data for other Latino groups during the 1970s. However, such data are available for 1985 and, at that time, the cumulative national admission rates of Chicanos (67%) and other Latinos (69%) are similar, so a chart displaying law school data for all Latinos combined would look similar. In other words, for the most part, the difference between the level of access to medical schools and law schools is not attributable to slippage between categories.

14. Representative of the strong criticism of *Hopwood* in the legal academy is Torres' remark that the decision "was breathtaking in its disdain for the Supreme Court's educational equal protection jurisprudence" (Torres, 2003, p. 1596).

15. This statistic reflects several trends. First, the driving force behind the one-quarter increase in overall J.D. enrollments was the rise in ABA-accredited law schools from 163 in 1976 to 195 in 2006, with all of these new schools starting out

at the lower to lower-middle end of the prestige hierarchy. Second, the slight overall decline in J.D. enrollments at the top 20 schools appears to reflect a conscious policy choice at a few law schools (NYU, Georgetown, Boston University) to scale back enrollments (particularly evening/part-time programs) as a means of maintaining prestige and reputation with legal employers (i.e., it does not reflect a decline in interest in the top 20 law schools, where the applicant pools are as robust as ever).

16. I was not able to obtain Berkeley and UCLA American Indian data for this entire 1967 to 2006 period.

17. Whether this part of Justice O'Connor's *Grutter* opinion expressed an aspiration or was mandatory is a matter of dispute among constitutional scholars.

18. This is increased from a range of 4.5 to 4.8 schools per candidate from 1991 to 2001.

19. These arguments are described in more detail in Chambers et al. (2005) and Lempert, Kidder, Clydesdale, and Chambers (2006).

20. This section is adapted from Kidder (2006).

21. Similarly, Stephan and Abigail Thernstrom claimed in the *UCLA Law Review,* "When preferences are eliminated, they [AAPIs] derive the greatest benefit. Thus Asian American enrollment at the UCLA School of Law jumped by 73% when race-neutral admissions went into effect" (1999, p. 1629). This particular claim is presented in a manner likely to mislead policymakers, as the increase in AAPI enrollments in 1997 was principally a consequence of an anomaly in the UCLA Law School's yield rate that year, which caused the overall entering class (including AAPIs) to swell to about 380 students where it typically hovers close to 300 (Kidder, 2000).

References

Abel, R. L. (1989). *American lawyers.* New York: Oxford University Press.

American Bar Association. (1977). *A review of legal education in the United States—Fall 1977.* Chicago: American Bar Association.

American Bar Association. (2007). *Enrollment and degrees awarded.* Retrieved October 15, 2007, from http://www.abanet.org/legaled/statistics/charts/stats%20-%201.pdf

American Bar Association and Law School Admission Council (ABA and LSAC). (2007). *Official guide to ABA-approved law schools* (2008 ed.). Newtown, PA: Law School Admission Council. Retrieved October 16, 2007, from http://officialguide.lsac.org/Search/MainSearch.aspx

Asian American Law Students' Association. (1978). Report of the Boalt Hall Asian American special admissions research project. *Amerasia Journal, 5*(1), 21–37.

Association of American Law Schools. (1977). *Report of the special committee on future directions for minority group legal education. 1976 proceedings part two.* Washington, DC: Association of American Law Schools.

Ayres, I., & Brooks, R. (2005). Does affirmative action reduce the number of Black lawyers? *Stanford Law Review, 57,* 1807–1854.

Barnes, K. Y. (2007). Is affirmative action responsible for the achievement gap between Black and White law students? *Northwestern University Law Review, 101,* 1759–1809.

Boalt Hall School of Law. (1977). Report on special admissions at Boalt Hall after *Bakke. Journal of Legal Education, 28,* 363–402.

Brief for the Petitioner in *Grutter v. Bollinger* (2003). Retrieved November 20, 2007, from http://www.umich.edu/~urel/admissions/legal/grutter/grupet-supct.pdf

Chambers, D. L., Clydesdale, T. T., Kidder, W. C., & Lempert, R. O. (2005). The real impact of eliminating affirmative action in American law schools: An empirical critique of Richard Sander's study. *Stanford Law Review, 57,* 1855–1898.

Cho, S., & Westley, R. (2000). Critical race coalitions: Key movements that performed the theory. *UC Davis Law Review, 33,* 1377–1427.

DeFunis v. Odegaard, 416 U.S. 312 (1974).

Dreyfus, J., & Lawrence, C., III. (1979). *The Bakke case: The politics of inequality.* New York: Harcourt Brace Jovanovich.

Edwards, H. T. (1971). A new role for the Black law graduate: A reality or an illusion? *Michigan Law Review, 69,* 1407–1442.

Edwards, H. T. (1972). "Headwinds" minority placement in the legal profession. *Law Quadrangle Notes* [a University of Michigan Law School alumni-focused magazine], *16*(3), 14–18.

Espenshade, T. J., & Chung, C. Y. (2005). The opportunity cost of admission preferences at elite universities. *Social Science Quarterly, 86,* 293–305.

Evans, F. R. (1977). Applications and admissions to ABA accredited law schools: An analysis of national data for the class entering in the fall of 1976. In *Reports of LSAC Sponsored Research: Volume III, 1975–1977.* Newtown, PA: Law School Admission Council.

Graglia, L. A. (1970). Special admission of the "culturally deprived" to law school. *University of Pennsylvania Law Review, 119,* 351–363.

Gratz v. Bollinger, 539 U.S. 244 (2003).

Grodsky, E., & Kalogrides, D. (2007). *The declining significance of race: Race-based affirmative action in college admissions between 1986 and 2003.* [UC Davis Department of Sociology Working Paper]. Retrieved October 23, 2007, from http://repositories.cdlib.org/cgi/viewcontent.cgi?article=1002&context=ucd soc

Grutter v. Bollinger, 539 U.S. 306 (2003).

Handwerk, P. (2007). *National applicant trends—2006. Research paper.* Newtown, PA: Law School Admission Council. Retrieved November 14, 2007, from http://www.lsacnet.org/data/National-Applicant-Trends-2006.pdf

Heriot, G. (2007, August 26). Affirmative action backfires: Has affirmative action reduced the number of Black lawyers? *Wall Street Journal.* Retrieved November 29, 2007, from http://www.opinionjournal.com/editorial/feature.html?id = 110010522

Ho, D. E. (2005). Why affirmative action does not cause Black students to fail the bar. *Yale Law Journal, 114,* 1997–2004.

Hopwood v. Texas, 78 F.3d 932 (5th Cir.), *cert. denied,* 518 U.S. 1033 (1996).

Jacobs, L. A. (1998). Integration, diversity and affirmative action. *Law & Society Review, 32,* 725–746.

Johnson v. Board of Regents of the University System of Georgia, 263 F.3d 1234 (11th Cir. 2001).

Jones, D. L. (1969). The *Sweatt* case and the development of legal education for Negroes in Texas. *Texas Law Review, 47,* 677–693.

Karabel, J. (1999). *The rise and fall of affirmative action at the University of California.* Unpublished manuscript, UC Berkeley Institute for the Study of Social Change.

Kay, H. H. (2000). The challenge to diversity in legal education. *Indiana Law Review, 34,* 55–85.

Kearney, J. D., & Merrill, T. W. (2000). The influence of amicus curiae briefs on the Supreme Court. *University of Pennsylvania Law Review, 148,* 743–855.

Kidder, W. C. (2000). Situating Asian Pacific Americans in the law school affirmative action debate: Empirical facts about Thernstrom's rhetorical acts. *Asian Law Journal, 7,* 29–55.

Kidder, W. C. (2003). The struggle for access from *Sweatt* to *Grutter*: A history of African American, Latino and American Indian law school admissions, 1950–2000. *Harvard Blackletter Law Journal, 19,* 1–42.

Kidder, W. C. (2005). *Does affirmative action really hurt Blacks and Latinos in U.S. law schools?* [Policy Brief, Tomás Rivera Policy Institute]. Retrieved October 14, 2007, from http://www.trpi.org/PDFs/affirm_action.pdf

Kidder, W. C. (2006). Negative action versus affirmative action: Asian Pacific Americans are still caught in the crossfire. *Michigan Journal of Race & Law, 11,* 605–624.

Law School Admission Council. (1981). *The challenge of minority enrollment: Seeking diversity in the legal profession.* Newtown, PA: Law School Admission Council.

Law School Admission Council. (1987). *Law school admission data and developments: Analysis of minority law school applicants: 1980–81 to 1985–86.* Newtown, PA: Law School Admission Council.

Law School Admission Council. (1988–2007). National Decision Profiles [Memoranda distributed annually to law school admission officials covering the prior year's admission cycle].

Law School Admission Council. (2002). *Minority databook*. Newtown, PA: Law School Admission Council.

Lawrence, C. R., III. (1997). Each other's harvest: Diversity's deeper meaning. *University of San Francisco Law Review, 31*, 757–775.

Lempert, R. O., Kidder, W. C., Clydesdale, T. T., & Chambers, D. L. (2006). *Affirmative action in American law schools: A critical response to Richard Sander's "A reply to critics"* (University of Michigan John M. Olin Center for Law & Economics Working Paper Series #06–060). Retrieved November 20, 2007, from http://law.bepress.com/umichlwps/olin/art60/

Moran, R. F. (2006). Of doubt and diversity: The future of affirmative action in higher education. *Ohio State Law Journal, 67*, 201–243.

Nairn, A. (1981). Standardized selection criteria and a diverse legal profession. In D. M. White (Ed.), *Towards a diversified legal profession* (pp. 366–377). San Francisco: Julian Richardson Associates.

National Asian Pacific American Legal Consortium (NAPALC). (2003). *U.S. Supreme Court amicus brief in support of respondents in* Grutter v. Bollinger *and* Gratz v. Bollinger. Retrieved November 29, 2007, from http://www.vp comm.umich.edu/admissions/legal/gru_amicus-ussc/um/NAPALC-both.doc

Nelson, R. L. (1994). The future of American lawyers: A demographic profile of a changing profession in a changing society. *Case Western Reserve Law Review, 44*, 345–406.

Olivas, M. A. (2005). Law school admissions after *Grutter:* Student bodies, pipeline theory, and the river. *Journal of Legal Education, 55*, 16–33.

Ramsey, H., Jr. (1980). Affirmative action at American Bar Association approved law schools: 1979–1980. *Journal of Legal Education, 30*, 377–416.

Regents of the University of California v. Bakke, 438 U.S. 265 (1978).

Rothstein, J., & Yoon, A. (in press). Affirmative action in law school admissions: What do racial preferences do? *University of Chicago Law Review.*

Sander, R. H. (2004). A systemic analysis of affirmative action in American law schools. *Stanford Law Review, 57*, 367–483.

Sander, R. H., & Williams, E. D. (1989). Why are there so many lawyers? Perspectives on a turbulent market. *Law and Social Inquiry, 14*, 431–479.

Schmalbeck, R. (1998). The durability of law school reputation. *Journal of Legal Education, 48*, 568–590.

Schwartz, B. (1988). *Behind* Bakke: *Affirmative action and the Supreme Court.* New York: New York University Press.

Selmi, M. (1999). The life of *Bakke:* An affirmative action retrospective. *Georgetown Law Journal, 87*, 981–1022.

Simien, E. (1987). The Law School Admission Test as a barrier to almost twenty years of affirmative action. *Thurgood Marshall Law Review, 12*, 359–393.

Slocum, A. A. (Ed.). (1978). *Allan Bakke versus Regents of the University of California: The Supreme Court of the United States* (Volumes I–IV). Dobbs Ferry, NY: Oceana.

Smith v. University of Washington Law School, 233 F.3d 1188 (9th Cir. 2000).

Sweatt v. Painter, 339 U.S. 629 (1950).

Taylor, S. (2007, October 15). Affirming Justice Thomas. *National Journal.* Retrieved October 17, 2007, from http://nationaljournal.com/members/buzz/2007/openingargument/101507.htm

Thernstrom, S. A. (1998). Farewell to preferences? *Public Interest, 130,* 34–53.

Thernstrom, S. A., & Thernstrom, A. (1999). Reflections on the shape of the river. *UCLA Law Review, 46,* 1583–1631.

Torres, G. (2003). *Grutter v. Bollinger/Gratz v. Bollinger:* View from a limestone ledge. *Columbia Law Review, 103,* 1596–1609.

University of California. (1977). *Final report of the task force on graduate and professional admissions.* CA: Author.

University of California, Berkeley School of Law. (1993). *Boalt Hall annual admissions report.* Unpublished report, University of California, Berkeley School of Law.

University of California Office of the President. (2007). *UC law school statistics, 1993–2006.* Unpublished data.

Vernon, D. H., & Zimmer, B. I. (1987). The size and quality of the law school applicant pool: 1982–1986 and beyond. *Duke Law Journal, 1987,* 204–239.

Welch, S., & Gruhl, J. (1998a). *Affirmative action and minority enrollments in medical and law schools.* Ann Arbor: University of Michigan Press.

Welch, S., & Gruhl, J. (1998b). Does *Bakke* matter? Affirmative action and minority enrollments in medical and law schools. *Ohio State Law Journal, 59,* 697–731.

White, D. (1977). The *Bakke* case. *Politics & Education, 1*(1), 5–12.

Wightman, L. F. (1997). The threat to diversity in legal education: An empirical analysis of the consequences of abandoning race as a factor in law school admission decisions. *New York University Law Review, 72,* 1–53.

Wightman, L. F. (2003). The consequences of race-blindness: Revisiting prediction models with current law school data. *Journal of Legal Education, 53,* 229–253.

Wilder, G. Z. (2003). *The road to law school and beyond: Examining challenges to racial and ethnic diversity in the legal profession.* Law School Admission Council Research Report 02–01. Newtown, PA: Law School Admission Council.

Wilkins, D. B. (2005). A systematic response to systemic disadvantage: A response to Sander. *Stanford Law Review, 57,* 1915–1961.

Wilkins, D. B., Chambliss, E., Jones, L. A., & Adamson, H. (2002). *Harvard law school report on the state of Black alumni, 1869–2000.* Cambridge, MA: Harvard Law School Press.

9

INSTITUTIONAL DECISION MAKING AND THE POLITICS OF FEAR 30 YEARS AFTER *BAKKE*

Karen Miksch

I n the U.S. Supreme Court case *Regents of University of California v. Bakke* (1978), Justice Lewis Powell recognized the concept of promoting educational diversity as a compelling governmental interest. Since then, debate has continued among legal scholars regarding whether a majority of the Supreme Court in *Bakke* agreed with Justice Powell's opinion that promoting diversity is a compelling interest (e.g., Daniel, 1999; Liu, 1998; Moses, 2001; Philip, 2001; Schuck, 2002). It was not until 2003 that the U.S. Supreme Court again affirmed that colleges and universities could consider an applicant's race and ethnicity, along with other factors, to ensure a diverse student body (*Grutter v. Bollinger,* 2003). Rejecting race-blind and race-neutral approaches advocated by the plaintiffs and the U.S. government, the Court upheld the University of Michigan Law School's admission policy (*Grutter,* 2003) but struck down its undergraduate policy because it was not narrowly tailored to ensure the educational benefits of a diverse student body (*Gratz v. Bollinger,* 2003). According to the Court, affirmative action programs that promote diversity on college and university campuses are constitutional as long as individualized review is a component of the admissions process (*Gratz,* 2003; *Grutter,* 2003).[1]

Whereas the *Bakke* and *Grutter* cases focused on the consideration of race/ethnicity in higher education admission policies, the diversity rationale first enunciated in *Bakke* has had a wider reach than just college admissions. *Bakke,* for example, has been applied to scholarship programs (Miksch, 2007; Office for Civil Rights Guidelines, 1994) as well as to outreach and recruitment programs that are designed to increase access and retention for a diverse group of students (Miksch, 2007). Yet, even though *Bakke* remains the law of the land, colleges and universities across the U.S. are dropping race-conscious admission policies as well as "opening up" recruitment and retention programs so that they no longer include race/ethnicity as an admission criteria; some institutions are stopping all together scholarship and other programs initially designed to diversify the student body (Ancheta, 2007; Miksch, 2007; NAACP Legal Defense and Educational Fund [NAACP-LDF], 2005; U.S. Department of Education, 2003, 2004). This trend raises a number of important questions. Why, given *Bakke*'s affirmation in the *Grutter* and *Gratz* decisions, are institutions of higher education backing away from considering race/ethnicity in admissions and other programs designed to recruit and retain a diverse group of students? Did institutions stop race-conscious policies because of a thorough legal review, for example, or did the fear of unwanted public scrutiny or legal challenges inordinately affect their decisions? Perhaps most importantly, who is making these decisions?

This chapter seeks to understand such decisions by specifically examining the role of the general counsel's office at selective institutions of higher education in that administrative process. The general counsel's office houses the university's chief legal advisor and his or her staff attorneys. Increasingly, the office of the general counsel is being called on by faculty committees and administrators to answer a variety of educational policy questions including ones about programs designed to recruit, admit, and retain diverse students. Although faculty and administrators certainly play a principal role in the decision-making process to continue programs, I wanted to focus on what responsibility, if any, university counsel have in deciding when to halt, change, or keep race-conscious admission policies and other programs designed to recruit, admit, and retain a diverse student body.

My consideration of the role of the general counsel's office stems from an earlier study (Miksch, 2007) in which I was able to document 71 race-conscious scholarship, outreach, and retention programs at 53 separate institutions that had been changed during a 10-year period (1995–2005). Programmatic changes ranged from broadening the concept of diversity beyond race and ethnicity, to opening up the program to all races, to getting rid of the program all together. Even though "institutional review of programs" was cited as a reason for changing or discontinuing a race-conscious program, the most common explanation given was an investigation or a perceived threat of investigation by the Office for Civil Rights (OCR) in the U.S. Department of Education. Fear of publicity—based on reading about other programs in *The Chronicle of Higher Education*—was also mentioned. Finally, of note was the "unknown" category. Many staff members did not know why the program had been changed, nor was it apparent that the staff had been consulted before changing the eligibility criteria. When asked, many thought it was "the attorneys" making the determination. These findings, then, raised questions about the influence of both the general counsel's office and fears of campus administrators related to institutional decision making about race-conscious policies and programs.

This chapter is designed to build on that previous research by addressing two research questions: (1) What role does the general counsel's office play in decision making about institutional race-conscious policies? and (2) What role does the media play in institutional decision making about affirmative action policies and programs? I begin the chapter with a literature review that documents the increasingly legalized environment of higher education and the expanding role of the general counsel's office. Next, qualitative interviews with university attorneys at selective 4-year public institutions provide insights into the growing importance of the general counsel's office in determining whether to permit race-conscious affirmative action. I next provide a discussion of a "politics of fear" framework and how it is used for this analysis. To shed light on the "politics of fear" that influence university administrators (including attorneys) to end affirmative action, the chapter provides a preliminary content analysis of *The Chronicle of Higher Education*. Finally, I offer recommendations for university attorneys, administrators, faculty, and staff to work collaboratively to ensure well-informed campus decision making that embodies the spirit of *Bakke* and the diversity rationale. I now turn to a discussion of the legalized environment of higher education and the role of the general counsel within it.

The Role of University Attorneys in an Increasingly Legalized Environment

Thomas Wright, a former general counsel and secretary for Princeton University, has discussed the expanded role of the university attorney as a result of an "increasingly legalized environment" (1985, p. 378) as well as the positive and negative effects of such an environment. On the positive side, he listed the development of the legal principle of deference to academic judgments (for faculty under the principle of academic freedom and for academic institutions under the legal defense of institutional autonomy). On the negative, he noted that the law has a tendency to elevate process over substance. Wright (1985) goes on to discuss the role of higher education attorneys with respect to this negative attribute of the law:

> Anecdotal "worst case" examples are well known: affirmative action plans that are all process and no affirmative action. . . . This tendency is an unfortunate by-product of legal procedures, and needs to be guarded against, and resisted. No one can guard against the misuse of the legal process better than lawyers. That, too, should be a major objective of the academic legal profession. (p. 377)

Wright recognizes that separating the spirit of the law from the institutional context often leads to worrying more about whether all of the punctuation in an affirmative action plan is correct, for example, rather than whether the plan increases access. Along with other university attorneys, Wright argues that guarding against this reification of the law is a primary role for the general counsel's office.

The preventive function of a university attorney was discussed by Bickel as early as 1974 when he wrote, "The primary thrust of the attorneys' responsibility to the university and the primary definition of his or her role within the institution is the providing of preventive advice which will save the institution from formal litigation or other challenges" (p. 77). Daane (1985) further describes the essential roles of university counsel to include the role of legal advisor, educator, and administrator. By the 1990s, university attorneys recognized that the preventive function went beyond just keeping the institution out of court. Ruger (1997), elaborating upon Bickel's view, noted that the preventive function of university counsel includes two aspects. First, Ruger asserted that university attorneys should monitor the external legal environment, educate clients about new legal developments, and participate in revising practices as necessary. The second aspect of the job is to provide advice that is "understandable, relevant, and useful" (p. 183). No matter how competent the lawyer, Ruger noted, no one can prevent lawsuits from being filed against institutions of higher education. However, a preventive posture can improve the chances of a successful defense of the institution.

A 2000 *Journal of College and University Law* article further discussed the role of the university attorney. Vinik, Kumin, and O'Brien (2000) provide practical advice to institutions surrounding affirmative action and college admissions. The authors recommend that legal counsel take "the initiative to refine their goals and review their admission processes to better defend themselves if they become targets in litigation or the political arena" (p. 428). This appears to be a more proactive role for university attorneys than that espoused by earlier authors.

The role of the university attorney, then, has evolved and become multifaceted in an increasingly legalized environment. Informed by this literature, the chapter now turns to a case study of the general counsel's office to more fully understand its role in the decision-making process surrounding race-conscious policies.

The General Counsel's Office and Institutional Decision Making

What role does the general counsel's office play in determining whether to continue race-conscious policies? Is it part of the role of the general counsel's office to make these decisions, or are others in the institution deciding whether or not to continue race-conscious policies? This is a critical question because the general counsel may very well be the key administrator in the affirmative action debate. The documentation and archival sources used for this case study include university senate meeting transcripts[2] and law review articles. In addition, the case study includes qualitative interviews I conducted with university attorneys at three selective public institutions.

Before further discussion, several limitations of this study should be noted. There are limitations to any research that includes qualitative interviews and particular limitations when interviewing attorneys. It is unethical for attorneys to discuss actual advice given in a particular case or administrative decision. Attorneys refer to this as "work product," and it is a confidential communication between the university attorney and her or his client. Thus, I was not able to ask many specific questions about actual cases but, rather, relied more on hypothetical scenarios. Archival documentation provided additional insights into when and how race-conscious decisions were made by the attorneys I interviewed. Another limitation of this case study is that I focused on three institutions and therefore the attorneys I interviewed may not represent major trends in the role of university counsel in higher education. The attorneys' responses, however, were in line with the literature and appear to provide several models of how general counsel offices operate. Further interviews at additional institutions are warranted. Even with these limitations, however, using multiple sources of evidence allowed the development of converging lines of inquiry (Yin, 2003) and led to a more holistic picture of the role of the general counsel.

Are the Lawyers Running the Institution?

Whether higher education is "becoming a product of lawyers" (McPherson & Schapiro, 1994, p. 18) is not a new question. University lawyers themselves have been pondering and worrying about this question for at least 20 years (e.g., Ruger, 1997; Wright, 1985). I was, therefore, particularly interested in investigating how attorneys define their institutional role and how this may have expanded after *Bakke* to include making policy decisions related to affirmative action. My general theoretical proposition was that university attorneys are increasingly being asked to decide whether to continue race-conscious programs and that this type of decision making goes beyond the type of legal advice general counsels were asked to provide pre-*Bakke*. I also considered rival propositions. That is, that the role of the general counsel has not changed and that other actors, rather than legal counsel, have largely been the decision-makers concerning affirmative action policies.

I interviewed university attorneys at three highly selective public research institutions.[3] None of the institutions was currently involved in litigation regarding race-conscious admission practices or programming at the time of the interview, as it would be unethical for attorneys to discuss ongoing litigation or OCR investigations. I interviewed the general counsel and a staff attorney specializing in affirmative action at all three of the institutions. I asked about their perception of their role as university attorneys in general and about their responsibility surrounding race-conscious programs specifically. Each institution's attorneys perceived their roles differently, both broadly speaking as well as regarding their role in race-conscious decision making.

Preserving Institutional Autonomy and Avoiding Litigation

At the first institution, both attorneys viewed maintaining institutional autonomy as the primary role for university counsel. In the context of race-conscious decision making, both attorneys saw preserving autonomy as critical. For example, one explained, "Maintaining the university's ability to decide for itself what its [race-conscious] policies will be should be the role of the university attorney."[4] The other attorney (interviewed separately) said, "I see my role as primarily defending the right of the faculty to make [affirmative action] decisions." This attorney went on to talk about the need for the courts to give deference to the expertise of university administrators and saw university counsel's role as helping maintain the faculty and administration's ability to make education decisions.

Avoiding litigation was also mentioned as a primary role for these two university attorneys. For example, one attorney, in explaining why the institution had recently ended several race-conscious outreach programs, asserted, "Avoiding litigation should be the goal of every administrator. You don't want the courts making institutional decisions." The costs of litigation—monetary and time—as well as negative publicity were also cited as reasons to change policies that might come under legal attack. These attorneys' notion of a dual role—defending institutional autonomy and avoiding litigation—mirrors Wright's (1985) competing roles of an academic legal professional:

> Colleges and universities, and their faculties, must know, and must comply with, the law. College and university lawyers have seen this as their primary responsibility. But at the same time, and equally important, college and university lawyers have preserved for their faculties a maximum zone of freedom of self-determination in academic matters. In doing so, they have served their profession, the institutions who are their clients, the well-being of faculty members, and the public interest. (p. 379)

The two lawyers at this first institution viewed avoiding litigation and maintaining institutional autonomy as important roles and did not think the two were in conflict. Rather, their job was to keep the institution out of court and at the same time leave educational decisions up to faculty and administrators. When asked about who decides how to handle admission criteria, they independently answered, "The faculty."

Educating the Community

At the second institution, I interviewed two university attorneys who had a somewhat different view of their role than those at the first institution. They talked primarily about educating the university community about the legal environment so that faculty and administrators could make sound decisions. For example, one attorney said,

> I want to make sure we provide training for administrators. I see this as a
> big part of my role. I don't tell [administrators] how to decide, but I do
> want to make sure they have all of the information in front of them to
> make a good decision.

The other attorney I interviewed at this institution similarly stated, "Educating the university community on the legal implications of race-conscious policies is the primary role of university counsel."

Unlike the first institution, these two attorneys did not mention avoiding litigation as a primary goal; however, managing negative publicity and preventive law were discussed. As far as eluding negative publicity, one attorney at this institution specifically mentioned articles in *The Chronicle of Higher Education* that discussed institutions that had been contacted by the Center for Equal Opportunity (CEO) and the American Civil Rights Institute (ACRI).[5] The attorney said, "This isn't the type of publicity that any administrator wants." One attorney at this institution also talked about initiating reviews of existing programs after the *Grutter* case was decided as part of the preventative law function of a university attorney. The attorney said, "I wanted to make sure that we, as an institution, reviewed our programs, rather than waiting for somebody else to tell us what to do." This comment harkens to the need to preserve institutional autonomy also discussed by attorneys at the first institution.

Defending the Institution by Working Collaboratively

At the third selective public institution, both attorneys discussed their role in terms of "defending the institution." "My role is to support and defend the faculty and administration," said one lawyer. The other described, "My role is to work with experts on campus to make sure we have a policy that is based on the best available research." These comments are reminiscent of Alger's (1998) suggestions that university attorneys and administrators proactively research the potential educational benefits of a diverse student body and align policies with sound empirical data.

On some level, saying that the role of a university attorney is to defend the institution was an "easy" answer. Lawyers often talk about their role in relation to defending their client, which is a role that all attorneys understand. Each state has a professional code of conduct detailing the duty owed to a client. University attorneys, like all attorneys, have a duty to vigorously defend their clients. These attorneys went beyond a simple discussion of defending the client, however, and talked about the need to work collaboratively with researchers, administrators, and faculty. For example, one said,

> A university attorney should start by looking on his or her campus and see who is doing research on affirmative action. We have a tendency to always look for outside experts, but we should be sure to look on our own campuses, too.

The other attorney asserted, "Our role is to work collaboratively with faculty and administrators to defend sound legal policies." The institution where these two attorneys work has included experts on educational policy in its ongoing reviews of race-conscious outreach, recruitment, access, and retention programs. Perhaps encouraging the expansion of the role of university counsel to include this type of collaboration may provide insight into how other institutions can cultivate a sense of shared decision making in the affirmative action arena.

Are the lawyers running the institution? The answer to this question is not a simple yes or no. Although the actual role that attorneys play is much more complicated than described here, this examination does provide important insights. Although the attorneys in this case study perceived and defined their primary roles differently, all recognized that they carry multiple responsibilities. The university attorneys in this study often initiated reviews of race-conscious programs as required in *Grutter,* for example, but they did not have the sole authority to halt programs. All of the attorneys I interviewed were called upon by administrators and faculty groups to provide education and legal analysis of the *Bakke* and *Grutter* decisions. This interaction between university attorneys and administrators or academics may ultimately lead to decisions to stop race-conscious programs, but the decision, according to the attorneys I interviewed, was not exclusively in the hands of the general counsel's office.

Understanding the complex roles that university counsel play—preventive lawyer, educator, litigator, and collaborative administrator—provides researchers and administrators ideas of how to work with university counsel to ensure that decisions regarding affirmative action are based on sound empirical evidence and legal analysis rather than fear of litigation or negative publicity. All of the attorneys that I interviewed mentioned the hostile legal environment surrounding race-conscious decision making and how the fear of litigation and negative publicity provides the context in which institutional decision making currently occurs. These findings confirm earlier research (Miksch, 2007) that fear of negative publicity and avoiding litigation each often play a role in the advice provided to institutions. In addition, the attorneys I interviewed discussed their concern that nervous administrators were relying exclusively on legal advice, rather than also considering educational research and policy. This harkened back to my earlier research project (Miksch, 2007) where administrators said that fear of litigation was the primary reason that race-conscious programs were halted. Ultimately, then, was fear primarily driving race-conscious decision making? A further examination of the politics of fear as part of this study design was, therefore, needed.

What Are the Politics of Fear?

Altheide (2006) defines the politics of fear as "decision makers' promotion and use of audience beliefs and assumptions about danger, risk, and fear in order to achieve certain goals" (p. 1). Noting that Hobbes was the first theorist to see fear's galvanizing political potential, Robin (2004) underscores how elites, laws, and institutions like the media and education reinforce political fears. "Power is the ability to define a situation for self and others" (2006, p. 207), Altheide writes, and "Powerful people assert their will in the modern world through the politics of fear by being part of the communication process that defines social issues and social problems" (p. 207). Most current literature using the politics of fear framework point to the media, as well as education, as the primary institutions that are used to promote decision making based on fear.

   Political and media theorists have applied the "politics of fear" concept to a range of media coverage, including crime and the war on terrorism (Altheide, 2002; Barber, 2004; Furedi, 2007). Works such as Altheide's *Creating Fear: News and the Construction of Crisis* (2002) highlight how media coverage can lead to policies based on panic rather than empirical evidence. Adding to the discussion, Gonzales and Delgado (2006) argue that the fear of immigrants and racial minorities, fear of terrorism, as well as homophobia and anti-feminist rhetoric, have served as the most effective political tactics for neoconservatives. However, the practice of using fear to gain political ends is not restricted to a particular political party or ideology. According to Furedi (2007), the practice "has become institutionalized in public life" (p. 1).

In further examining institutional decision making, then, I apply the politics of fear framework—that organizations promote audience assumptions about danger and fear to achieve certain political goals—to the attacks on *Bakke*'s diversity rationale and institutional decision making about higher education race-conscious policies and programs. The *Bakke* decision has shaped how institutions of higher education think about how to create a diverse student body, and yet, many are halting affirmative action programs. If the U.S. Supreme Court had overturned *Bakke* when it decided the Michigan affirmative action cases in 2003, then it would be fairly easy to see that institutions were required to change or eliminate their programs based on the law. The *Grutter* decision, however, unequivocally upheld the *Bakke* decision. Legal scholars, even those who disagree with *Bakke*'s diversity rationale, concede that the *Grutter* decision ended all legal debate that diversity is a compelling interest (e.g., Mawdsley & Russo, 2003).[6] Why, then, are institutions of higher education moving away from *Bakke*?

Do the Politics of Fear Affect Higher Education Decision Making?

Considering the politics of fear and its potential influence on higher education decision making, I first returned to my earlier study documenting why institutions were halting race-conscious programs. Many of the administrators I interviewed mentioned a series of articles in *The Chronicle of Higher Education* (Miksch, 2007) in which the CEO and ACRI claimed to have contacted 100 institutions demanding that each halt its race-conscious programming (e.g., Schmidt, 2004). This led to my current analysis of how organizations have used publicity and the media, and whether that promotes the politics of fear.

Although my earlier research focused on the efforts of the ACRI and CEO, both of which are national organizations that similarly argue race-conscious affirmative action should be illegal, this study included the Center for Individual Rights (CIR) because the organization represented the plaintiffs in the Michigan affirmative action lawsuits (*Gratz,* 2003; *Grutter,* 2003) and the organization was mentioned by administrators I interviewed previously (Miksch, 2007). My review of these organizations' websites revealed that they use two primary strategies to persuade institutions of higher education to stop employing *Bakke*'s diversity rationale: the threat of civil rights complaints and publicity via the media (see, also, Miksch, 2007; NAACP-LDF, 2005).[7] Further, the findings of a national survey examining administrators' knowledge of higher education law indicated that a substantial number (44%) of the 250 deans and administrators surveyed listed using *The Chronicle of Higher Education* "often" or "always" as a legal resource (Schimmel & Nolan, 2005). As such, I decided to examine the extent to which these various organizations (ACRI, CEO, and CIR) were achieving publicity through *The Chronicle* and, as a result, the type of resource it might serve for higher education leaders as they make decisions on race-conscious policies and programs.

I selected the period from 1996 through 2007 for my analysis.[8] Of the 80 articles published in *The Chronicle* that directly mentioned *Bakke,* 26 cite someone from the CIR as a source for the proposition that affirmative action is illegal. In these same 80 articles, the next most highly cited organizations were the CEO (with 16 attributions to support the position that affirmative action is illegal) and the NAACP-LDF, cited 16 times for the proposition that affirmative action is constitutional. When reviewing all stories dealing with race-conscious affirmative action during the 10-year period, the contrast is even starker. Of the 460 stories related to race-conscious admission policies and other programs designed to admit and retain a diverse group of students, the most highly cited sources include the CIR (with 79 attributions) and the CEO (with 78 attributions). Compare this with the 50 times that the NAACP-LDF was cited during the same time period in articles regarding race-conscious affirmative action.

In addition, I reviewed whether additional organizations researching the impact of diversity were cited as authorities by *The Chronicle.* I found, for example, that the American Educational Research Association (AERA) and The Civil Rights Project at Harvard University (both research organizations that have publicly supported affirmative action policy) were only cited 6 and 10 times, respectively. Suffice it to say, when looking at sheer volume, the CIR and CEO, affirmative action opponents, are more frequently quoted by *Chronicle* reporters than are supporters of affirmative action, questioning the utility of *The Chronicle* as a balanced source of information upon which to make institutional decisions.

In addition to being cited as sources in articles written by *Chronicle* journalists, the CIR and CEO often published opinion pieces and letters-to-the-editor with titles such as "The Demise of Race-based Admissions Policies," written by then CIR director Michael S. Greve (1999) and "Time Has Not Favored Racial Preferences," written by Roger Clegg (2005), director of the CEO. Of course, individuals and organizations that disagree with the CIR and CEO also write opinion pieces. For example, an opinion piece written by Ian F. Haney L'Pez (2006), a professor at the Boalt Hall School of Law at the University of California, Berkeley, strongly criticized the CEO in the *Chronicle Review,* the opinion section of the newspaper. However, in my previous study (Miksch, 2007) when I interviewed administrators about why a race-conscious outreach, access, or retention program had been changed, it was not the opinion section of *The Chronicle* that was mentioned. Rather, several articles in *The Chronicle* were specifically mentioned by respondents (e.g., Healy, 1999; Schmidt, 2004; Schmidt & Young, 2003) who listed fear of litigation and the concomitant negative publicity as a primary reason for halting diversity programs. The threats of imminent litigation described in those articles, however, do not appear to be based on court opinions, laws, or current regulations (e.g., Ancheta, 2005, 2007; Miksch, 2007).[9] For example, the U.S. Supreme Court has never ruled on race-conscious summer programs, and lower courts have found no constitutional injury when colleges and universities use race-conscious outreach and recruitment strategies (Ancheta, 2007). In addition, the OCR guidelines approve race-conscious scholarships designed to ensure a diverse student body, and the courts have never ruled that diversity is not a compelling interest in the area of scholarships and other types of retention programs (Ancheta, 2007; Miksch, 2007). Although the ACRI and CEO demands to end affirmative action are not based on U.S. Supreme Court precedent, these threats appear to carry weight (Miksch, 2007; NAACP-LDF, 2005). These findings support the concerns of the attorneys I interviewed by highlighting the potentially skewed perspective on affirmative action being presented through media outlets. I now offer recommendations for administrators and educational researchers as they work with university attorneys to make decisions about race-conscious policies and programs.

Recommendations for Institutional Practice

This chapter urges thoughtful consideration about the future of institutional practice in the context of *Bakke.* I do this by considering several different influences on institutional decision making. The multifaceted role of the general counsel's office to avoid litigation and negative publicity while preserving institutional autonomy and educating the university community appears to exert an influence on institutional processes. This influence is particularly evident in the increasingly hot-button area of race-conscious decision making. The politics of fear has been used as a framework to understand why colleges and universities may be moving away from *Bakke.* Ultimately, how can administrators and faculty obtain the best information about their institution's race-conscious policies, the law, and their options? These recommendations are based on my belief that, by working together, higher education leaders can make better informed decisions.

Knowledge Is Power

At a minimum, this case study documents why administrators and faculty members should not use *The Chronicle of Higher Education* as a legal resource. Schimmel and Nolan (2005) published the results of a national survey of academic administrators and noted that many did not have adequate knowledge of higher education law. Schimmel and Nolan recommend every campus provide a "crash course" in legal literacy. In addition, they recommend that institutions hire campus counsel who can teach laypersons about the law. Several of the attorneys interviewed for this study concurred with this notion that part of their job is as an educator. Administrators, who lack legal literacy, appear to defer to legal expertise when the topic is affirmative action (Schimmel & Nolan, 2005). Whether administrators actually defer to legal expertise in affirmative action decisions is an area that calls for further research. Further, I believe that teaching administrators about higher education law may lead to less decision making based on fear. Ideally, when administrators are getting a "crash course" on higher education law, education and public policy research should also be presented. As Schimmel and Nolan (2005) note, most administrators do not have degrees in higher education, yet, they are making important policy decisions. Most administrators, therefore, also need education policy literacy. If only the legal implications are discussed with administrators, the danger is that legal concerns will be primary, while sound educational policies will be seen as secondary, if they are considered at all. Ultimately, teaching and learning across disciplines, whether it be law, policy, or educational research, is one way to begin to ensure that when legal and policy decisions need to be made, a variety of perspectives will be explored to make an informed decision.

Publish (or Perish)

Another way to make sure that affirmative action decisions are based on research, rather than fear, is to publish in venues that reach lawyers. For example, social scientists should consider coauthoring an article with an education law scholar in a law review or legal magazine. The legal scholar can help write and explain the research in a format that lawyers (and judges) will understand and recognize. For example, unlike peer-reviewed education journals, law review articles and legal briefs rarely include sections on "methods" or "theoretical perspective." Educational researchers may find that relegating a discussion of methodology to an appendix is a more effective way to explain the importance of findings to a legal audience. In addition, both attorneys writing for education audiences and social scientists writing for lawyers will have to "translate" specialized language so that readers outside of their field will understand the import of the findings. Having someone outside of your field edit your manuscript is always useful.

In addition to publishing education research in legal publications and legal analysis in education journals, workshops and forums with university attorneys and educational researchers each presenting their work are beneficial. After the *Grutter* Supreme Court decision, for example, I presented at a number of forums and committee meetings, along with members from the general counsel's office. These presentations afforded a somewhat informal way to discuss the legacy of *Bakke* and recent educational research on diversity. Having research, policy, and legal perspectives presented at the same time generates a more collaborative and fully informed approach to affirmative action decision making.

Power of the Press

Last, but not least, the findings presented here point to the importance of access to the media to combat the politics of fear. Although it is sometimes difficult to find the time, working with journalists to make sure important legal analysis and research findings are reported, and reported accurately, is a critical way to ensure that policy decisions are based on sound evidence. Again, most administrators obtain knowledge about the law surrounding affirmative action from *The Chronicle of Higher Education* (Schimmel &

Nolan, 2005). Thus, it is important for university counsel, education researchers, and policy experts to work with reporters of *The Chronicle* and other media sources to ensure that stories include the most up-to-date legal analysis and educational research.

There are a number of ways to work with the press. In addition to writing opinion pieces and responding to articles in a letter-to-the-editor, researchers should consider sending a press release to *The Chronicle* when publishing research findings that affect institutions of higher education. Many colleges and universities have an office that helps with press releases and contacting the media. Absent this resource, researchers can contact local reporters who cover education issues.

The politics of fear surrounding affirmative action can be partially addressed in the media through sound empirical evidence, clearly explained. Training researchers about how to work with the media in constructive ways is an important undertaking that can result in a richer and accurate discussion regarding race-conscious decision making. This case study points to the need for media workshops on how to translate educational research findings so that they will more readily reach policymakers including higher education administrators, university attorneys, and elected officials. Balanced articles, specifically in *The Chronicle,* and on-camera interviews in local and national media outlets, are also needed to provide decision-makers with accurate and up-to-date research to inform race-conscious policies.

Conclusion

The following quote from an administrator demonstrates the fear that surrounds law and higher education:

> I worry that overemphasis on lawsuits can prevent administrators from doing their job. We live in a very litigious society . . . it does make an administrator very cautious and nervous and worried when weighing in on contentious issues. (Schimmel & Nolan, 2005, p. 466)

The increasingly legalized environment of higher education, and the concomitant expanding role of the general counsel's office, means that university attorneys are key actors in the affirmative action debate. One hopes that keeping in mind the multiple roles university attorneys play—

preventive lawyer, educator, administrator—will assist administrators and faculty in understanding how to work with lawyers in more collaborative and proactive ways. Currently, institutions appear to be reacting to the politics of fear. To proactively work on the critical issues of access and equity so that the benefits of diversity described in *Bakke* might be realized, institutional leaders in higher education need to operate from a more accurate perspective. Eliminating the fear that contextualizes decision making surrounding race-conscious policies should be our goal. Access to higher education is much too important to be marginalized by the politics of fear.

Notes

1. See Joint Statement of Constitutional Law Scholars (2003) for a detailed discussion of the *Gratz* and *Grutter* opinions.

2. A 2-year review of the minutes of senate committee meetings at the three public institutions I studied revealed that university attorneys were being asked to sit *ex officio* on, or were regularly invited to attend meetings of, university committees that consider equity and access issues.

3. As Kane (1998) documented, race-conscious affirmative action admission policies are located in highly selective institutions of higher education. This study, therefore, focuses on elite institutions. In this case study, I focus on selective 4-year public universities. Using the Integrated Postsecondary Education Data System (IPEDS), a group of institutions were selected. The characteristics included public, 4-year, degree-granting, Carnegie Classification of Doctoral/Research Universities-Extensive, with research expenditures of more than $100 million, and with a comparable number of enrolled undergraduate and graduate students.

4. The statements used in this section of the chapter are from interviews with university attorneys. To protect the confidentiality of the respondents, no identifying information is provided.

5. The Center for Equal Opportunity (CEO), the American Civil Rights Institute (ACRI), as well as the Center for Individual Rights (CIR) discussed later in the chapter, are national organizations that argue race-conscious affirmative action should be illegal.

6. Most recently, in the 2007 voluntary desegregation court cases (*Parents Involved in Community Schools v. Seattle School District No. 1*, 2007; *Meredith v. Jefferson County Board of Education*, 2007), the Supreme Court left *Bakke* standing with regard to higher education.

7. Another strategy used by opponents to ban the use of affirmative action is ballot initiatives. Ballot initiatives in California, Washington, and Michigan have led to a ban on all consideration of race in higher education, among other institutions. Although this strategy certainly fits within the conceptual framework of the politics

of fear, ballot initiatives were not being conducted in the states where the attorneys reside and were not mentioned by the attorneys that I interviewed as reasons for stopping race-conscious policies. They are, therefore, outside the scope of this project.

8. I started my review of *The Chronicle* with 1996 because that is the year that the Fifth Circuit Court of Appeals ruled in *Hopwood v. Texas* that diversity is *not* a compelling interest. The U.S. Supreme Court refused to hear the *Hopwood* case on appeal, and it remained controlling precedent in the Fifth Circuit until 2003. In 2003, the *Hopwood* decision was overturned by the U.S. Supreme Court's opinion in *Grutter*. I concluded my review of *The Chronicle* with 2007, 4 years after the Supreme Court opinion in *Grutter* upheld the diversity rationale.

9. In one recent case, however, the CIR filed a lawsuit against the Dow Jones Fund and Virginia Commonwealth University (Schmidt, 2007). The CIR contended that the Dow Jones Fund summer program for prospective journalists violated Title VI of the Civil Rights Act. The fund's guidelines for newspapers and colleges involved in its summer workshops required each participant to "be a minority (defined as U.S. citizens who are black, Hispanic, Asian or Pacific Islander, American Indian, or Alaskan Native)" (Schmidt, 2007, p. 18).The case settled in 2007 and the Dow Jones Fund agreed to change the name of the program and open it to all students, regardless of race.

References

Alger, J. R. (1998). Unfinished homework for universities: Making the case for affirmative action. *Washington University Journal of Urban & Contemporary Law, 54,* 73–92.

Altheide, D. L. (2002). *Creating fear: News and the construction of crisis.* New York: Aldine de Gruyter.

Altheide, D. L. (2006). *Terrorism and the politics of fear.* Lanham, MD: Rowman Altamira.

Ancheta, A. N. (2005). After *Grutter* and *Gratz*: Higher education, race, and the law. In G. Orfield, P. Marin, & C. L. Horn (Eds.), *Higher education and the color line: College access, racial equity, and social change* (pp. 175–196). Cambridge, MA: Harvard Education Press.

Ancheta, A. N. (2007). Antidiscrimination law and race-conscious recruitment, retention, and financial aid policies in higher education. In G. Orfield, P. Marin, S. M. Flores, & L. M. Garces (Eds.), *Charting the future of college affirmative action: Legal victories, continuing attacks, and new research* (pp. 15–34). Los Angeles: The Civil Rights Project at UCLA.

Barber, B. (2004). *Fear's empire: War, terrorism, and democracy.* New York: W.W. Norton.

Bickel, R. D. (1974). The role of college or university legal counsel. *Journal of Law and Education, 3,* 73–80.

Clegg, R. (2005, January 14). Time has not favored racial preferences. *The Chronicle of Higher Education,* p. 10.

Daane, R. K. (1985). The role of university counsel. *Journal of College & University Law, 12,* 399–414.

Daniel, T. K. (1999). The rumors of my death have been exaggerated: *Hopwood's* error in "discarding" *Bakke. Journal of Law and Education, 28,* 391–418.

Furedi, F. (2007). *The politics of fear: Beyond left and right.* London & New York: Continuum International.

Gonzales, M. G., & Delgado, R. (2006). *The politics of fear: How Republicans use money, race, and the media to win.* New York: Paradigm.

Gratz v. Bollinger, 539 U.S. 244 (2003).

Greve, M. S. (1999, March 19). The demise of race-based admission policies. *The Chronicle of Higher Education,* p. B6.

Grutter v. Bollinger, 539 U.S. 306 (2003).

Haney L'Pez, I. F. (2006, November 3). Colorblind to the reality of race in America. *The Chronicle Review,* p. 6.

Healy, P. (1999, February 5). A group attacks affirmative action and seeks help from trustees and students. *The Chronicle of Higher Education,* p. A36.

Hopwood v. Texas, 78 F.3d 932 (5th Cir.), *cert. denied,* 518 U.S. 1033 (1996).

Joint Statement of Constitutional Law Scholars. (2003, July). *Reaffirming diversity: A legal analysis of the University of Michigan affirmative action cases.* Cambridge, MA: The Civil Rights Project at Harvard University.

Kane, T. J. (1998). Misconceptions in the debate over affirmative action in higher education. In G. Orfield & E. Miller (Eds.), *Chilling admissions: The affirmative action crisis and the search for alternatives* (pp. 17–31). Cambridge, MA: Harvard Education Publishing Group.

Liu, G. (1998). Affirmative action in higher education: The diversity rationale and the compelling interest test. *Harvard Civil Rights—Civil Liberties Law Review, 33,* 381–342.

Mawdsley, R. D., & Russo, C. J. (2003). Supreme Court dissenting opinions in *Grutter:* Has the majority created a nation divided against itself? *Education Law Reporter, 180,* 417–435.

McPherson, M. S., & Schapiro, M. O. (1994). Governing the university in a litigious age. *New York State Bar Journal, 66,* 18–21.

Meredith v. Jefferson County Board of Education, 127 S. Ct. 2738 (2007).

Miksch, K. (2007). Stand your ground: Legal and policy justifications for race-conscious programming. In G. Orfield, P. Marin, S. M. Flores, & L. M. Garces

(Eds.), *Charting the future of college affirmative action: Legal victories, continuing attacks, and new research* (pp. 57–78). Los Angeles: The Civil Rights Project at UCLA.

Moses, M. S. (2001). Affirmative action and the creation of more favorable contexts of choice. *American Educational Research Journal, 38*(1), 3–36.

NAACP Legal Defense and Educational Fund, Inc. (2005, June 23). *Closing the gap: Moving from rhetoric to reality in opening the doors to higher education for African-American students.* Retrieved October 12, 2007, from http://www.naacpldf.org/content/pdf/gap/Closing_the_Gap_-_Movingefrom_Rhetoric_to_Reality.pdf

Office for Civil Rights Guidelines, 59 *Fed. Reg.* 8756 (Feb. 23, 1994).

Parents Involved in Community Schools v. Seattle School District No. 1, 127 S. Ct. 2738 (2007).

Philip, E. (2001). Diversity in the halls of academia: Bye-bye *Bakke? Journal of Law and Education, 31,* 149–166.

Regents of the University of California v. Bakke, 438 U.S. 265 (1978).

Robin, C. (2004). *Fear: The history of a political idea.* New York: Oxford University Press.

Ruger, P. H. (1997). The practice and profession of higher education law. *Stetson Law Review, 27,* 175–198.

Schimmel, D., & Nolan, L. (2005). Academic administrators, higher education and the practice of preventive law. *West's Education Law Reporter, 194,* 461–472.

Schmidt, P. (2004, March 19). Not just for minority students anymore. *The Chronicle of Higher Education,* p. 17.

Schmidt, P. (2007, February 23). Dow Jones Fund opens journalism programs to White students after lawsuit. *The Chronicle of Higher Education,* p. 18.

Schmidt, P., & Young, J. R. (2003, February 21). MIT and Princeton open two summer programs to students of all races. *The Chronicle of Higher Education,* p. 31.

Schuck, P. H. (2002). Affirmative action: Past, present, and future. *Yale Law and Policy Review, 20,* 1–96.

U.S. Department of Education, Office for Civil Rights (2003). *Race-neutral alternatives in postsecondary education: Innovative approaches to diversity.* Washington, DC: U.S. Department of Education. Retrieved August 1, 2007, from http://www.ed.gov/about/offices/list/ocr/raceneutral.html

U.S. Department of Education, Office for Civil Rights (2004). *Achieving diversity: Race-neutral alternatives in American education.* Washington, DC: U.S. Department of Education. Retrieved August 1, 2007, from http://www.ed.gov/about/offices/list/ocr/raceneutral.html

Vinik, D. F., Kumin, L., & O'Brien, J. P. (2000). Affirmative action in college admissions: Practical advice to public and private institutions for dealing with the changing landscape. *Journal of College and University Law, 26,* 395–428.

Wright, T. (1985). Faculty and the law explosion. A twenty-five year perspective (1960–1985) for college and university lawyers. *Journal of College and University Law, 12,* 363–379.

Yin, R. K. (2003). *Case study research: Design and methods* (3rd ed.). Thousand Oaks, CA: Sage.

10

BAKKE AND STATE POLICY

Exercising Institutional Autonomy to Maintain a Diverse Student Body

Patricia Marin and Stella M. Flores

I
n *Regents of the University of California v. Bakke* (1978), the matter before the Court was the constitutionality of the admissions policy of the
medical school at the University of California, Davis (UC Davis). Of
the various rationales put forward to justify this admissions policy,[1] the only
one acknowledged in Justice Lewis Powell's deciding opinion as a compelling state interest was "obtaining the educational benefits that flow from an
ethnically diverse student body" (*Bakke,* 1978, p. 306).[2] Although Powell's
opinion was the subject of debate for many years, his conclusion was decidedly affirmed in the *Gratz v. Bollinger* (2003) and *Grutter v. Bollinger* (2003)
Supreme Court opinions.[3]

Although many recognize *Bakke* as the Supreme Court case that secured
the "benefits of diversity" rationale for higher education, it is not as well
known that Justice Powell supported this conclusion employing the principle of academic freedom (also known as institutional autonomy when refer-
ring to institutions). In his opinion, Justice Powell suggested that higher
education institutions are unique and, therefore, must have the ability to
make their own academic decisions. Providing a specific example, he
explained,

> Academic freedom, though not a specifically enumerated constitutional
> right, long has been viewed as a special concern of the First Amendment.

> The freedom of a university to make its own judgments as to education
> includes the selection of its student body. (*Bakke,* 1978, p. 312)

Drawing from *Keyishian v. Board of Regents of the University of the State of New York* (1967), he further emphasized his point by acknowledging "our national commitment to the safeguarding of these freedoms within university communities" (*Bakke,* 1978, p. 312). Ultimately, he concluded that UC Davis "must be viewed as seeking to achieve a goal that is of paramount importance in the fulfillment of its mission" (p. 313). Twenty-five years later, Justice Sandra Day O'Connor, writing for the *Grutter* majority, supported Powell's conclusions and reinforced the importance of "giving a degree of deference to a university's academic decisions" (2003, p. 328)—what she refers to as "educational autonomy" (p. 329).

Although Justices Powell and O'Connor asserted that, because of academic freedom, an institution should be allowed to admit its own student body, this autonomy was not offered without restrictions. Of course, institutions are governed by more than just their own missions and academic freedom. For example, the *Grutter* Court talked about autonomy "within constitutionally prescribed limits" (2003, p. 328). In fact, an institution is governed and affected by a whole host of parameters including federal, state, and local laws and policies (Kaplin & Lee, 1995) that may work in concert with, or against, the goals of an institution. Abiding by all of these laws and policies, while remaining true to their institutional missions and their desired outcomes, therefore, can be quite a challenge for colleges and universities. As a result, campuses intentionally exercising institutional autonomy to create the diverse student body they have asserted is necessary to achieve their missions occurs in the larger context of supporting and competing external policy. This also contributes to and affects institutional decision making.

This chapter considers some of the external limits on an institution's academic freedom and what colleges and universities have to or can do to creatively exercise their autonomy, within these existing parameters, to admit a diverse student body as per *Bakke*. In doing so, we ask the question: what affect can state policy have on an institution's ability to admit a diverse student body as afforded in *Bakke*? To begin this examination, we provide a brief discussion of academic freedom, particularly defining the concept of institutional autonomy. Then we examine how the law can affect an institution's academic freedom, focusing on state policy because of its central role in public higher education (McGuinness, 1994). In the next section we provide two examples of current state policies that directly hinder or enhance an institution's ability to achieve a diverse student body. We follow by providing two examples of state policies that may indirectly support or interfere with an institution's implementation of diversity goals.[4] In the final section, we discuss why the intersection of institutional autonomy and state policy continues to be relevant to campuses and their decision making. In the current climate that is generally hostile to race-conscious policies, we argue that institutions interested in reaping the benefits of a diverse student body must act intentionally to successfully achieve their institutional missions.

Academic Freedom

Academic freedom, considered "a safeguard essential to the aims of the university and to the welfare of those who work within it" (Bok, 1982, p. 20), refers "to the custom and practice, and the ideal, by which faculties may best flourish in their work as teachers and researchers" (Kaplin & Lee, 1995, p. 299). Although a more specific definition is elusive (Kaplin & Lee, 1995), higher education most often uses the 1940 Statement of Principles on Academic Freedom and Tenure, developed by the Association of American University Professors (AAUP) and the American Association of Colleges and Universities (AAC&U), to explain this unique concept (Springer, 2006). The 1940 Statement of Principles indicates,

> Teachers are entitled to full freedom in research and in the publication of the results. . . . Teachers are entitled to freedom in the classroom in discussing their subject. . . . When [teachers] speak or write as citizens, they should be free from institutional censorship or discipline. (AAUP & AAC&U, 2006, p. 3)

In addition to its relevance for individual faculty members, academic freedom also has meaning at the institutional level.

Institutional Academic Freedom

Sweezy v. New Hampshire, a 1957 Supreme Court decision,[5] provides "the basis for the academic freedom of institutions" (Euben, 2002, n.p.). Institutional academic freedom, similar to individual academic freedom, is considered a First Amendment right by the Court (Euben, 2002). Most often quoted in this matter is Justice Felix Frankfurter's concurring opinion in *Sweezy.*[6] In writing about "the dependence of a free society on free universities," he indicates, "This means the exclusion of governmental intervention in the intellectual life of a university" (1957, p. 262). Expanding on this notion, he quotes from a statement of South African scholars who at that time were fighting for open universities:

> It is the business of a university to provide that atmosphere which is most conducive to speculation, experiment, and creation. It is an atmosphere in which there prevail "the four essential freedoms" of a university—to determine for itself on academic grounds who may teach, what may be taught, how it shall be taught, and who may be admitted to study. (p. 263)

Overall Justice Frankfurter believed that "political power must abstain from intrusion into this activity of [academic] freedom, pursued in the interest of wise government and the people's well-being, except for reasons that are exigent and obviously compelling" (1957, p. 262). Guided by the Supreme Court, the AAUP "has concluded that institutions have academic freedom when a challenged decision involves educational or academic policy and functions (as opposed to other nonacademic decisions)" (Euben, 2002, n.p.). Therefore, the educational aspects of college and university decision making, such as faculty hiring and academic requirements, fall under the umbrella of institutional autonomy. Nevertheless, this autonomy is not without limits, mainly as a result of government intervention. The chapter now turns to this issue.

State Action Intersects With Institutional Autonomy

Scholars have argued that "if a college or university is effectively to define its goals and select or invent the means of attaining them, it must have a high degree of substantive autonomy" (Berdahl & McConnell, 1994, p. 56). Because of the public interest in higher education, especially public higher education, however, we are witnessing increasing involvement in the matters of colleges and universities by both the federal and state governments (Berdahl & McConnell, 1994). Sometimes this involvement provides added support to an institution as it attempts to successfully reach particular goals; other times this involvement works against an institution's interests (Berdahl & McConnell, 1994). Derek Bok, former president of Harvard University, has argued, "Professors and administrators have both been losing some of their independence to the mounting requirements of the state," and "Universities find themselves subjected to a host of rules covering a long and growing list of campus activities" (Bok, 1982, p. 37).

It comes as no surprise that state action affects whether or not an institution meets its goals, especially as the public has become more aware of higher education institutions and their important role in society (Berdahl & Mc-Connell, 1994; Bok, 1982; McGuinness, 1994). This has led to suggestions of strained relations between a state government and the public colleges and universities within the state (McGuinness, 1994). Given a steady erosion of institutional autonomy (Berdahl & McConnell, 1994), then, it is important to have a general understanding of these "external sources of law" (Kaplin & Lee, 1995, p. 13) and how they relate to each other and to an institution's autonomy.[7] Although a detailed discussion of these "external sources of law" is beyond the scope of this chapter, we provide relevant highlights and focus on the *Bakke* Supreme Court case and its intersection with state policy.

The U.S. Constitution "is the highest legal authority that exists" (Kaplin & Lee, 1995, p. 13). As such, any law that conflicts with it is "subject to invalidation by the courts" (Kaplin & Lee, 1995, p. 13), including provisions in any state constitution, considered the highest legal authority in a state, or any state statute or law. Although many laws affect higher education without specifically addressing matters of education (e.g., fair hiring practices, anti-discrimination laws, etc.), we are most interested in examples of state policy that focus directly on colleges and universities.

Although governmental bodies at all levels may enact legislation specifically related to higher education, the states provide most of these statutes (Kaplin & Lee, 1995). This is both because the U.S. Constitution does not provide specifically for higher education and the Tenth Amendment reserves powers not delegated to the federal government to the states (Gladieux, Hauptman, & Knapp, 1994). As such, higher education is considered the responsibility of the states (Kaplin & Lee, 1995). Under this context, "federal law establishes a 'floor' upon which state law may, in appropriate circumstances, 'build' " (Coleman, Palmer, Sanghavi, & Winnick, 2007, p. 4). Specifically related to *Bakke,* then, the Supreme Court decision does not "*mandate or require* that higher education institutions use race or ethnicity in their admissions programs. Rather, [it] *permit*[*s*] institutions to use race and ethnicity in limited ways in admissions decisions" (Coleman et al., 2007,

p. 4). This lack of mandate, for example, then, allows for "state constitutional, statutory, or regulatory provisions that forbid the use of race or ethnicity in public higher education" (2007, p. 4). In such situations, institutions that want to assert their institutional autonomy to determine "who may be admitted to study" (*Sweezy,* 1957, p. 263) would be prohibited from implementing a race-conscious admissions plan. This is only one example of how external laws and policies can limit the ability of colleges and universities to completely self-govern.

Ultimately, the goal must be "to decide how government and universities can work in harmony so that higher education will be able to make its greatest contribution" (Bok, 1982, p. 39).[8] The challenge in accomplishing this relationship, in part, lies in acknowledging the importance of institutional autonomy, recognizing the role of the states in developing higher education policy that addresses and protects local interests and needs, and establishing the requisite balance between the two. With this in mind, we now discuss two examples of instances where state policy intersected, either positively or negatively, with an institution's ability to recruit and enroll a diverse student body in efforts to fulfill its educational mission.

Considering State-Level Policy

A range of state-level policies can affect an institution's ability to determine "who may be admitted to study" and, thereby, affect the admission of a racially/ethnically diverse student body. Although some are clearly written to directly address higher education admissions decisions and may affect the enrollment outcomes of a student body, other state policies do not have as specific a connection. Yet, these latter public policies, by their design, also may have the power to alter enrollment outcomes. Further, although some policies are race-conscious or specifically bar the use of race, others do not address issues of race specifically but still may affect racial/ethnic outcomes.

In this section, we detail examples of state admissions-specific policies that can directly affect the racial/ethnic diversity of an institution's student body. Those we consider to have direct effects on student body diversity by either attempting to prevent the loss of racial and ethnic representation in college admissions or barring the consideration of race/ethnicity in decision making include (1) the Top Ten Percent Plan in Texas, a state legislative initiative that grants automatic admission to the top 10% of a graduating class in any Texas high school to public colleges and universities in the state, and (2) Proposition 209 in California, the voter referendum that banned the use of race in admissions, employment, and financial aid decisions by public state entities.

State Policies With Direct Effects on Student Body Diversity

Public postsecondary institutions in Texas and California have each experienced limitations on their autonomy to admit a diverse student body through distinct legal and policy mechanisms. In Texas, a federal court ruling banned the use of race and ethnicity in college admissions in states in the Fifth Circuit Court of Appeals (Texas, Louisiana, and Mississippi).[9] In California, a voter-approved constitutional amendment banned the use of race/ethnicity in college admissions. What these states similarly demonstrate, however, is the use of institution-level action as a response to those external limitations on autonomy to admit and retain a diverse student body. Texas, in seeking to uphold the ability to achieve the educational benefits of student body diversity outcomes as outlined in *Bakke,* used legislative action via the Texas Top Ten Percent Plan, supported and supplemented by institutional-level university investment in programmatic and publicity efforts, to counteract federal limits on institutional autonomy. California has employed multiple methods to counteract state imposed limits on institutional autonomy over admissions decisions as a result of Proposition 209. These include a University of California system initiative modeled after the Texas percent plan and supported by California state leaders—Eligibility in Local Context (ELC)—and significant state investment in college outreach to underserved areas with low college enrollment rates. We discuss each of these examples, in turn, below.

Texas' Top Ten Percent Plan

Institutional autonomy in Texas was limited by the *Hopwood v. Texas* (1996) decision—a federal court ruling barring the use of race/ethnicity in college admissions in the Fifth Circuit. As a result, state policymakers in Texas (with the support of academics and community members), concerned about the potential loss of underrepresented students in the state's public higher education institutions, legislated an admissions bill that would counteract such losses in racial and ethnic diversity. House Bill 508, known as the Top Ten

Percent Plan, guarantees admission to the top 10% of a high school graduating class to any public higher education institution in the state. The automatic admissions plan was designed as a viable option to replace the loss of the use of affirmative action in the state (Montejano, 1998) and was written acknowledging the educational benefits of diversity expressed in *Bakke.* For Texas, this meant that there were benefits to admitting a pool of students from various geographic areas across the state because that also represented various racial, ethnic, and income groups; the plan has been successful largely because of demographic distribution (Tienda & Niu, 2004).

Legislative action to replace the loss of affirmative action in Texas, however, was not the only tool designed to meet this goal of achieving a racially diverse student body. Instead, for example, the University of Texas at Austin, followed by Texas A&M University, supplemented the state automatic admissions plan at their respective institutions with specific scholarship and retention programming designed to attract a diverse student body (Horn & Flores, 2003). The Longhorn Opportunity Scholarship (LOS) available at the University of Texas at Austin targeted low-income students in the top 10% of their high school graduating class in schools that had low rates of college enrollment at the University of Texas (Horn & Flores, 2003). LOS students were further supported by retention services once they enrolled on campus. Texas' other flagship institution also initiated a similar scholarship program, although without specific income requirements. In sum, each institution designed particular scholarship and retention programs connected to the state percent plan but particular to their contexts and recruitment needs.

By the time the *Bakke* principles were reaffirmed in *Grutter,* enrollment by almost all underrepresented racial and ethnic groups, which initially saw declines, had risen to near pre-*Hopwood* levels at the University of Texas at Austin. The same was not true at Texas A&M, however, signaling different levels of institutional involvement and success with recruiting and admitting a diverse student body (Chapa & Horn, 2007). Rising enrollment of racial and ethnic minorities at the University of Texas at Austin before the reinstatement of affirmative action has been attributed to the strategic implementation of an institutional-level response coordinated with state legislation post-*Hopwood* (Domina, 2007; Horn & Flores, 2003). Selective institutions in Texas, therefore, used their autonomy to directly link programmatic services likely to recruit a diverse student body with state policy (the Top Ten Percent Plan) to offset the Fifth Circuit's retraction of affirmative action and enhance the implementation of the state-mandated percent plan. Texas presents a distinct and successful story regarding the assertion of academic freedom via institutional-level responses to maintain the ability to admit a diverse student body.

California's Proposition 209

California, through Proposition 209, was the first state to specifically use state policy to ban the use of race, sex, color, ethnicity, and national origin for all public education, employment, and public contracting decisions, including college admissions (Chavez, 1998; Coleman et al., 2007; Pusser, 2004). The new state constitutional amendment was a result of a voter referendum instigated after the University of California system's Board of Regents voted on resolutions—SP-1 and SP-2—to prohibit the use of race in college admissions, employment, and contracting (Horn & Flores, 2003). Although these were not institutional-level decisions but, rather, university system initiatives, the vote approving SP-1 and SP-2 represented the decision of the UC system's governing board; all institutions in the public state system were obliged to abide. In 2000, the UC Board of Regents voted to repeal SP-1 and SP-2, although the vote was considered largely symbolic because Proposition 209 had already been in place for 3 years and the regent vote would have no effect on this state law (Pusser, 2004).

Proposition 209, the most formal, longest standing, and permanent state action on higher education admissions, offers a second example of the complex relationship between state policy and college and university institutional autonomy. Before Proposition 209, the California state constitution provided language directing universities to admit classes that reflected the gender, racial, and ethnic diversity of the state (Pusser, 2004), a provision that coincided with the goals of the institutions. Actually, despite the regents' vote on SP-1 and SP-2, some members of the university faculty and administration, including UC System President Richard Atkinson, had opposed SP-1 and SP-2 and continued to voice support for diversity-enhancing initiatives (Pusser, 2004). Regardless of the extent to which they opposed bans on race-conscious initiatives and wanted to preserve their institutional autonomy regarding admissions decisions, public universities' actions were legally limited.

Once Proposition 209 became official state policy that governed all public college and university systems, the implications for college access for particular student groups became more pronounced. As a remedy to the restrictive state law, state and university leadership at that time (e.g., Governor Gray Davis and UC President Atkinson) offered an alternative UC system admissions plan called "Eligibility in Local Context" to address potential losses in student body diversity (Ball, 2000). In 1999, this new admissions plan was passed by an overwhelming majority of the members of the UC Board of Regents, the same group that voted to dismantle the use of race in college admissions, with the intention of mitigating some of the loss of racial and ethnic diversity resulting from Proposition 209 (Pusser, 2004).

ELC differed from the Texas initiative in that it only allowed admission to those graduating in the top 4% of any high school graduating class in California to the UC system (and not the institution of choice). However, the plan was designed with the intention of evaluating a student based on the opportunities afforded by his or her local high school context (Student Academic Services, 2002). Other requirements specific to California's ELC not present in the initial Texas percent plan included required high school course taking and recommendations to take the range of required UC tests to become UC-eligible (University of California, 2003). In general, the plan was designed to identify students who were within reach of achieving UC eligibility the summer after their junior year of high school so that individual UC campuses could make concerted efforts to advise students regarding their course-taking patterns as well as remain connected throughout the college application process.

Another attempt to mitigate the potential decline in minority enrollment after Proposition 209 became investment in college outreach programs through state-mandated legislative funding. Legislative action in this circumstance involved carefully targeted and, initially, generous budgetary commitments that included funding for K–12 outreach, university and K–12 partnerships, and the creation of summer training academies (Pusser, 2004). Although funding proposals for college outreach were as much as six times the amount of any funds spent on these activities before the 1995 passing of SP-1 and SP-2 (Ristine, 2000), this form of response proved to be temporary and vulnerable. Conflict between other state economy needs and changing gubernatorial administrations led to significant decreases in state support for this remedy (Schevitz, 2004). In California, therefore, we see that attempts to exercise institutional autonomy did not have lasting state support. As a result, these efforts have not proven a strong counterbalance to the state constitutional law banning race-conscious admissions.

Data reflecting the policy implementations of SP-1, Proposition 209, and ELC do not tell a tale of full recovery. By 2003, underrepresented minority enrollment at the UC system-level had dropped significantly from 1995 enrollment levels. In fact, the UC system saw its most dismal level of underrepresented minority enrollment upon the implementation of Proposition 209 in 1998. Enrollment overall began a climb upon the implementation of various outreach programs, but the trends at the individual campus level could not boast much, if any, steady increases. Although the UC system showed some recovery by 2003 at the system level post-ELC, most campuses had not recovered to the 1995 levels of underrepresented minority applicants and enrollees (University of California, 2003). In any case, much of the gain could be simply a result of the growing proportion of underrepresented minority groups in California's pool of graduating high school seniors (Horn & Flores, 2003; University of California, 2003).

State Policies With Indirect Effects on Student Body Diversity

The Texas and California examples of how admission policies and limits on them can affect an institution's ability to achieve a diverse student body are fairly straightforward. It is not hard to understand how directly relevant admissions legislation is likely to affect admission outcomes. What may be less obvious is that non-admissions policies may also have an effect on student diversity. In these instances, the outcomes of state policy, rather than the policy itself, can have an effect on the institution. Examples are policies that serve as financial incentives to apply to and enroll in an institution including the following: (1) the HOPE Scholarship, a merit-based financial aid program in Georgia (one of at least 14 states to provide such an incentive), and (2) an in-state resident tuition (ISRT) policy, House Bill 1403, which provides an in-state resident tuition discount to high school graduates in Texas (one of 10 states that offers the discount). Further, although these policies are facially race-neutral, targeting students, whether by citizenship status or grade point average, is likely to have an effect on the racial and ethnic makeup of a student body.

The HOPE Scholarship

State merit-aid programs are examples of policies that have an indirect effect on the student body of institutions.[10] Although these scholarship programs do not dictate or limit institutional action, they affect institutions because of the funds provided to students, the criteria used to distribute those funds, and the choices students make in using the funds. As a result, different students may be accepting admission to colleges and universities in Georgia in different ways than in the past. Georgia's Helping Outstanding Students Educationally (HOPE) Scholarship is one example of such a state merit-aid program.

The Georgia HOPE Scholarship, instituted in 1993 and funded by state lottery revenue, is "the largest state-financed, merit-based aid program in the U.S." (Cornwell-Mustard HOPE Scholarship Page, 2007, n.p.), having disbursed more than $3.61 billion dollars to more than 1 million students.[11] It has served as the model for more than a dozen similar scholarships around the country (Heller & Marin, 2004). The Georgia program, the longest in existence, is also the most studied, thereby offering extensive information to examine the potential effects of such a financial aid incentive.

To be eligible for the HOPE Scholarship, a student must have Georgia residency and "have graduated from an eligible Georgia high school since 1993 with at least a 'B' (3.0 grade-point) average" (Cornwell-Mustard HOPE Scholarship Page, 2007, n.p.). The original program design included an eligibility income cap of $66,000 that was increased to $100,000 in the second year; the cap has now been eliminated altogether. HOPE Scholars can use the aid at either a public or private degree-granting institution.[12] Finally, to maintain the scholarship, students are required to have at least a 3.0 college GPA (Cornwell-Mustard HOPE Scholarship Page, 2007).

It seems hard to argue against a merit-based scholarship that provides financial support to students who have demonstrated some level of academic achievement as defined by the program's criteria, especially "given the popularity of these programs among middle-class citizens" (Doyle, 2006, p. 260). Yet, a closer examination of many of these scholarships has demonstrated that they tend to be awarded to those who would already attend higher education rather than to underrepresented students whose opportunity to attend college might be enhanced as a result of such a financial incentive (see Heller & Marin, 2002, 2004; Marin, 2002). As Dynarski (2004) notes, although the programs are facially race-neutral, these "scholarships flow disproportionately to white, non-Hispanic, upper-income students" (p. 68). Specifically examining the HOPE Scholarship, Dynarski found that it "has increased racial and ethnic gaps in college attendance in Georgia" (2004, p. 82). These results, though unintentional, are nevertheless significant for institutions interested in admitting and retaining a diverse student body. Further, these outcomes take on even greater importance for states where race-conscious policies are barred by state law or in states with low college attainment for its minority groups.

The use of state merit aid programs "represents one of the most pronounced policy shifts in higher education in the last 20 years" (Doyle, 2006, p. 259), with an increase in the proportion of all state aid going to merit-based programs and a simultaneous decrease in the proportion of all state aid funding need-based programs (Doyle, 2006). This type of massive state policy overhaul, especially given who tends to benefit from merit aid programs, must be examined in light of institutional goals to admit a diverse student body. For example, as per its mission, the University of Georgia (UGA) "seeks to foster the understanding of and respect for cultural differences necessary for an enlightened and educated citizenry. It further provides for cultural, ethnic, gender and racial diversity in the faculty, staff and student body" (University of Georgia, 2005, n.p.). As such, the institution, and others with the same interests, may need to exercise its institutional autonomy to implement policies and programs that would still allow it to achieve its goal of admitting a diverse student body.

In-State Resident Tuition Legislation

Another example of state policy gaining both prominence and controversy across the United States is that of in-state resident tuition (ISRT) legislation. These policies are designed to provide an in-state tuition discount to any student who graduates from a state's secondary school system and has lived in that state for a particular number of years. This includes undocumented immigrant students who meet these requirements. The legislation has, in effect, mirrored a proposed federal law that would allow undocumented immigrant high school graduates to pay in-state resident tuition, among other provisions. In addition to the tuition discount, the proposed federal act, called the Development, Relief, and Education for Alien Minors Act (DREAM), would allow undocumented students to begin the path toward obtaining U.S. citizenship and gaining legal employment if they go to college or serve in the U.S. military (Olivas, 2004). The state versions, however, are limited in scope because they cannot override federal immigration law and are, therefore, in the form of a basic tuition discount. ISRT legislation grants undocumented immigrant students, as well as any other student who moves to an ISRT state, the same in-state resident tuition discount as legal residents, if they meet specific residency and graduation requirements (Olivas, 2004). As out-of-state rates are significantly higher than in-state rates, the tuition discount is particularly significant for students who do not qualify for federal aid because of citizenship status (Olivas, 2004).

ISRT policies are controversial in nature because of those students they are likely to serve—undocumented high school graduates of a racial/ethnic minority status. Most undocumented individuals in the United States are of Latin American origin, and a number of the states with tuition legislation represent regions of the country with the highest number of Latino-origin individuals and undocumented immigrants (Passel, 2005; Passel, Van Hook, & Bean, 2004). As such, the likelihood that an individual benefiting from such a policy is of Latino origin is relatively high. Texas, which has the oldest ISRT policy in the nation, has documented the increase of students identified as ISRT policy-eligible from approximately 1,488 students in fall 2001 to almost 9,000 in fall 2005 (Texas Higher Education Coordinating Board, n.d.). Although in most cases community college entrance makes up most of the ISRT higher education enrollment, there was a steady increase in 4-year enrollment by this category of students from 2001 to 2005, a number of whom entered the University of Texas at Austin, one of the state's flagship institutions (Texas Higher Education Coordinating Board, n.d.).

This resulting trend represents a unique opportunity for colleges and universities to exercise their institutional autonomy with regard to how the outcomes of these state ISRT policies may contribute to a potential increase in the racial and economic diversity of their incoming students. Although the policies may not have been designed with *Bakke* principles in mind, the mission to provide access through a financial aid discount to students who likely cannot afford high tuition and are barred from all forms of federal financial aid likely yields an economically and racially diverse pool of students entering higher education.[13] In states where the tuition discount is available, institutions may use this policy mechanism as a diversity-enhancing tool and implement methods successful to their particular context to recruit and retain these students. As the pool of students likely to be undocumented will vary based on geographic region, some institutions may have to make more concerted efforts than will others. A number of institutions in Texas, for example, have partnered with local community, nonprofit, and religious organizations to publicize the rights afforded by the tuition legislation to immigrant families (Flores, 2007; Rincon, 2005). Such methods of creative partnerships may serve as a lesson to other institutions in states where the benefit is available but the take-up rate of the policy does not reflect the number of students who may be eligible.

State policy in this area, however, is not static; several states have had to adjust to legislative changes regarding the college access opportunities for undocumented immigrants. While 10 states to date have ISRT policies, Arizona, for example, through a voter referendum known as Proposition 300, has barred undocumented students from receiving any state financial aid benefits such as those accorded by an in-state resident tuition law (Redden, 2007). In addition, a number of other states with ISRT legislation have introduced bills to repeal any financial discounts supported by state funds and offered by these policies to undocumented students (Redden, 2007). Thus, although the discount was originally approved by various state legislatures around the country, it appears that voters in at least Arizona have taken active initiative to oppose this practice for a particular category of students— undocumented immigrants. As state reaction to this type of tuition legislation continues to unfold across the country, institutions should remain vigilant and creative about how to take advantage of policy windows of access for students who contribute to their overall mission of diversity.

Exercising Institutional Autonomy

Mounting state policy related to postsecondary education confirms the increasing interest the public has in higher education and the "right" to a college degree. As long as this interest remains, state policy will continue to intersect with institutional autonomy and colleges and universities will need to determine if, how, and when to exercise their academic freedom to achieve their institutional missions.

As a result of the defense of the University of Michigan undergraduate and law school admissions policies in the *Gratz* and *Grutter* cases, it became more evident than ever that higher education institutions believe, as affirmed in *Bakke,* that a racially/ethnically diverse student body is an essential component in achieving their educational missions. However, obtaining a diverse student body remains a matter of concern despite the 2003 upholding of *Bakke* in *Gratz* and *Grutter*. For example, three states to date—California,

Washington, and Michigan—have barred the use of race/ethnicity in college admissions through referenda and campaigns are underway in five more states—Arizona, Colorado, Missouri, Nebraska, and Oklahoma—to have citizens vote on anti-affirmative action ballot measures in November 2008 (Schmidt, 2007). The affirmative action initiatives have also been increasingly associated with issues of illegal immigration, bringing any policies that may benefit immigrants in a state to even greater visibility (Schmidt, 2007). Of the five states with potential referenda votes, two—Oklahoma and Nebraska—have in-state resident tuition policies and Arizona already has implemented a ban on use of the state tuition discount for undocumented students.

Research has shown a drop in the percentage of racial and ethnic minority applications and enrollment in states that prohibit the use of race/ethnicity in college admission (Horn & Flores, 2003; Long, 2004). Although we have seen a partial recovery of underrepresented minority enrollment in some institutions where state-level policy has restricted the consideration of race, the rise has been only partially the result of alternative admissions plans such as a percent plan and these results vary even by institution within a state. Instead, lessons in California and Texas have shown that creativity in exercising institutional autonomy, which has included partnerships with external agents such as the legislature, is essential to enrolling and serving a diverse student body and attempting to reverse the negative trends caused by policies that prohibit the use of race/ethnicity in decision making.

With regard to policies that are not directly admissions-related but instead affect outcomes of student body enrollment by their design, it will be increasingly important for institutions to acknowledge and assess the indirect affects of these policies and to exercise their institutional autonomy to mitigate any negative effect on student diversity.

Conclusion

Institutions that believe in the *Bakke* principle that diversity is a compelling state interest must be prepared to exercise their institutional autonomy, sometimes creatively, to admit and retain a racially/ethnically diverse student body. Institutions cannot be passive, especially when state policy negatively affects their desired goals. Of course, this is a complex endeavor because institutions have multiple missions and many goals, and even these sometimes internally conflict (see Marin & Yun, 2005). Nevertheless, institutions must serve as policy evaluators, assessing the impact state policy will have on their interests, as well as policy actors, actively developing solutions to the challenges they face. Remaining committed to *Bakke* will increasingly require institutions to exercise their institutional autonomy to intentionally address obstacles to their diversity goals.

Notes

1. The other rationales presented by UC Davis but discounted by Justice Powell include reducing the scarcity of underrepresented minorities in both medical schools and the medical profession, addressing the effects of societal discrimination, and increasing the number of doctors who would practice in underserved communities. See Ancheta, this volume, for further discussion on Justice Powell's review of these rationales.

2. Although Justice Powell supported this rationale, he did not support the specific admissions policy in question at UC Davis. Therefore, the admissions policy at Davis was deemed unconstitutional.

3. The 2007 *Parents Involved in Community Schools v. Seattle School District No. 1* and *Meredith v. Jefferson County Board of Education* cases involving voluntary elementary and secondary desegregation plans also left *Bakke* standing.

4. Because public universities are accountable to the state in ways that private universities are not (Berdahl & McConnell, 1994), our examples focus only on public institutions.

5. This Supreme Court case considered whether New Hampshire's attorney general could prosecute a professor for refusing to answer questions about a lecture delivered at the state university.

6. Concurring opinions generally agree with the decision of a court case, but usually provide alternative reasoning. Even though they are not binding in any way, they can have influence on future decisions, as is the case with Justice Frankfurter's concurring opinion in *Sweezy,* as well as in the public arena.

7. For a detailed explanation, see Kaplin and Lee (1995).

8. For a discussion of the moral disagreement present in the affirmative action debate, see Moses, this volume.

9. At the time of the *Hopwood v. Texas* ruling, public colleges in Louisiana and Mississippi struggled to interpret the limits set by this Court decision because these states were under federal desegregation court orders (Healy, 1998).

10. These scholarship opportunities are generally available to any state resident who meets the established award criteria. Award criteria, based on measures of academic merit such as grade point average or test score, vary by state (Heller, 2002).

11. In addition to the HOPE Scholarship, the HOPE Program also includes the HOPE Grant, which does not have any merit requirements and can be used for

nondegree programs at technical schools (Cornwell-Mustard HOPE Scholarship Page, 2007). This chapter does not discuss the HOPE Grant.

12. For HOPE scholars using their scholarship at degree-granting public institutions, "the program covers tuition, HOPE-approved mandatory fees and a book allowance. The value of the award is about $5,000 for the 2006–2007 academic year" (Cornwell-Mustard HOPE Scholarship Page, 2007, n.p.). Those students using their scholarships at private, degree-granting institutions receive $3,000 per academic year to use toward tuition (Cornwell-Mustard HOPE Scholarship Page, 2007).

13. One assessment limitation of this analysis is the lack of demographic data that include accurate and detailed citizenship status. No government agency in the United States, including public higher education institutions, collects data solely on undocumented immigrants (Passel, 2005). Therefore, directly studying how the role of citizenship status, by race/ethnicity, affects student diversity outcomes poses different and more complex challenges than does studying other higher education policies that affect racial and ethnic minorities.

References

Association of American University Professors (AAUP) & American Association of Colleges and Universities (AAC&U). (2006). *1940 statement of principles on academic freedom and tenure.* Washington, DC: AAUP.

Ball, H. (2000). *The* Bakke *case.* Lawrence: University of Kansas Press.

Berdahl, R. O., & McConnell, T. R. (1994). Autonomy and accountability: Some fundamental issues. In P. G. Altbach, R. O. Berdahl, & P. J. Gumport (Eds.), *Higher education in American society* (3rd ed., pp. 55–72). Amherst, NY: Prometheus Books.

Bok, D. (1982). *Beyond the ivory tower: Social responsibilities of the modern university.* Cambridge, MA: Harvard University Press.

Chapa, J., & Horn, C. L. (2007). Is anything race neutral? Comparing "race-neutral" admissions policies at the University of Texas and the University of California. In G. Orfield, P. Marin, S. M. Flores, & L. M. Garces (Eds.), *Charting the future of college affirmative action: Legal victories, continuing attacks, and new research* (pp. 157–172). Los Angeles: The Civil Rights Project at UCLA.

Chavez, L. (1998). *The color bind: California's battle to end affirmative action.* Berkeley: University of California Press.

Coleman, A. L., Palmer, S. R., Sanghavi, E., & Winnick, S. Y. (2007, March). *From federal law to state voter initiatives: Preserving higher education's authority to achieve the educational, economic, civic, and security benefits associated with a diverse student body.* New York: College Board.

Cornwell-Mustard HOPE Scholarship Page. (2007). *Georgia's HOPE scholarship.* Retrieved November 4, 2007, from http://www.terry.uga.edu/hope/gahope.html

Domina, T. (2007). Higher education policy as secondary school reform: Texas public high schools after *Hopwood. Educational Evaluation and Policy Analysis, 29*(3), 200–217.

Doyle, W. R. (2006). Adoption of merit-based student grant programs: An event history analysis. *Educational Evaluation and Policy Analysis, 28*(3), 259–285.

Dynarski, S. (2004). The new merit aid. In C. M. Hoxby (Ed.), *College choices: The economics of where to go, when to go, and how to pay for it* (pp. 63–97). Chicago: University of Chicago Press and the National Bureau of Economic Research.

Euben, D. R. (2002, May). *Academic freedom of individual professors and higher education institutions: The current legal landscape.* Washington, DC: AAUP. Retrieved November 17, 2007, from http://www.aaup.org/AAUP/protect/legal/topics/AF-profs-inst.htm

Flores, S. M. (2007). *The effect of in-state resident tuition policies on the college enrollment of undocumented Latino students in Texas and the United States.* Unpublished doctoral dissertation, Harvard University, Cambridge, MA.

Gladieux, L. E., Hauptman, A. M., & Knapp, L. G. (1994). The federal government and higher education. In P. G. Altbach, R. O. Berdahl, & P. J. Gumport (Eds.), *Higher education in American society* (3rd ed., pp. 125–154). Amherst, NY: Prometheus Books.

Gratz v. Bollinger, 539 U.S. 244 (2003).

Grutter v. Bollinger, 539 U.S. 306 (2003).

Healy, P. (1998, April 24). Affirmative action survives at colleges in some states covered by *Hopwood* ruling. *The Chronicle of Higher Education.* Retrieved December 5, 2007, from http://chronicle.com/che-data/articles.dir/art-44.dir/issue-33.dir/33a04201.ht m

Heller, D. E. (2002). State merit scholarship programs: An introduction. In D. E. Heller & P. Marin (Eds.), *Who should we help? The negative social consequences of merit scholarships* (pp. 15–24). Cambridge, MA: The Civil Rights Project at Harvard University.

Heller, D. E., & Marin, P. (Eds.). (2002). *Who should we help? The negative social consequences of merit scholarships.* Cambridge, MA: The Civil Rights Project at Harvard University.

Heller, D. E., & Marin, P. (Eds.). (2004). *State merit scholarship programs and racial inequality.* Cambridge, MA: The Civil Rights Project at Harvard University.

Hopwood v. Texas, 78 F. 3d 932 (5th Cir.); *cert. denied,* 518 U.S. 1033 (1996).

Horn, C. L., & Flores, S. (2003). *Percent plans in college admissions: A comparative analysis of three states' experiences.* Cambridge, MA: The Civil Rights Project at Harvard University.

Kaplin, W. A., & Lee, B. A. (1995). *The law of higher education* (3rd ed.). San Francisco: Jossey-Bass.

Keyishian v. Board of Regents of the University of the State of New York, 385 U.S. 589 (1967).

Long, M. C. (2004). College applications and the effect of affirmative action. *Journal of Econometrics, 121,* 319–342.

Marin, P. (2002). Merit scholarships and the outlook for equal opportunity in higher education. In D. E. Heller & P. Marin (Eds.), *Who should we help? The negative social consequences of merit scholarships* (pp. 111–116). Cambridge, MA: The Civil Rights Project at Harvard University.

Marin, P., & Yun, J. T. (2005). From strict scrutiny to educational scrutiny: A new vision for higher education policy and research. In G. Orfield, P. Marin, & C. L. Horn (Eds.), *Higher education and the color line: College access, racial equity, and social change* (pp. 197–218). Cambridge, MA: Harvard Education Press.

McGuinness, A. C., Jr. (1994). The states and higher education. In P. G. Altbach, R. O. Berdahl, & P. J. Gumport (Eds.), *Higher education in American society* (3rd ed., pp. 155–180). Amherst, NY: Prometheus Books.

Meredith v. Jefferson County Board of Education, 127 S. Ct. 2738 (2007).

Montejano, D. (1998). On *Hopwood:* The continuing challenge. In N. Foley (Ed.), *Reflexiones 1997: New directions in Mexican American studies* (pp. 133–156). Austin, TX: CMAS Books.

Olivas, M. A. (2004). IIRIRA, the Dream Act, and undocumented college student residency. *Journal of College and University Law, 30,* 435–464.

Parents Involved in Community Schools v. Seattle School District No. 1, 127 S. Ct. 2738 (2007).

Passel, J. S. (2005, March 21). *Estimates of the size and characteristics of the undocumented population* (Pew Hispanic Center). Retrieved September 1, 2005, from http://pewhispanic.org/reports/report.php?ReportID = 44

Passel, J. S., Van Hook, J., & Bean, F. D. (2004). *Estimates of the legal and unauthorized foreign-born population for the United States and selected states, based on Census 2000* (Report to the Census Bureau). Washington, DC: Urban Institute.

Pusser, B. (2004). *Burning down the house: Politics, governance, and affirmative action at the University of California.* New York: State University of New York Press.

Redden, E. (2007). An in-state tuition debate. *Inside Higher Education.* Retrieved March 1, 2007, from http://www.insidehighered.com/news/2007/02/28/immigration

Regents of the University of California v. Bakke, 438 U.S. 265 (1978).

Rincon, A. (2005). *Paying for their status: Undocumented immigrants and college access.* Unpublished doctoral dissertation, University of Texas at Austin, Austin, Texas.

Ristine, J. (2000, January 21). UC's efforts to boost minority admissions hit. *San Diego Union-Tribune*, p. A3.

Schevitz, T. (2004, January 27). College outreach imperiled: Budget ax may hit programs helping disadvantaged students. *San Francisco Chronicle*, p. A1.

Schmidt, P. (2007, October 19). 5 more states may curtail affirmative action: Ballot measures pushed by Ward Connerly are likely to win passage. *The Chronicle of Higher Education, 54*(8), p. A1.

Springer, A. (2006). Academic freedom of students and professors, and political discrimination. Washington, DC: AAUP. Retrieved November 17, 2007, from http://www.aaup.org/AAUP/protect/legal/topics/PolDivDiscrim.htm

Student Academic Services, Office of the President at the University of California. (2002, February). *Eligibility in Local Context program evaluation report.* Retrieved June 14, 2002, from http://www.ucop.edu/news/cr/report02.pdf

Sweezy v. New Hampshire, 354 U.S. 234 (1957).

Texas Higher Education Coordinating Board. (n.d.). *HB 1403 students, 2001–2004* [Data file]. Austin, TX: Author.

Tienda, M., & Niu, S. (2004). *Capitalizing on segregation, pretending neutrality: College admissions and the Texas Top 10 Percent law.* Retrieved August 22, 2005, from http://www.texastop10.princeton.edu/reports/forthcoming/capitalizing_on_segregation.pdf

University of California Office of the President. (2003, March). *Undergraduate access to the University of California after the elimination of race-conscious policies.* Retrieved December 5, 2007, from ucop.edu/outreach/aa_finalcx%202.pdf

The University of Georgia. (2005). *The mission of the University of Georgia.* Retrieved November 4, 2007, http://www.uga.edu/profile/mission.html

11

THE FUTURE OF *BAKKE*

Patricia Marin and Catherine L. Horn

To many, *Bakke* may seem superfluous or even invisible in the context of the 2003 *Grutter* decision, but as this book has demonstrated, it actually continues to have a ubiquitous and significant presence in higher education. The contributors to this volume have, through multidisciplinary approaches and with attention to our country's multiracial context, represented a kaleidoscope of voices on the continued significance of *Bakke* and issues of access and equity in postsecondary education. As racial divisions in the country are sharpening and as educational outcomes continue to be directly related to race and poverty, this volume helps inform and further the discussions and decisions necessary to bring about the changes that lead to equal opportunity.

In specifically considering *Bakke*'s influence on the discussion of the use of race/ethnicity as a factor in admissions decisions, remember that most colleges and universities in this country admit virtually all qualified applicants without regard to such issues. Research has shown that for less-selective schools, race/ethnicity plays little, if any, role in determining whether an applicant will be admitted. Nevertheless, in efforts to create a racially/ethnically diverse student body at the most selective schools, admissions officers often consider race/ethnicity as a "plus factor" in deciding whom to admit. And attendance at those elite schools has profound positive effects on the personal and professional pathways of their graduates, leading to increased societal benefits.

The complexity of race, equity, and access in America's postsecondary schools, however, expands *Bakke*'s relevance far beyond the admission door.

Institutions do not operate in a vacuum. The broader local, state, and federal policy and political context highlighted by authors throughout the book represent real and profound influences on capacity to realize institutional mission. For example, states in recent years have substantially cut funding to public higher education institutions, forcing universities to make hard choices because of very limited resources. Additionally, substantial demographic shifts in the college-going population (e.g., California's massive influx of college students known as Tidal Wave II) will increasingly put pressure on the infrastructure of institutions and, coupled with an increasing awareness across the board of the importance of a college degree to life chances, keep at the forefront this fundamental question of who deserves the right to a college degree. What *Bakke* tells us, then, is in many ways more relevant today than 30 years ago.

Postsecondary Education's 21st Century Landscape

Although the *Bakke* case affirmed the ability of higher education institutions to employ race-conscious policy, many colleges and universities are retreating from the race-conscious tools afforded them by this Supreme Court decision. Specifically, we are witnessing institutions eliminate the use of race/ethnicity in campus policies and practices, even when this may not be required by the law or state policy. Research presented in this book and elsewhere provides evidence of the negative outcomes associated with the absence of race-conscious admissions policies, including decreasing access for underrepresented students and not affording all students the benefit of experiencing a diverse student body in their educational environment.

Amid all the reversals, however, the University of Michigan serves as an exemplar of one institution's efforts to both acknowledge and defend its commitment to racial/ethnic access and equity. Making the decision to take a stand for their belief in the educational benefits of a diverse student body as articulated in *Bakke,* institutional leaders mounted a defense of the university's law school and undergraduate affirmative action programs. Ultimately, the end result was the 2003 *Grutter* opinion, which strongly affirmed *Bakke*'s fundamental tenets. What is perhaps equally important to note, however, is that throughout this legal process, an unprecedented collaborative of the higher education community, civil rights advocates, and a broad constituency of allies—including *Fortune* 500 companies and high ranking retired military leaders—stood publicly to defend *Bakke* alongside the University of Michigan.

We celebrate the affirmation of *Bakke* that came with *Grutter,* but the higher education community must acknowledge that the victory is fragile. Ongoing legal challenges to affirmative action policies, particularly in the context of an increasingly conservative Supreme Court, continue to put at risk the tools education communities have used to help create diverse learning communities. Most recently, the Supreme Court's 2007 ruling in *Parents Involved in Community Schools v. Seattle School District No. 1* maintained *Bakke*'s relevance to postsecondary settings but made very clear that the balance of support has tipped toward an opposition of race-conscious policies. This sentiment seems to be seeping into the public forum as well. Even after winning its extensive legal battle in *Grutter,* for example, the University of Michigan has been barred from using race as a result of Proposal 2, a ballot initiative passed by voters in 2006. Similar ballot initiative campaigns are underway in five additional states—Arizona, Colorado, Missouri, Nebraska, and Oklahoma—and could appear on the 2008 ballot. Fundamental issues of access and equity are at stake, and the higher education community can neither rest on its laurels nor can it retreat, as some institutions unfortunately have already done, from what will surely be a volatile path down which progress may be made or lost.

Looking to the Future

We hope that this book has identified some useful ideas for areas to be addressed, questions to be researched, and policies to be implemented or amended to better ensure access and equity for traditionally underrepresented students to higher education. Even in its thorough consideration, though, the book is truly only a snapshot of what continues to be important in discussions of access and equity. Building on the research presented in these chapters, ongoing discussion and further exploration among and between a wide range of constituencies is required to continue to expand an understanding of the issues at hand, challenges faced, and effectiveness of efforts that ultimately may allow the benefits of a diverse campus to be reaped. This chapter takes a moment to offer possibilities for deliberation in several arenas.

Legal Theory and Effective Defense

Justice Lewis Powell's opinion reshaped the discussion of race/ethnicity in college admissions from one of remedies for past institutional discrimination to one of educational benefits of diversity. While recognizing the utility of the latter, legal scholars and higher education attorneys must continue recognizing the legal validity of the former. Establishing a legally compelling rationale for race-conscious decision making is not an either/or proposition because, as Justice Sandra Day O'Connor notes in her majority opinion in *Grutter,* both are permissible under the law. Further, the time is ripe for legal scholars to consider new defenses and, particularly in the context of O'Connor's 25-year admonition, question whether a sunset clause applies to the educational benefits of diversity.

Social Science Research

Continued social science research is essential for us to improve our understanding of the central issues relevant to *Bakke* and faced by higher education today. Although a comprehensive list would be too long to include here, we offer several suggestions as starting points. Continued work understanding the educational benefits of a diverse student body is essential if institutions hope to legally ground themselves for challenges to race-conscious programs and policies. Such studies may consider the extent to which those benefits are enjoyed, by whom, under what circumstances, and to what end. Further, studies on the outcomes of race-conscious supplemental programs (e.g., summer bridge and targeted retention programs) and, related, the outcomes when such programs are modified or made race-neutral are also needed. It is particularly important to consider these questions over time, as the journey into and out of college is a complex one.

One of the foundational arguments by the defendants in *Grutter* was the notion that a "critical mass" of students of color is a necessary precursor to the educational benefits of diversity. This condition allows an environment in which students can avoid being stereotyped or viewed as wholly representative of a cultural perspective and thus feel more comfortable openly sharing opinions. Much research is needed to better understand this concept and its influence on the educational experiences of students. In particular, studies are needed that explore how critical mass at the classroom level intersects with similar conditions at the campus level to ultimately affect educational outcomes.

Social scientists need to continue to document the effects of race-neutral and alternative admissions policies across racial/ethnic groups. Additionally, further empirical work should be conducted analyzing the effects of the interaction of admissions variables on predicted (and actual) admissions decisions. The process of admitting a student body is always, to some degree, subjective and complex. It is improbable, then, that predictors acting alone realistically represent the process. Perhaps most importantly, continued research needs to be done looking at the factors that most greatly affect an admitted student's decision to enroll at and graduate from a particular university. If the desire exists to create and maintain a diverse campus, careful attention must be paid to what influences enrollment and retention practices. Although much work has been done in this area, especially as it relates to enrollment, sustained efforts need to also be made assessing the effectiveness of various programs and interventions (including those begun pre-college) and supplemental policies (e.g., race-conscious scholarships) in retaining traditionally underserved minorities.

Institutional Policy and Practice

As they consider race-conscious policy and programs on their campuses, higher education leaders are faced with a complex set of circumstances in which to make decisions. It is essential that the practitioner role be one of policy evaluator as well as policy advocate in this process. As the *Grutter* decision identified, campuses now have a profound legal responsibility to actively document the extent to which race-conscious programs and policies are achieving their intended goals as well as justify that such outcomes could not be achieved in a race-neutral manner. The enduring legacy of *Bakke* compels campuses to be self-reflective and actively (rather than passively) claim the legal rights granted under the decision. In this self-reflection, institutions have an opportunity to educate themselves about the clarity and complexity in the law as well as to understand the broader context that brings influence to bear.

2028

The 50th anniversary of *Bakke* will coincide with the conclusion of O'Connor's 25-year sunset admonition. We are left, at the conclusion of this book, with great concern about where the higher education community will be at that time with respect to access and equity for traditionally underserved students. Some of what has been discussed should offer hope. But much of what we have documented suggests that profound work remains to be done in the work toward real access and equity in higher education. Our hope is that this volume will help expand discussions and inform decisions by federal and state policymakers, educational providers, civil rights advocates, and other interested stakeholders to bring about the changes that lead to equal opportunity. In that equal opportunity, we all reap benefit.

ABOUT THE AUTHORS

Angelo N. Ancheta is an assistant professor of law at the Santa Clara University School of Law. He has also been a faculty member at the Harvard Law School, the NYU School of Law, and the UCLA School of Law, and, from 2000 to 2004, he was the legal director for The Civil Rights Project at Harvard University. His research and teaching focus on constitutional law, voting rights, and immigrants' rights. He has written extensively in the area of civil rights and affirmative action law, and among his most recent publications are the books *Scientific Evidence and Equal Protection of the Law* (Rutgers University Press, 2006) and *Race, Rights, and the Asian American Experience* (Rutgers University Press, 1998; 2nd ed. 2006). Before teaching, Ancheta was a legal services and civil rights attorney in California, specializing in immigration law, civil rights, and appellate advocacy. He continues to practice appellate advocacy and has represented national organizations as *amici curiae* in U.S. Supreme Court appeals involving affirmative action in higher education and voluntary desegregation in K–12 education. He received his A.B. in 1983 and his J.D. in 1986 from UCLA, where he was Chief Managing Editor of the *UCLA Law Review,* and his M.P.A. in 2000 from Harvard University.

Erika Felts is a doctoral student in sociology at the University of California, Davis. Her research interests include quantitative methods, social stratification, and education policy. She is currently working on projects exploring the distributional effects of class size, the interactive effects of race and socioeconomic status, and affirmative action. Erika received her B.A. from the University of Missouri.

Stella M. Flores is an assistant professor of public policy and higher education at Vanderbilt University. Her research investigates the impact of state and federal policies on college access for low-income and underrepresented student populations. She has written on the role of alternative admissions plans in college admissions, demographic changes in higher education,

Latino students and community colleges, and the impact of in-state resident tuition policies on the college enrollment of undocumented immigrant students. Flores received her Ed.D. from Harvard University. She is coauthor of *Percent Plans in College Admissions: A Comparative Analysis of Three States' Experiences* (with C. L. Horn, 2003) published by The Civil Rights Project at Harvard University, coeditor of *Legacies of Brown: Multiracial Equity in American Education* (with D. J. Carter and R. J. Reddick, Harvard Education Press, 2004), and *Community Colleges and Latino Educational Opportunity* (with C. L. Horn and G. Orfield, Jossey Bass, 2006). Her research has been funded by the Spencer Foundation, the National Association of Student Financial Aid Administrators, the Association for the Study of Higher Education, Lumina Foundation for Education, and Time Warner, Inc.

Donald E. Heller is professor of education and senior scientist at The Pennsylvania State University where he also serves as director of the Center for the Study of Higher Education. He teaches and conducts research on higher education economics, public policy, and finance, focusing on college access and choice for low-income and minority students. He has consulted on higher education policy issues with university systems and policy organizations in California, Colorado, Kansas, Massachusetts, Michigan, New Hampshire, Tennessee, Washington, and Washington, D.C., and has testified in front of congressional committees and state legislatures and in federal court cases as an expert witness. Heller earned an Ed.D. in higher education from the Harvard Graduate School of Education. Before his academic career, he spent a decade as an information technology manager at the Massachusetts Institute of Technology. Heller is the editor of the books *State Postsecondary Education Research: New Methods to Inform Policy and Practice* (with K. Shaw, Stylus Publishing, 2007), *The States and Public Higher Education Policy: Affordability, Access, and Accountability* (Johns Hopkins University Press, 2001), and *Condition of Access: Higher Education for Lower Income Students* (ACE/Praeger, 2002). He received the 2002 Promising Scholar/Early Career Achievement Award from the Association for the Study of Higher Education.

Catherine L. Horn (editor) is an assistant professor of educational psychology at the University of Houston. Her work, discussed by national and regional media outlets, addresses issues related to high-stakes testing, higher education access, affirmative action, and diversity. She has written on the effectiveness of alternative admissions policies in creating racially and ethnically diverse student bodies. She received her Ph.D. from Boston College. Horn coedited (with P. Gándara and G. Orfield) a special volume of *Educational Policy* (2005) and *Expanding Opportunity in Higher Education* (SUNY Press, 2006), both of which analyze the educational access and equity crisis in California. She is also coeditor of *Higher Education and the Color Line* (with G. Orfield and P. Marin, Harvard Education Press, 2005) and *Community Colleges and Latino Educational Opportunity* (with S. M. Flores and G. Orfield, Jossey Bass, 2006). Horn is the associate editor of the *Review of Higher Education.* Her work has been cited in numerous *amicus curiae* briefs submitted to the U.S. Supreme Court in the *Gratz* and *Grutter* cases and cited in Justice Ginsburg's dissenting opinion.

William C. Kidder is the special assistant to the Vice President-Student Affairs for the 10-campus University of California system, where he provides research and consultation on a broad range of educational policy issues. Previously, he served as a senior policy analyst at UC Davis and as a researcher at the Equal Justice Society. Kidder has written extensively about higher education affirmative action, entry into the legal profession, and standardized testing. His work has appeared in the *California Law Review, Law & Social Inquiry, Harvard Blackletter Law Journal,* and *Yale Journal of Law & Feminism.* His recent research includes a *Stanford Law Review* essay and a working paper (coauthored with D. L. Chambers, T. T. Clydesdale, and R. O. Lempert) that critically examines some of the empirical flaws underlying claims that affirmative action "mismatches" African American students academically and depresses the resulting number of Black lawyers. Kidder has written about the unique higher education issues associated with membership in federally recognized American Indian tribes, and his scholarship is also critical of the many unsupported claims about Asian Pacific Americans in the affirmative action debate. Kidder has a B.A. and J.D. from UC Berkeley, where he won the prize for law journal writing.

Michal Kurlaender is an assistant professor in the School of Education at the University of California, Davis. Her areas of research include access and persistence in higher education for underrepresented groups, K–12 school desegregation and integration, and bringing innovative quantitative methods to bear on issues of education policy. She has published in a variety of academic journals in the fields of education and sociology, including most recently, "The Limits of Income Desegregation Policies for Achieving Racial Desegregation" in *Educational Evaluation and Policy Analysis* (with S. Reardon and J. T. Yun, 2006) and "Measuring School Racial Composition and Student Outcomes in a Multiracial Society" in the *American Journal of Education* (with J. T. Yun, 2007). She is currently coediting a book (with E. Grodsky) on the impact of California's Proposition 209 on access to the University of California. Kurlaender has received research grants from institutions including the Spencer Foundation, the American Educational Research Association, and the Institute for Education Sciences of the U.S. Department of Education. She received her Ed.D. in education policy from the Harvard Graduate School of Education in June 2005.

Chungmei Lee is a research associate at The Civil Rights Project. She received her M.Ed. in administration, planning, and social policy from the Harvard Graduate School of Education in 2001. In her capacity as a researcher, she has written on issues of equity and desegregation in K–12 education, and her work has been cited extensively on this topic, including by the U.S. Supreme Court. Before joining the Project, she worked with Harvard's Programs for Professional Education (PPE) and helped train education leaders around the world in Education Management Information Systems (EMIS). At PPE, she also worked on issues relating to the professional development of teachers. As an independent consultant for the National Bureau of Economic Research (NBER), she examined issues such as the financing of higher education and its impact on middle- and low-income students' access to higher education.

Patricia Marin (editor) is a researcher and lecturer in the Gevirtz Graduate School of Education at the University of California, Santa Barbara (UCSB). She studies issues of inclusion and equity in higher education for underrepresented students. In particular, her work examines issues of diversity, affirmative action, and college access. Before joining the Department of Education at UCSB, she worked for The Civil Rights Project (CRP) at Harvard University and the American Council on Education in Washington, D.C. She is coeditor of *Higher Education and the Color Line* (with G. Orfield and C. L.

Horn, Harvard Education Press, 2005) and *Moving Beyond* Gratz *and* Grutter: *The Next Generation of Research* (with M. Moses, 2006), a special issue of *Educational Researcher,* which received the Outstanding Publication Award of the American Educational Research Association's Division J (Higher Education). Her Ph.D., from the University of Maryland, College Park, is in higher education policy. She received her M.Ed. in higher education and student affairs administration from the University of Vermont and her B.A. in Spanish from the University of Pennsylvania.

Karen Miksch is an assistant professor in the Department of Post-secondary Teaching and Learning (PsTL) in the College of Education and Human Development at the University of Minnesota. She is also an affiliate faculty member in the law school. She received her J.D. in 1989 from the University of California, Hastings College of the Law and is a member of the American Educational Research Association (AERA), the Association for the Study of Higher Education (ASHE), and the Education Law Association. She is on the editorial review board for the *Education Law Reporter,* and the AERA and ASHE Monograph series. Miksch's research focuses on access, persistence, and success in higher education, particularly for low-income, first generation, and underrepresented students of color. She is the coauthor of the law field review for the Social Science Research Council's Transition to College project. Her current projects include an access to higher education case study of selective 4-year public research universities.

Michele S. Moses is associate professor of educational foundations, policy, and practice at the University of Colorado at Boulder and is affiliated with the Education and the Public Interest Center. She specializes in philosophy and education policy studies. Her research centers on issues of educational equality and social justice within policies related to race, class, and gender, such as affirmative action. Her work has appeared in journals such as the *American Educational Research Journal, Educational Researcher, Journal of Social Philosophy, Journal of Philosophy of Education, Philosophy and Public Policy Quarterly,* and *Educational Policy.* In addition, she is the author of *Embracing Race: Why We Need Race-Conscious Education Policy* (Teachers College Press, 2002). In an effort to gain a deeper understanding of the roots of the political debates about such race-conscious policies as affirmative action that profoundly affect meaningful opportunities for higher education, she is examining the nature of persistent moral disagreement about controversial education policies in the United States, as well as the relationship between moral disagreement and theories of justice. She recently was awarded the Early Career Award by the American Educational Research Association's Committee on Scholars of Color in Education and was a Fulbright New Century Scholar.

John T. Yun is an assistant professor in the Gevirtz Graduate School of Education and director of the Center for Educational Leadership and Effective Schools (CELES) at the University of California, Santa Barbara (UCSB). His research focuses on issues of equity in education, specifically: patterns of school segregation, the effects of school context on educational outcomes, the importance of integrating evaluation into everyday school practice, and the educative/counter-educative impacts of high-stakes testing. His work has been featured in journals such as the *American Journal of Education, Educational Evaluation and Policy Analysis, Educational Researcher,* and *Sociology of Education.* It has also been widely cited by researchers around the country and used in multiple *amicus curiae* briefs in the *Gratz* and *Grutter* cases, as well as in several school desegregation cases argued before the U.S. Supreme Court. He is coeditor of *The Complex World of Teaching* (with E. Mintz, Harvard Educational Review, 1999), winner of the 2000 AESA Critics Choice Award, and a former solicitations editor at the *Harvard Educational Review.* He received his Ed.D. in administration, planning, and social policy research from Harvard University in 2003.